INSTIGATOR OF JOY

INSTIGATOR OF JOY

Becoming my own fairy godmother

NANCY C. ILLMAN

JOYFLY PRESS

For more information, contact Joyfly Press, 7417 Cedar Avenue, Takoma Park, MD 20912

FIRST EDITION

ISBN: 979-8-9873425-0-3

Cover art by Nancy Illman

Cover design by Renee Duran

Interior design by Duane Stapp

To Miriam Spears

☆ ☆ ✩☆ ☆
        ☆

It is never too late to be what you might have been.
—GEORGE ELIOT

No one saves us but ourselves. No one can and no one may.
We ourselves must walk the path.
—BUDDHA

Who acts from love is greater than who acts from fear.
—TALMUD

☆

It's not so much what we have in this life that matters.
It's what we do with what we have.
—FRED ROGERS

☆

What do you do with a BA in English?
—JEFF MARX, LYRICIST, *AVENUE Q*

TABLE OF CONTENTS

PREFACE

"Write what you know, because it will help others."

I lost track of how many times I received this instruction, but I began hearing that I would someday write a book back in the 1990s, from a series of psychic advisors and friends. I knew from a young age that I was good with words, but I wasn't sure I had anything worth saying. When my freshman writing instructor at Harvard, Nancy Piore, scrawled on the back of my first assignment. "A rose is a rose is a rose; your prose flows," her encouragement made all the criticism that followed easier to swallow. At the end of the course, I had no idea how to write a book, and by the time I graduated college, I was pretty sure nobody would want me to.

Several years later, I won a writing award at Fordham Law School. The emptiness of that honor helped me get clear about my goals: I didn't want to write persuasive legal briefs; I wanted to tell a true story in a way that would touch people's hearts. For many years, though, I had more pressing things to do. It was so easy to put off writing a book, or discovering what the story of my life would be about.

I am the mother of three children, who, together, were my primary excuse for the "delay" in publishing my story. In fact, the truth went much deeper and would take many years to discover.

In 2009, a journalist came to my home in Wyoming, Ohio, to interview me for a profile in the *Tri-County Press*, a local newspaper, for an article unrelated to authorship. At the time, as she noted in her piece, my family held center stage in my life. Some women manage to inhabit their biggest, brightest selves while living under the same roof as their children. I was not that kind of mother, but that was never my kids' fault. Parenting was where I found my value, because for a long time, I couldn't find it in myself. To earn money, I created all sorts of programs that were essentially me parenting other people's kids—people too busy with their own careers to spend much time with their own children.

I lavished my energy, talents and attention on those kids, creating beautiful bedroom murals and custom-painted furniture, teaching them to play the violin and the ancient history of art, and teaching them how to "fish," so that one day they could make art of their own. I instructed them on the practice of yoga, the value of journaling and of nutrition—everything I had found to be vital and enriching for my own children.

As my kids grew up and left home, I had no choice but to take center stage and let the follow spot shine on me. It took some getting used to, but I finally claimed the time and space to focus on myself and reflect on my journey.

Back when the *Tri-County Press* article was published in 2009, the journalist mentioned that I was working on a memoir entitled *Princess in Recovery*. The shift in my self-image since then, as reflected in the current book title, is not insignificant.

When I began working on the earliest iteration of my memoir, I couldn't have claimed the title *Instigator of Joy*—much less that of fairy godmother. I was still wending my way into those roles. The former title was apt at the time, because I was still rehabilitating myself—unpacking decades of messaging and actions that had silenced me, stifled me, shrunk me, imprisoned me in darkness as effectively as any fairy tale princess locked in a tower or sentenced to a deep sleep.

Through the very process of writing this book, with the goal of helping others, I found my way back into the light I was born to inhabit. When I shared my writing endeavors, wise people would sometimes say, "Oh, that will be so therapeutic!" I hoped I was polite enough to hide my annoyance, but I was secretly thinking: "I am not writing for therapeutic reasons, damn it; I am creating literature!" I had no idea what sort of lessons lay ahead for me.

I received enthusiastic responses in sharing snippets of my story, with many demanding that I tell more. Once I managed to believe I had a story worth telling, the hard work began. I had to dig deep to excavate scenes and dialogue from the dustiest corners of my memory and the rustiest crevices of my psyche. Once they reached the surface, these memories needed to be processed—in writing workshops, yes, but also in writing groups with friends, as well as on the yoga mat, and at retreat centers.

Eventually, armed with notebooks full of new insight and inspiration, as well as stacks of journals I'd filled with emotive scribblings since the age of sixteen, I had to make myself sit down, and stay seated, day after day, to write that lonely, lousy first draft. Early readers offered encouragement and instruction—like author Katharine Hikel and performer Ann Randolph—and more came later from those I hired—teachers, coaches, editors. I spent time developing my craft at Antioch College and at a place in Cincinnati called Women Writing for (a) Change. I took deep dives into my soul at Hope Springs Institute, in meditation, and with my therapists. It was a long and winding path before I could hire a developmental editor.

It was during that developmental edit that the real mining began. As I responded to editorial comments in the margin of the most recent draft one day, my dear friend Alison called to ask me how it was going.

"It sucks," I told her.

"I'm sorry," she said.

"It's like you're an archaeologist," I said, "and you're working at an excavation site and you say to your boss, 'How am I doing?' and they say, 'Well, do you see all these areas where you're starting to uncover things? So…you have to go back to all of those areas and keep brushing and keep scraping and see what else is revealed.'

So, I've done that a couple of times, and now I'm going back to my boss and saying, 'Am I done digging yet?' and my boss is like, 'Okay…that's very, very good but look, over here, at this pile of steaming shit! So…you need to climb down here and keep digging in this pile, all the way down until you reach the bottom.'

That's how it's going.

I'm in the shit hole."

But there was gold in that there pile of shit!

It was the slow-burning magic of excavating memory that enabled me to fully inhabit my role center stage and claim the title of fairy godmother. I'm so glad I didn't know it would take this many years or this much work, but I am grateful for every step along the way.

I believe the book culled from those memories can and will help others—that's what kept me in my seat. I recommend memoir writing to anyone needing to make sense of their past—and everyone who wants to create their best possible future.

AUTHOR'S NOTE

On a soul level, I think I always knew I was going to write this book. I began making audio recordings of myself at age four. I briefly kept a *Harriet the Spy*-style notebook in elementary school, full of snarky observations of my classmates, but quickly learned that if people *know* you keep a journal, they *will* read it. Oopsie.

When I left home at sixteen, I felt compelled to record what was happening in my life, as reference material for my future self. Knowing what I know now, I would say I was guided to do so. I knew I was going to change, that life would change me, and that I would want to be able to review the process.

I used my writing to process my feelings in response to situations and events, to integrate my experience of them. I have scrawled and printed in more than twenty journals, filling them with recollections, reflections, and ruminations. With the sole exception of a kitchen encounter with my mother in 1985, which was transcribed in real time, right in front of her, my journal entries were written at my earliest convenience, but without the benefit of an audio device.

My memory has been one of my greatest strengths and one of my greatest sources of pain my entire life. Fictional coach Ted Lasso teaches the players on his team to "be like a goldfish," which he claims is the happiest animal because of its short memory span. Fortunately, finding myself close to the opposite end of the spectrum has not doomed me to being the unhappiest person. When I was fifteen, I painted elephant toenails on the cuffs of my jeans because, while I was model-slim at the time, it felt like I was continually being told that my memory was elephantine, and this was my way of embracing that strange remark.

My specialty lies not in reciting the digits of pi or the capitals of states, but in being able to reproduce utterances—both from conversations and lectures. I love the English language, and I appreciate eloquence. When I hear a turn of phrase I find particularly entrancing, I tend to remember it. Some of the loveliest things my professors said in lecture found their way from my memory down through my pen onto paper, prompting more than a few people to scrawl, "This sounds familiar!" in the margin of a bluebook while grading my essay. The more emotional impact a conversation has upon me, the more likely I am to remember every word of it. If it rises to the level of trauma, it's engraved in stone. This quirk of my mind has astounded friends and teachers; it has caused no end of annoyance in couples counseling. It would inspire one of my bosses to send me to the Soviet Union to walk around, listen to conversations, and report back.

I am not a journalist. I did not take notes with the conscious intention of publishing them someday. My journal entries are true to the extent they reflect my feelings in response to events, conversations, and even dreams that took place in the past, but I do not claim they are objectively true. Together, they inform my story, as honestly as I can tell it. The words herein comprise my experience.

Some names have been changed, as a courtesy.

ACKNOWLEDGEMENTS

I must begin by thanking my husband and three children, whose faith in me is both humbling and inspiring. Many have encouraged me over the years to share my story—so many, that it is impossible to name them all.

I am grateful to my fellow practitioners of Soul Empowered Hypnosis, especially Rita Lampe, who has held space for me to receive guidance from spirit. I know that support and awareness of what we do here on Earth extends well beyond the time and space of our planet and its atmosphere. By telling the truth and embracing forgiveness, we heal the wounds of generational trauma, for both our ancestors and our descendants.

Dozens of people are mentioned by name in this book; if you are one of them, know that I am so grateful for your contribution to my life. As for those whose names I changed, you are also essential, but I did not think you would want credit. I hope you find the concealment of your identity in these pages to be sufficient. If you have wronged me, I forgive you, along with everyone else who has ever hurt me, inadvertently or otherwise. We are all doing the best we can in this challenging classroom called life.

The first teachers to encourage my writing were at Little Flower Montessori. Later, my AP English teacher, Mr. Doherty at Massapequa High, and Nancy Piore, my freshman writing instructor at Harvard, helped me believe that my writing is a pleasure to read, and Lynn Hugo, at Antioch College, strengthened my belief in the healing value of writing my truth.

The late Miriam Spears never stopped reminding me to write and publish this book, which is why I dedicate it to her. Because she lacked awareness of how many times she had said this, she also lacked the fear of pestering me to the point of irritation. When Miriam finally heard my overwhelm, she urged me to write nothing but my own story, and to proceed with the pure and simple intention of helping one person.

Thanks to Karen Gooen, who directed me to her editor, Alice Peck, who—after instructing me what to do back at the drawing board—sent me to the brilliant Crystal Sershen, from which moment something magical has been at play. Crystal demonstrated a stunning ability to say precisely the right thing at each juncture, as if she knew me forever. As an editor, she completes me. I am also grateful to Duane Stapp for ensuring that the book is an aesthetically pleasing experience for the reader.

Alison Weikel provided me the precious gift of hospitality in her home, welcoming me to stay long enough to produce an early draft of this book. Her company, over morning coffee and during walks in the woods, was a precious bonus. I will never forget how Alison read the entire book in one sitting, taking just a few hours' break to sleep late one night before finishing it the next morning, then insisting in her bleary-eyed stupor that she loved it. I can only hope to be worthy of this level of friendship.

Acknowledgements

The following year, Ivana Adler invited me to stay in her home with three cats and a well-stocked refrigerator, during which time I was able to produce yet another iteration of this book. Ivana has borne wise and loving witness to the goings-on of my household over the course of many years, and her insight has been invaluable to me.

My home-based writing retreat with Renee Sopala may not have produced as many written words as we had hoped, but it proved invaluable in other ways. Procrastinating with her led to my reconnecting with Miriam. It also shed a light on Renee's powerful gift of mediumship, which I hope she will continue to cultivate. Renee adapted my mural of Artemis to become the perfect cover art for this book.

As the book evolved through its various gestational stages, my husband, Paul, has been the greatest constant, rolling with everything, including dramatic changes in my mood after a deep dive into one of my journals. Paul has a cherished dream of burning all my journals once their purpose has been served. Now that the most salient points in each have been poured into this book, perhaps we will hold a bonfire ritual...just as soon as I organize all the ingredients for vegan s'mores.

Thanks to Nancy Covello Murray and our classmate, sci-fi fantasy author Tom Doyle, for helping me envision what it looks like to show up at Harvard as a Joy Professor. I will never forget standing in the Science Center with you, filling up a chalkboard with the collective wisdom of our class in every color of the rainbow, then turning to lead a chorus of *Let it Go!* in my loudest singing voice. Truly the stuff of sci-fi fantasy, but together, we manifested our shared vision into the dimension of Earth. Because we did that, I believe anything is possible.

Other folks not mentioned elsewhere, whose belief in me adds fuel to my engine, include, but are not limited to: the Waits family, the Weikel family, the Jaroszewicz family, the Bakshi family, the Shaeffer-Allen family, the Brochstein family, the Kerchner family, Larry Appleblatt, Jeffrey Chappell, Renee Devigne, Maja Brlecic, Gülsun Gull, Tessa Vermaeren, Kathie Murren, Amy Linker, Kristin Lewis Haight, Jordana Carmel, Laura Beasley, Jane Green, Holly Lennihan, Jade Drakes, Mira Gurarie and Warren Arenstein, Charlotte Schoeneman, Gina Weathersby, Ilene Mitz, Juli Argerakis, Jeff and Amy Jarkow, Deb Zane, Spring Starr Pillow, Amanda Spivack, Kira Starhill, Geneva Watenpaugh, Lacy Barkley, Lisa Zeidman, Lisa Apfelberg, Rachel Stern, Berti Helmick, Barb Howard, Shawn Charton, Bennett Lowenthal, Salvatore Valentino, Sue Feldman, Naomi Kline, Sandey Fields, Claire Newman, my late father-in-law, Edward, my sisters and brothers-in-law, my nieces and nephews, my Reiki clients, my mural clients, my hypnosis clients, every musician in Seven Hills Sinfonietta and Tempo Giusto, members of the Harvard graduating classes of 1987 and 1988, French Woods Festival of the Performing Arts, the Valley Temple, Living and Giving in Takoma Park, and the Dragonfly Hummingbird Joy Posse on Facebook.

I am grateful for my newly discovered cousins, and all they have enabled me to learn about myself and whence I came. This process of discovery began with Trish Collins, who responded with kindness to my SOS message on ancestry.com, connecting me to her sister, Nancy, and our cousin Stephen, who opened his heart and home to me, and connected me to his sister, Elisabeth, who hosted me, Paul, and our cousin Caroline, at her home, and showed me my paternal grandfather's face for the first time, as well as our great grandparents, photographed with extended family at their fiftieth wedding anniversary. Thanks to Keith Clark, my closest relative on 23andMe, who shared ancestry stories and connected me to our cousin Richard, who showed me the beautiful portrait of our great grandmother, Helen Lancaster. Thanks to genealogist Chris Child, who identified my paternal grandfather, and to Scott Steward, who assigned my case to Chris, and to my friend, Gillian Benet Sella, who intuited the *Mayflower* mystery and connected me to Scott. In my next book, I may take a deeper dive into the ensuing discoveries of my true ancestral origins, which I am still processing.

Instigator of Joy
A Prayer for the Reader

I am here to help increase joy on this planet
As a priestess of love and compassion, as a healer,
I must begin by looking inward and healing myself
Healing work is founded upon care, love, and compassion
These three elements are the bedrock of my practice

I pray that by telling you what I have learned
I may show you how to walk your path with joy
I cannot go back in time and apply new wisdom
To soften the sharp edges of my own past
But I can hold my younger self more tenderly
I can step into my future shining more brightly
Having uncovered my light, I can raise it for you
I pray that you will never again feel alone,
That you understand you are cherished and adored
That you become aware of the guidance that surrounds you

16

After a tumultuous journey to midlife and beyond
I now embody how to access joy and self-love
And I am excited to show and tell you all about it
Invite "little you" to read along; my wish is that
You will find gifts to lavish upon yourself

Chapter 1

METAMORPHOSIS

A Real Live Fairy Godmother

In a magical land not so far away, a giant fairy alighted in the garden of a courtyard of an old stone church.

In broad daylight.

With her long legs, she strode past a wooden boat not much taller than herself, and a freight train that reached the height of her shoulder. With a few powerful steps—a giant sack trailing behind her along the ground—she reached a door at the rear corner of the garden.

With a wave of her hand, a small red light on the door went dark, then blinked green, and she floated through the door into the building. The fairy made her way down a dimly lit hall and entered a huge underground room full of children.

Their faces lit up when she entered, their eyes grew wide, their mouths opened, and their voices rang out in a five-syllable chorus:

Hello, Miss Nancy!

They flocked to her then, curious to see what magic lurked inside the enormous bag.

Miss Nancy didn't resemble the grown-ups who spent long days with the children at school. They'd noticed that she was taller than any of the teachers—one of the ways they knew she was not, in fact, a fairy. But they kept quiet about that. For perhaps…she was a fairy godmother.

Miss Nancy dove into the bag of tricks, letting them touch the things she brought to share, without their having to ask permission. She allowed—no, *encouraged*—them to be messy, and never told them their way of being creative was wrong. She gave them big piles of colorful pom-poms, bottles of sticky drippy glue, and cans of fluffy white shaving cream. And she sprinkled glitter all over their artful projects (even though glitter was a microplastic and therefore banned from the school). *Shhhhhh.*

But these weren't the only reasons the children expected Miss Nancy might be a fairy godmother: her hair always changed color from one visit to the next, and she wore clothes unlike any they had ever known a grown-up to wear.

On this particular summer day, Miss Nancy appeared in their classroom sporting lavender-, silver-, and rose-colored hair, fastened with white silk daisies into two pigtails! She wore a pale pink A-line dress embroidered with flowering vines and butterflies of every color—like the ones you would find in an enchanted garden.

Miss Nancy dug down deep in the big, dark, mysterious bag and began to pull out…plastic bottles?

"I found all of these in the park this weekend," she explained. "Some were thrown away, and others were left on the ground. But today," she announced, "we are going to transform them into a beautiful chandelier, which we will hang from the ceiling of this room." The children were wide-eyed as she distributed paint, brushes, and scissors and showed each of them how to perform the requisite magic, and they all passed a happy hour working to make it so.

When the magic chandelier was complete, Miss Nancy stood on a chair, and, reaching overhead with her extra-long arms, attached each of the children's colorful artworks to the wire clothing hangers she had hooked into the basement's tiled ceiling. She hugged the smallest children and high-fived the older ones, congratulating them all for making their classroom so beautiful and unique. As the children gazed up at the chandelier, marveling at their creation, Miss Nancy vanished into thin air.

Returning home from her time with the children, Miss Nancy was spotted by one of her neighbors on the sidewalk in front of her home. The woman complimented her creative outfit and asked if she could share a secret.

"Why, most certainly," Miss Nancy said, leaning in, assuring the woman she would keep the information confidential.

"Well, the fact is," murmured the woman, "you remind me of a tall Tinker Bell."

Miss Nancy grinned from ear to ear. This was very valuable information indeed.

"Perfect," Miss Nancy replied, "that's what I was going for."

"Oh good," the neighbor said. "Well…you're nailing it."

I have a small confession to make.

I am Miss Nancy.

Yes, yes, yes…creator of found-object chandeliers, wearer of fanciful frocks and unicorn locks, resident of a rainbow cottage.

I am all those things.

But I wasn't always.

In fact, I was quite like the Tinker Bell who got shut up in a tiny lantern, captured and held against her will—her magical powers extinguished, left to die alone…until the audience affirms its belief in fairies by clapping their hands and bringing her magical being back to life.

My dear reader, clap your hands.

For this is the story of a metamorphosis—my journey from a captive, caterpillar-like girl to a full-blown fairy godmother—hair and clothes and pixie dust and all.

You see, I had to become my own fairy godmother to get where I got.

And this is my story.

A Magic Potion for Accessing Joy

If I were *your* fairy godmother, here's what I'd whisper in your ear:

What did "little you" most love to do?

What would you do to amuse yourself before you were introduced to those dark knights: fear and limitations? Before you learned to be ashamed, to follow the rules and dial it down?

Before your parents and teachers and society taught you what you ought *not* to do and be?

Remember who you were before you were shown what was

wrong with you—before you were told what special part of yourself you had to suppress or hide, before you were scolded to stop doing or stop being.

Dig down deep and figure that out, without further delay.

Go ahead. Do it now. I'll be here waiting, magic wand poised.

If you feel tingles all over your body, you've succeeded.

Now: feel yourself anointed with fairy dust and *resume*— start doing it again, start being the real you, *right away*, because life is too short *not* to.

I know. Because that's how I transformed from a slow-crawling caterpillar into a free-flying *Instigator of Joy*.

Instigator of Joy

I have not always been an instigator of joy. Well, I was *born* to be, and tried to be a living breathing agent of joy, but by the time I left home at sixteen, my spirit had been crushed under the heels of propriety and expectation. Confused by messages suggesting that my regular self was not good enough (in spite of the lyrics on my well-loved Mister Rogers records), I tried to be what my parents asked me to be instead. I learned to dim my light, silence myself, put others' needs ahead of my own, and *cut myself off from joy*. I stashed my fondest dreams away, went off to Harvard at sixteen, married at twenty-three, and became a mother at twenty-seven. Spirit appropriately stowed. I went from riches to rags (or some people's version of it, anyway), and kept myself small...until one day, I threw off all the "shoulds" that had been threatening to break me, like a proverbial camel under a load of straw, and I got down to reclaiming my full, true authentic self. It was a steep and rocky road, but I resurrected my spirit and made it through the dark night to shine my light, dance in the rain, sing out loud, and paint the rainbow.

The Birth of the Joy Lab

I came out as a Joy Professor at my thirty-fifth college reunion (Class of 1987) in a science classroom within the hallowed halls of Harvard University—though my history as a Harvard student was anything *but* joyful.

On the first Friday morning of June 2022, I awakened in a dormitory bed, full of excitement and anticipation—in the very place I had struggled with shame, self-loathing, insecurity, and loneliness as a co-ed. I'd come a long way since my parents controlled every facet of my life—sending me to Harvard because they believed it was my best chance at landing an appropriate husband, and putting me on prescription medication to stunt my growth.

Ten years earlier, I'd attended our twenty-fifth reunion with trepidation—concerned the familiar faces and places would revive that old trauma from my college days. But instead of hurtling myself back in time to a void of misery, I wound up making new friends and having a wonderful time.

Then, at our thirtieth reunion, I met Nancy Covello Murray. Nancy and I had a few friends in common during college, but our paths never really crossed. We lived at opposite ends of campus. She studied economics while I drifted from fine arts to English literature. Nancy played flute in the marching band and managed the men's swim team. I played violin in a student-run chamber orchestra, hung out at Hillel and the Hasty Pudding Clubhouse, and often traveled to MIT on Wednesday evenings for Israeli folk-dancing classes. But as the years went by and the twentieth century wound to an end, Nancy and I each pivoted, and our paths began to converge. She walked away from a career in accounting and became a yoga teacher. Eight years after college, in 1996, I left my first marriage and the legal profession in one fell swoop—to pursue my true calling as an artist and a healer.

It wasn't that we hadn't found success within our original professions—Nancy excelled as a certified public accountant, and I had great potential as a lawyer. But our souls longed to break free of their conventional restraints and embark upon our spiritual journeys. Living 800 miles apart, without any awareness of one another's existence, we had both become healers and teachers—working with individual clients and creating retreats and workshops where we guided people toward greater peace, self-love, and joy. There, at our thirty-fifth reunion, five years after finally meeting, Nancy and I were poised to share our unique talents with our Harvard classmates as experts in connecting with joy.

Struck by the momentousness of the occasion while packing for that thirty-fifth reunion, I decided to bring a long, colorful patchwork robe I'd purchased years earlier, during a memoir-writing workshop at Antioch College. When I'd modeled the robe for my fellow workshop attendees, they'd exclaimed with delight—predicting I would wear it on *Oprah* to promote my memoir. That manuscript went into a drawer, so Oprah never heard about it. But now, wearing the Nepalese robe for the debut of our Joy Lab felt right, and meaningful: the garment had merely been waiting for me to fill it—to stand in my power, ready to share my wisdom with the world.

Our Joy Lab was an enormous success. We had curated a magical concoction of essential oils, film score melodies, soap bubbles, beach balls, colorful hair wax and face paint, crayons, stickers, and a big bag full of musical instruments designed for preschoolers—all to encourage our fifty-something classmates to excavate and discard inhibiting thought patterns and to embrace and celebrate their inner children.

After we sprang a pop quiz on them and collected the bluebooks, we invited people to call out their joy triggers as they swatted at colorful beach balls sailing around the room. Next, we invited them to call out their impediments to joy. As I turned to the chalkboard to make a mural out of the common obstacles to joy people encounter, something magical happened—the obstacles floated through the air to me as I stood at the front of the room and each took shape as part of a colorful word cloud I was creating on the chalkboard. Then, a boy with whom I once race-walked across the yard to see *Splash*, a movie about a mermaid, shared what it was like to find himself at middle age, consumed by bitterness and regret ever since his divorce. Chalk still in hand, I whipped around to face him and without hesitation, I responded from the most secret, saddest parts of my past. It was as if our last conversation had taken place only yesterday, instead of almost forty years ago. It was as if—instead of dozens of attentive classmates—no one but the two of us were in the room. It was a stunning moment of group intimacy, and it encouraged others to speak their truth openly too.

Even before we received feedback about the lab's success—how it helped people release old ways of thinking and open themselves to new possibilities, before we returned home and learned that our session had altered the course of some of our classmates' lives—Nancy and I felt exhilarated. Our Joy Lab had exceeded our expectations. Our hearts were full as we collected crayons and castanets, and cleared the space for the next alumni panel. For the next two days, we were greeted all over campus with cries of "Hey, Joy Lady!" and heard people exclaim "I wanna dance with joy!" as they approached us on the dance floor. At the closing brunch, so many classmates thanked us for transforming the weekend—our little experiment had created a ripple effect that imbued the entire reunion with pure, sweet, exhilarating joy.

Are you feeling those tingles again? I know I was. Pleased with our accomplishment, I sent my mother a photo of me writing on a chalkboard in a Harvard classroom, along with the note "We did it!"

I blinked at my iPhone in dismay. Instead of returning her congratulations, I received a seven-word reply from my dear mother: "What is that thing on your back?"

I did a double take—zooming in on the photo to see what it was—and realized she was criticizing my colorful Nepalese robe. Then I remembered something I learned in therapy: "Happy adults do not seek validation from their children or their parents." A lesson I had been learning, over and over, time and again. But I wasn't about to let anything prevent me from celebrating my accomplishment and the pleasure it brought me. Not this time.

We'd all done a lot of living since graduation—twice as much as we had before starting college. Most of our classmates launched themselves out of Harvard Yard in 1987 hoping to achieve the great success bequeathed upon us by our Ivy League degrees—through impressive job titles, lucrative salaries, or powerful positions in our professional and social circles. Indeed, many of us had gone on to sit on the boards of major corporations, build vast fortunes, serve on presidential cabinets, and lead major universities. Others were disappointed when we didn't achieve the goals to which we had once aspired.

Just five years ago at the thirty-year reunion, as we navigated the hump of turning fifty, many (including myself) were wrestling with the midlife spiritual trifecta: "Who am I? Why am I alive? What shall I do with the rest of my time on this earth?"

While we were similar in many ways, my objectives when I first arrived at Harvard were different from what I imagined most of my classmates' had been. At age twelve, I had been an accomplished violinist with professional aspirations, already navigating my freshman year of high school, when I was pulled out of class for an impromptu meeting with my guidance counselor and my mother. Once I took a seat in the guidance office, I was admonished that I had better get my grades up to reflect my true abilities. When I got home, my mother explained the reason this was so important was that I would have serious difficulty finding a husband if I did not get into Wellesley or Harvard. Among the Harvard male student population, Mommy advised, I would have the best chance of meeting a qualified Jewish man, able to deal with all of me, which was quite a lot. Harvard summer school was where my mother—then a lanky, twenty-two-year-old dance instructor—had met the tall, handsome, athletic, ostensibly Jewish medical resident who became my father—and thus was spared the looming prospect of spinsterhood.

As the next segment of a multi-pronged strategy to "fix me up" for success, I was prescribed a growth-stunting medication to prevent me from becoming unmarriageably tall. It also kept me thin enough to spend my thirteen-year-old year of Saturdays modeling at Saks Fifth Avenue (more about that later). Seeking my parents' approval, I did as I was told. My entire life was prescribed: where I went, with whom, what I did, and what I put in my mouth.

At sixteen, I surrendered my orange plastic bottle of amphetamines, along with my dreams of Juilliard training, and found myself stranded on the Harvard campus, where my father had studied more than three decades earlier. Like so many of my classmates, I was at Harvard to fulfill my parents' dreams for me, eager to make them proud, desperate to earn their love.

Both of my parents phoned my freshman dorm often—my father advising me what classes to take and which clubs to join, my mother checking in every Friday to ask why I still didn't have a date. And while she hoped I was watching my weight and not overserving myself at the buffet, she never bothered to warn me about the inevitable effects of going off my medication.

As I turned seventeen, my newly rediscovered appetite developed a routine that included Sunday night study breaks at our proctors' suite (featuring cookies), rehearsing with the Bach Society Orchestra on Monday nights (more cookies), playing violin in the Gilbert and Sullivan pit orchestra (ice cream afterwards), and availing itself every Thursday of the open bar at the Hasty Pudding Social Club (gin and tonics, olives, crackers with brie, mixed nuts)—which also organized black-tie events on weekends for every conceivable occasion, many invented merely as another excuse to dress up, eat, drink, and dance.

My resurrected appetite helped me pack many a pound onto my tall, lean frame during my first two months away from home, but at a certain point, I declared war on it by drastically restricting my eating, and I managed to lose most of the weight. By the time I returned home for Thanksgiving break, one week after my birthday, I was only seven pounds heavier than when I had left.

My mother's reaction was brutal. She gaped at me like a goldfish as I removed my coat, finally finding her words.

"Oh my God, Nancy! What's happened to you? You've blown up! You look just like Cousin Florence!"

I wanted to tell her that what happened to me was that I had been reunited with my dormant appetite, given unfettered access to rich food, and allowed my seventeen-year-old body to soften into a more adult shape. Specifically, I had sprouted breasts—something no one had apparently anticipated, since my mother and her sister together *might* have had just enough soft tissue to fill an A-cup. Their own mother's breasts had been surgically removed, in a full-frontal assault on the cancer that threatened her life well before I was born. My mother's kind, affectionate, older cousin—Florence, whom I now apparently resembled—was unacceptably zaftig; in my mother's opinion, she took up entirely too much space.

Soon after that visit home, I became bulimic, and by the end of freshman year, I could have written a paper on the pros and cons of each brand of laxative sold at Store 24 in Harvard Square. I learned the location of every public bathroom in and around Harvard Yard, including the basement of the Science Center, where I now found myself, almost forty years later—not suffering from explosive diarrhea and self-loathing, but inflating beach balls, sorting decorative stickers, and unwrapping sidewalk chalk—getting ready to help my classmates access joy and let their inner children roam free.

At eighteen, I got myself kicked out of college for plagiarizing a homework assignment in my Shakespeare class. After receiving the news, I held court in the Cabot House dining hall for a few days, eating ice cream from a bottomless bowl and sharing my woes with anyone curious to know why I was wearing pajamas. Some of the students were shocked to learn there could be such a harsh penalty for a first offense. Others were amazed I hadn't known my section leader, Elizabeth Goodenough, was notorious for being the plagiarism exterminator. Soon, I would be banished from campus—isolated from my friends, classes, activities, and any sense of purpose—to endure the most challenging year of my young life, living with parents who let me know each and every day how horribly disappointed they were in me.

Part of my family's fabricated grandiosity stemmed from a legend that none of us required mental health services; they were for other people. For months, I was forbidden from seeing any sort of mental health professional or telling anyone why I was home from school. As my shame grew, my weight skyrocketed. I had no access to a scale at home, so I don't know what my top weight was, but on the day I got busted, I had been able to throw myself to the floor for a quick pelvic tilt—thus zipping myself into a size-eight pair of designer jeans—and a few months later, I had expanded past ladies' clothing sizes ten and twelve until I was unable to sit down in a size fourteen skirt without blowing the fastener off the waist band. I only resumed normal eating and returned to a healthy weight after seeking the help of a group of doctors at Columbia University who advertised in the Yellow Pages. These kind men let me tell them what I had done to get kicked out of Harvard, and the compassionate way they listened to my story let me know how normal this sort of thing was.

From that day on, I no longer needed to "eat my feelings," because telling my story obliterated my shame. For decades afterward, I would draw upon the wisdom I acquired during that difficult year to offer support to friends and clients alike—anyone who confided that they felt they'd disappointed their parents, or themselves. Over the years, I have learned that as a species, we are suffering from an epidemic deficit of self-compassion. And sharing our stories is powerful healing for what ails us.

At the thirty-fifth reunion of Harvard's Class of 1987, Nancy and I faced a room full of folks who might make such a confession. Some still remembered me from the wintry week back in the eighties when I chose not to shower or get dressed, the week I gained eight pounds eating nothing but ice cream. They marveled at the person I'd become, and they were curious to know my story.

With this book, I am making good on my promise to share that story, and I am also following orders, repeated over the course of my twenty-five-year relationship with a gifted psychic named Miriam: "Write what you know, because it will help someone."

The rest of this book describes the arc of my path to becoming a Real Live Fairy Godmother, an Instigator of Joy—both how I cut myself off from joy and how I found my way back. I pray that the telling of my journey will help you instigate joy, for yourself and for others.

Phoenix Rising

Do not think of me as having been born from a flower,

emerging to gradually unfurl my wings

and fly off to sprinkle fairy dust on the heads of mortals.

Rather, think of me as being born from fire,

rising like a Phoenix,

nourished from the ashes of destruction to feed the world.

I may have been born to channel joy,

but I stumbled many times before finding my footing

and becoming able to follow my true path, as you are invited to see.

My So-Called Charmed Life

Many people believe I am living a charmed life, and if that is true, I attribute much of it to my willingness to receive guidance from the dedicated team of loving protectors in spirit who watch over me and nudge me toward being my best, happiest, most generous and loving self. They help me function as a channel of love—because that is what I signed up to be in this life, and they won't let anything stand in my way. At least, not for long. When I stumble, when I lose my footing, they help me pick myself up and get back on track. My work is to remember that all the help I need is available to me. To receive it, to benefit from it, I must get still and quiet, listen, and follow the promptings I receive.

Something I simultaneously love and hate about life is that we can never see more than one step ahead on our path; and yet we try to, don't we? Like walking through a dense fog, we can perceive only the next step as it appears before us, and the best we can do is open our hearts and minds (and wings), trusting that we are well guided, and follow the promptings of our soul as we go along.

Who Am I To Be?

My childhood was spent trying to earn approval from stern, taciturn parents—a roller coaster ride of expectation and failure, hope and despair. My mother was capricious, with an emotional dial vacillating between cooing sweetness and screaming rage, with intermittent doses of haughty criticism; my father could be sardonic, withholding, even downright cruel. Pitted against my little sister, I lived in hope of earning a slice of what I was taught to perceive as a finite love pie. I would have done almost anything to be the good girl. As it was clear that only one of us (at most) could be in my parents' good graces, my efforts to earn their love (and dessert) often included betraying my little sister. I tried in vain to follow all the many rules, much as a fairytale princess must do, so that she can marry in a way that makes everyone else happy, so she may live out her days in safety and security—and not burden or humiliate her family. This is what I was taught to aspire to.

It may have seemed, to an outsider—because I was attractive and well dressed, lived in a big house on the water, was driven to school in a fancy car and always returned to classes after winter vacation with a tan—as if I had it all. But I sought approval and praise to counteract the dichotomy of my parents' estimation that I was both not enough and too much. Rather than empower me with strategies, my mother castigated me for my forgetfulness, blamed me for not being better organized or careful enough with my belongings, for not keeping quiet, or keeping my hands and clothing clean, for not keeping my hair free of tangles, or taking enough pride in my appearance. It was a long list.

When I was called downstairs to the kitchen every evening to section the grapefruit halves and set the table for dinner, I typically entered the room with my head down, hair hanging loose, trying to hide my face, but my mother invariably noticed spots of blood blooming on my cheeks—and rather than recognize this as *dermatillomania*, or excoriation disorder (a mental health condition requiring professional treatment), I was scolded for my failure to properly appreciate and care for the perfect skin with which I had been blessed. As I grew older, Mommy told me I wouldn't be able to support myself; I would need a husband to enjoy a decent quality of life. At the same time, my oversized appearance and outsized personality were deemed intimidating and overwhelming; I would need to cultivate modesty, forbearance, and greater self-control.

And Daddy warned me when I was young that I would follow in his footsteps in becoming one of the world's great underachievers. By all accounts, he was a busy, successful surgeon; I was never sure why he thought so little of his accomplishments. Perhaps they weren't enough to fill the mysterious emptiness inside him—an insight that escaped me until almost a decade after his demise.

As a hardworking doctor, Daddy was less involved in parenting, day to day, than Mommy, but when he returned from the hospital at night—if she was playing the piano in the living room—he would sometimes feel inspired to contribute to my development. Daddy would come upstairs and enter my darkened bedroom, the door to which was always kept open (house rules). If I was already asleep and remained so, I'd be regaled the next day at dinner with Daddy's story about the absurd response I gave to a question he posed while I slept. Other times, though, I'd be lying there in my bed on the verge of sleep, and Daddy would stand at my bedside, encircle his left wrist with his right thumb and fingers and announce: "It's time for The Hand. Ready?"

Regardless of my answer, he would curve the fingers of his

left hand to form a claw, then, guiding it with his right hand, slowly lower it toward my abdomen while repeating one word, softly but sternly: "Control." All I wanted was his approval. Even during this stressful, vaguely disturbing ritual, I was grateful for the attention and hoped each time that I would pass muster. If I laughed or spoke, wriggled or squirmed, I would be admonished. Daddy would then raise "The Hand" even higher and begin again. In this manner, I was trained to lie still and suppress my instinct to respond or react in any way to the anticipation of being touched.

The Hand visits began sometime before I was six—I know, because I distinctly remember that the random bedtime questions morphed into my being quizzed (both awake and asleep) on my multiplication tables, which I was assigned to memorize near the beginning of third grade, some weeks before my seventh birthday.

This mysterious practice trained me to become silent and submissive, and not react to being touched, whether said touching was done by a stranger rubbing his erection against my teenage ass while we stood pressed together on a crowded New York City subway, or by a guy I was dating. It is the reason my boyfriends were confused when they would try to make out with me. My words and actions while standing or sitting indicated willingness, even eagerness to engage. But once in a horizontal position, my body would revert to the immobilized silent state I had been trained to adopt in my childhood bed. The man who would become my first husband tried to make a joke of it by saying I seemed to be impersonating a log, albeit a beautiful one, but he didn't know what to make of my log-like behavior and I didn't know what to tell him.

It would take quite a bit of reprogramming work for me to unlearn this lesson, but I never understood why I had to endure these experiences. Why did my father want to train me to be silent and submissive? Did he believe I would need to behave this way to please a man? After Daddy died, and it was time to choose what words were to be engraved on his headstone, my mother told me she had selected the phrase "Loving and Loved"; then she said she wanted to check with me about it. Did I agree that this was the best thing to say about him? I was silent for a moment, and I was grateful we were on the phone, that I didn't have to moderate my facial expression. Noting my hesitation, she told me that everything Daddy did, he had done to try to prepare me for a cold, cruel world, because that was what his uncle Nat had done for him. That was the reason, she said, that he had always been so hard on me. I expect that I will never really know why Daddy trained me not to react to The Hand, but I must believe he meant well.

When we were little, Daddy took wonderful photographs of my sister and me, and later in life, his five grandchildren became his favorite subjects. I suppose I felt the most love from my father when I saw myself in his pictures, the way he'd seen me through his camera lens: picture perfect. He never gave compliments, he was not affectionate, nor did he ever say "I love you"—until I trained him to do so as a teenager when I worked part-time in his medical office. I would tell him I loved him in front of other people as if it were natural and commonplace—

pushing through the awkwardness. He would respond by echoing the phrase. And that was what it sounded like—an echo, hollow and imitative. In this way, I was able to achieve some small part of what I longed to have with my father.

My mother, while she took pride in having produced a child who was more intelligent, attractive, charming, and talented than she was, advised me from adolescence onward that I was "too much." Instead of a true feeling of emotional connection, Mommy offered me a poor substitute for closeness when she instructed me to keep secrets from my father—whether that was hiding the packages of new clothes from our shopping trips to Loehmann's or urging me to remove any trace of the makeup that briefly transformed my freckled face during my Saturday mornings modeling at Saks. She also said things to alienate me from my father in a variety of ways—such as when she confided, upon learning I had qualified for a national merit scholarship—that Daddy would be surprised to learn I was quite so intelligent, but she was not at all surprised. My mother seemed somehow jealous of me, which was confusing and hurtful. I sought her approval and longed for her affection, but the emotional connection was never there.

My parents each projected their own feelings of inadequacy, insecurity, and scarcity onto their two children. Of course, I was too young to understand the family dynamics as I was growing up. My parents each had a narcissistic view of me, as an extension of themselves—a reflection of their worth as parents and as people, such that they were unable to see me as a distinct individual, much less validate or celebrate my unique gifts. My mother would have found it gratifying if I married an ambassador or perhaps a captain of industry. My father would have liked to mentor me in becoming a surgeon or see me become the chief executive of a major corporation. But none of those things was my calling.

Both my parents were disappointed by what they saw as my choice not to follow the paths they envisioned for me. I would need to discover my distinct gifts and learn to value them on my own.

In Judaism, the faith tradition in which I was raised, there is a signature theme conveyed by the Hebrew phrase *Tikkun Olam*. As Jews, we are taught that the world was created for us to improve upon—that it is our duty to contribute in some way to the common good. We must each do something in the world that will not only fix its imperfections, but make it better in a way that only we, as individuals, can fashion. Each of us is born with a unique gift—our own way to repair or improve the unfinished creation of the world, and it is up to each of us to discover the answers to the questions: Who am I to be? What is mine to do?

As we seek to discover these answers, we experience varying degrees of ease and difficulty in our search. Our unique gift may be hidden in plain sight; it often turns out to be that which we love to do as soon as we stumble upon it, yet it is not always recognized as such. Actors and astronauts alike report, in interviews and award acceptance speeches, that they knew their calling at a young age; there was nothing else they ever wanted to do with their lives. Others, including many artists, take a more circuitous route to self-discovery—trying this, that, and the other thing until they wend their way to their life's work. Still others say they are initiated into their highest calling by the transformative fires of life.

What I have learned as a member of this latter group is that when life seems broken, we need not try to transcend or ignore the pain, trauma, and loss. Rather, we should embrace all the brokenness, turmoil, and change. We should nourish ourselves upon the ashes of destruction and rise, like the phoenix, ready to soar in strength and beauty, poised to fly high. We can grow from our catastrophes and find we are strengthened by them, ready to feed the world.

Chapter 2
JUVENESCENCE | RAPUNZEL

Early Childhood | Bedtime Stories

When I was very small, my mother read to me every night, from one of five hardcover anthologies: *The Lore of the Old Testament* (1966), *D'Aulaires' Book of Greek Myths*, *Classic Fairy Tales*, *The Adventures of K'Tonton* (a 1930s Jewish Tom Thumb that blends fairy tales with Jewish values), and a 1955 edition of *The Illustrated Treasury of Children's Literature*. By the age of five, impatient with my mother's pace, I began reading these stories to myself before drifting off to sleep each evening, thus absorbing the patriarchal messaging that a girl must shrink herself and follow society's rules to be considered worthy of love and marriage, safety and security.

I would later devote my college thesis to examining how classic fairy tales promote the idea of love as a scarce, precious resource—something to be earned through tremendous effort. A fairy tale protagonist must overcome obstacles, hindrances, and trials to win love, wealth, and power. In order to be worthy of marriage, the hero must be daring, clever, brave, and kind. The girl is an object to be won—a prize whose beauty comes with a bundle of wealth, status, and power that attaches to the suitor through marriage. To be worthy of such valiant pursuit, a princess must be beautiful, small, silent, subservient, virginal, and demure—kept securely under lock and key, preferably in a castle or a high tower, ideally falling somewhere on the consciousness spectrum between asleep (Aurora, Briar Rose, Sleeping Beauty) and resembling a corpse (Snow White).

Greek myths present the female paradigm with an equally fervent but varied misogyny. To have value, a Greek girl must be virginal, youthful, and beautiful—but she is never to be trusted. Men are cursed with the need to produce heirs from a creature whose seductive beauty conceals her unreliability, her greediness, her inherent uselessness. We find evidence of this type of misogyny in a poem by Semonides, written in the seventh century BC. In the poem, Zeus is described as having created a catalog of ten types of wives, based upon animals, with corresponding stereotypes to address the negative impact women can have upon men through uncontrollable sexual desire, continuously changing moods, and a penchant for nagging. Women's charms are suspect; they are a necessary evil. The only type of woman considered capable of making a good wife is rare indeed, and modeled after the chaste, industrious bee.

In Judaism, there is a traditional weekly blessing of a wife, by her husband, taken from a poem called "Woman of Valor" ("Eishet Chayil" in Hebrew), found in Proverbs 31:10. In it, the ideal woman is praised as a wife who works ceaselessly, rising before dawn to feed her family and working by lamplight well into the night. She makes everything her household needs—

clothing, food, warm blankets. She even produces a surplus, which she sells at a profit so that she may share her earnings with the poor. This virtuous woman eschews grace and beauty; she speaks wisdom and fears the Lord.

No matter from which of these cultures we might wish to derive a feminine ideal (or not), virtuous women are consistently portrayed as modest, hardworking, well-behaved wives who follow all the rules. Selflessness is extolled as the greatest virtue of all. Rebecca of the Torah is praised for seeing a stranger at the well and giving water to the old man and his animals before taking care of her own needs. The man is a servant to Abraham, and her kindness qualifies her to marry Isaac and become a matriarch of the Jewish people. As a young girl, I was encouraged to dress up as Rebecca for the Jewish festival of *Purim* and attend a costume carnival at our temple while balancing on my shoulder the drawing of a pitcher of water my mother had made and cut out from shirt cardboard. Rebecca is not a character in the story traditionally told at *Purim*, but more than any character in the Book of Esther, Rebecca—the Jewish paradigm of putting others' needs before one's own—is whom my mother most wanted me to emulate.

My parents—especially my mother—should not have been surprised, then, much less dismayed or enraged, when I came home from Montessori school at age four without any of the six shiny brass buttons that had adorned my new Florence Eiseman plaid wool jumper earlier in the day. My friend and classmate, Lillian, had admired the buttons and asked if she could have them. I felt no attachment, and they served no practical purpose, so I gave Lillian permission to remove the buttons and stood patiently while she pulled them, one at a time, from my dress. My father turned the incident into a euphemism and right up until the last season of his life, he would caution me not to give away my buttons.

Whenever I tell my mother I have a new client or job, she asks in a certain tone whether I'm being paid. Whether she fears I lack self-respect, knows I have a history of being charitable, is aware that artists are often asked to work for free, or suspects my work lacks value, I can't be sure. But it is an unpleasant reminder of the anger she expressed when I came home from Montessori with loose threads dangling from the front of my dress at each of the spots where six shiny buttons had been when she sent me off to school that morning.

As for the impact of *The Illustrated Treasury of Children's Literature*, I was stunned to revisit the first poems in this book recently and recognize the fertile seeds of shame that had been planted in my mind by a nursery rhyme. The pain I have experienced from struggling to keep track of my personal possessions—the pattern of being rewarded for good behavior with dessert as a substitute for love—all of it came flooding back as I scanned page four: the drawing featuring three little kittens who are alternately good or naughty—which characterization determines who shall or shall not receive pie from their mother, depending on whether they manage to keep track of their mittens. The finite love pie writ small. I have carried this verse with me all my life.

The idea, held by much of Harvard's English Department when I was a student there, that children's literature was not worthy of serious academic inquiry is patently absurd. It's the stuff that fills our imagination; it shapes our very psyche.

Starting School

As noted in my mother's handwriting below my photograph in the blue leather photo album, embossed on the cover with the words "Our Girls," I know that I began student life at the age of two years and ten months. More than half a century later, I can see that I looked like a living doll—standing outside the red-and-yellow house with my big brown eyes and sweet smile, my hair combed into a neat side part. I'm wearing a white blouse and navy-blue skirt, both trimmed with red rickrack. White knee socks cover the bottom half of my long, sturdy legs, and saddle shoes adorn my feet.

My teachers adored me—my quick mind, warm smile, my eagerness to please—and I loved being dropped off early at Little Flower Montessori, so I might have time alone with my favorite teacher, Miss Queenie, who lived upstairs, above the classrooms. Miss Queenie was from India, and she came down to teach us every day wearing a beautiful silk *sari*. When I was lucky, I would arrive in time to go upstairs and see her apply a *bhindi*, a small perfect circle between her brows, using one of the many-colored powders inside her special compact. Being welcomed into Miss Queenie's private space made me feel special and loved; the warmth of being included in her moments of personal preparation meant the world to me—the kinds of moments that seemed so natural, yet I somehow never experienced with my mother.

Before I was big enough to attend school, I loved to read books and listen to records. I adored playing with my slightly bossy five-year-old friend, Alison, who lived next door. But I may have loved drawing and coloring more than anything in the world. I would sit at the kitchen table and carefully crayon patterns of pink and purple—or yellow, green, and orange—on the white paper my mother provided. One day, when I was almost three, Mommy delighted me by complimenting my designs, saying they would make wonderful wallpaper. She said we should show them to Ruth, the decorator who was coming to help design my bedroom. My heart leapt at the praise; feeling excited and inspired, I continued drawing until I had amassed a thick stack of designs.

The day of the meeting, I headed upstairs for my nap, filled with happy anticipation of presenting my artwork to Ruth, whom I trusted would select the best design and take charge of having it applied to the walls of my bedroom. I was bewildered when I awoke from my nap, got out of bed, and descended the stairs to the kitchen, only to find the design meeting well underway—without me. When I politely reminded Mommy about the designs I had created to give to Ruth for my walls, the two adults laughed.

I was stricken with betrayal. My colorful crayon drawings were never seen or mentioned again.

I realized that Mommy had lied to me. Soon, I learned that

a misguided color scheme of yellow and white—which the two women considered cheerful—had been chosen for my bedroom without my input. My bedroom walls and doors would be covered with a paper patterned in yellow-and-white gingham, overlaid with a glossy white grapevine silhouette. Rather than granting any respite from the checkered monotony, my wide front window, with its oblique view of the bay—even the smaller one over the driveway—would be subsumed in a sea of yellow and white, covered with curtains and valances sewn from matching fabric and trimmed with a white eyelet ruffle. Wall-to-wall yellow shag carpeting would cover the wooden subfloor. My headboard and footboard would be covered in shiny white vinyl trimmed in bright yellow piping, and a yellow-and-white metal light fixture would hang from the ceiling above my wall-papered closet doors. Fifteen years later, I would read Charlotte Perkins Gilman's indictment of Victorian patriarchy, *The Yellow Wallpaper*, with a horrified sense of recognition.

At night, I would lie in my custom bed—its mattress both extra-long and extra-narrow, for aesthetic reasons—with my face lined up beside a particular part of the glossy white grapevine that terrified me. I saw in the silhouette of the leaves and fruit what appeared to be a witch on a broomstick. Once seen, I could not unsee it. I would shut my eyes tightly and try to think about the story I had read before bedtime, so as not to give attention or power to the witch next to my head. I also did my best to ignore the monsters that may or may not have been hiding in my closet. I believed none of these creatures would harm me unless they knew I was aware of them.

I bring the tenderness of this memory with me to every mural I design for a child's bedroom, bathroom, or playroom; if the child's active participation in the meeting is not possible, I insist on obtaining their consent to my design before I begin painting. Unless they are one of those rare children lucky enough to have a treehouse in the backyard, or perhaps a clubhouse over the garage, there is typically no space other than their bedroom where a child can hope to have any sense of dominion. My painting business is called Magic Wand Murals, because magic is what happens when you utter words, wave a wand, and something transforms. It is my job to listen to the words my clients speak, wield my paintbrush as their personal magic wand, and transform surfaces or spaces in a way they find gratifying. I love that one of my earliest memories inspired me to turn the experience on its head and make a mission of creating magical, personal spaces for children three decades running. From Connecticut to Kentucky, I have had the privilege of showing children of all ages that they are powerful. I help them perform magic.

Where Did I Come From?

As a toddler, out in the world with Mommy, I was fascinated to overhear people asking if I had been adopted. My mother was tennis-tournament slim, a Virginia Wade look-alike, but taller—with dark brown eyes and brown curly hair. Her college roommate had grown up in Alabama and never known a Jew before; when they first met, she had asked if she might see the horns she imagined were hidden among my mother's dark curls. My own hair was auburn with a glint of gold, as fine as silk, with a slight wave. Along with my robust toddler body and apple-cheeked face, my hair was an object of curiosity among the other parents. As I squatted near other children, coaxing fistfuls of sand through a series of brightly colored plastic objects in the sandbox, the mothers sat on the benches of Massapequa's playgrounds, cataloguing what their children ate and drank, comparing when we had taken our first steps, spoken our first sentences, or any other developmental milestones that seemed worth noting. The other mothers were amazed by my height and weight—both off the growth chart—and even more so when my mother revealed that her almost-three-year-old daughter was already reading books.

Mommy thought I was too young to pay attention to these conversations—or to remember them—but I would hear her brag to my father at the end of the day about how the other mothers wanted all the details of my diet, how they demanded to know what vitamins she gave me to make me so tall and sturdy. Mommy never repeated the other question she fielded, about whether I had been adopted, to which she would reply "Of course not!"—as if her interlocutor must be confused or crazy. Years later, I would hear her rebuff the same inquiry at Beth Sholom, the synagogue our family joined in Amityville. The reason for the query would remain a mystery for many years.

My Montessori report card described me the previous year as "a brilliant child who could achieve even more if she were not so easily drawn into socializing with other children." I had been learning in three languages: reciting French poetry, singing songs in Spanish, and writing all my letters in upper and lowercase, even mastering a childish-looking cursive. I could count into the hundreds, work the abacus to perform basic arithmetical functions, and was able to draw all my geometric shapes, including the trapezoid and rhombus. It never occurred to my teachers that my love of connecting with others might be my most special gift of all. In my mind, I was behaving admirably—I wasn't merely socializing, but rather helping and encouraging my friends in their work, after I had completed my own.

My teachers paid attention to me; they observed me closely. They noticed the way I took care of everyone around me, and they documented how my attention was carefully divided between the people sharing space with me and my assigned work. They judged what they saw with eyes and minds poisoned by the timeworn values of school and society. It would take many years for me to free myself from these values, to stop judging myself by the same rubric, and to appreciate the rare gift I have to offer.

Because of my memory, reading fluency, and poise, I was given the lead role in the school's play about personal hygiene—I played the Chairman of the Board—tasked with explaining the importance of brushing one's teeth and washing one's hands. I took great pride in my role, and unfortunately this led to my First Great Public Mortification. At the end of the performance, which was attended by the majority of our parents, the principal gave a congratulatory speech. He then placed into my arms a dozen long-stemmed red roses, in a moment similar to what I had seen happen onstage with prima ballerinas at the New York City Ballet and to Dame Joan Sutherland at the Metropolitan Opera House.

I was so giddy with delight after the performance, I mistook the bouquet as a tribute for me, the star of the play, and received it as such. Beaming, I began to execute a graceful curtsy, when the principal whispered from beneath his judgmental mustache that I was to carry the flowers across the stage and present them to Miss Queenie, whom he wished to honor for her diligent work as our director. I felt the blush rise in my cheeks, embarrassed at my blunder, feeling an extra dose of humiliation because I had made the mistake in front of a massive audience. On stage. I crossed to Miss Queenie, curtsied deeply this time, and presented the flowers to my beloved teacher; she accepted them with a sympathetic smile. The moment became indelible in my memory, along with the sense of shame that I had thought I really was the chairman of the board—the star of the show—but I wasn't. I lugged around a heavy dose of self-judgment for some time afterward, along with the note to myself that I must be modest, and never expect accolades for my contributions to a performance.

When I was five years old, I was taken out of Little Flower Montessori and placed into Birch Lane Elementary, a public school about a mile down the street from our home in Massapequa. For my mother, this change meant she no longer had to drive me all the way to Amityville every morning. For me, it meant my fondest dreams were coming true—I was finally able to ride the coveted yellow school bus, from a bus stop I walked to all by myself, around the corner from our house. But it also meant I was spending six hours each day in a classroom with many rules, one authoritarian teacher, and about two dozen other children. Most of my classmates had already been there for a year, accustomed to marching to a completely different tune from the one I knew and loved at Montessori.

In order for me to be placed in the new school, I was given an assessment—on which I performed so well, the test administrator suspected I'd read the answer key backward and upside down from across the table. It was the first time I was accused of cheating rather than being praised for my talent.

I also confounded my test givers by reading at a third-grade level, yet being unfamiliar with the words "steeple" and "leisure," which perplexed the principal but delighted my mother, who felt proud to have provided books and life experience that had insulated me from both Christianity and idleness. And then, there was my size: I was as tall as the biggest seven-year-olds in the second grade, but only as old as the average kindergartner. As a compromise, my first week of public school was spent alone in the back row of a first-grade classroom, trying hard to ignore the teacher coaxing my classmates to learn the ABCs while I read my way through all the books on the back shelf, including the entire Dick and Jane series, and about as many from Dr. Seuss. The next week, Principal Young herself took me by the hand and led me down what felt like an endless corridor, all the way to Mrs. Ullmeyer's second-grade classroom, where I was presented as the "new student."

Some of the other second-grade students at Birch Lane were suspicious of my appearance—a round baby face atop a tall, sturdy body, more formally dressed than anyone else in the class. Also suspect among a sea of Long Island accents was my Southern drawl, an enduring souvenir of having learned to speak on an Air Force base in Arkansas while my father was in the service. A rumor began to circulate that I was "retarded" and had either been left back to repeat second grade or sent down from a higher grade. I was teased on the playground. In response, I stood up straight, trying to muster an air of dignity, but inwardly felt mortified, bewildered, insulted, and hurt. How I missed my friends and teachers at Montessori, where I had felt so accepted. I still remember the loneliness of those long, solitary sessions of recess—wandering the perimeter of the Birch Lane playground, utterly alone.

Eventually, I managed to befriend two lovely girls in my class—Kimberly and Pamela—to whose houses my mother would drive me, on an alternating basis, to borrow whichever book I needed to do my homework, as I would invariably leave mine in my desk at school. I also set my cap for my new teacher, Mrs. Ullmeyer—doting on her, writing poems for her, illustrated in crayon—and at Christmas, gifting her a tube of her favorite Zinc Pink lipstick, which I considered the ultimate in sophisticated loveliness.

Music Soothes the Saddest Child

My mother had taken me to the Young People's Concerts with Leonard Bernstein at Lincoln Center for as long as I could remember, and I had fallen in love with the idea of becoming a violist. It was difficult to find a viola teacher who would take on a young student unless they first received a year of instruction in piano—a sensible requirement, but one I was not interested in fulfilling. Most teachers who took on viola pupils younger than age six taught them using the Suzuki method, which requires a parent to learn and practice daily along with the child; my mother had less interest in doing this than I had in learning to play the piano.

Finally, Mommy was led to Patty Kopec, a twenty-six-year-old Czech immigrant who came to America via Israel to study viola at Juilliard. Because I was already reading books, Patty agreed to take me on as a student as soon as I turned six and a half. Through her, I would meet my first two musical idols: Pinchas Zukerman and Itzhak Perlman, whom she knew from their days as music students in Israel. I surprised Patty by showing up for my first lesson with a violin rather than a viola, but she took it in stride, and laughed when she heard how the change had happened. When I had gone with my mother to be sized for a rental instrument, either I was too impatient to wait for Mr. Huggler to switch out the strings on the half-size fiddle and restring it as a viola, or maybe I just didn't want to put him to any trouble. Perhaps my mother had a preference for violin over viola. In any case, the violin became my instrument, but I still don't like playing high notes on the E string.

Though Patty yelled at me often, I knew this was just her teaching style. And I was quite accustomed to being yelled at. I loved her fiercely and tried hard to live up to her expectations, even though it was difficult to focus on practicing when left alone in my bedroom each day. I lived for the recitals: the shining moment of making music in the spotlight, followed by bowing, applause, cake, cookies, ice cream, and kind remarks from other people's parents.

Another sanctuary was literature. I devoured books like frosting on a cake.

I read all the 1930s Nancy Drew and Hardy Boys mysteries I found on the shelves in the basement, then demanded more. My mother's childhood friend, Joan—a teacher in Forest Hills, Queens—caught wind of my voracious appetite for books and gave me volumes of stories about Mrs. Piggle Wiggle and Pippi Longstocking. These kind, clever, and unconventional protagonists ignited my imagination and encouraged my nonconformist behavior—though the psychic damage done by the traditional literature I had consumed would not be so easily repaired. Besides, Pippi (practically an orphan) and Mrs. Piggle Wiggle (a widow) both lived alone, which didn't seem like something to aspire to—at least not without a fortune and a good house, which they both happened to have. After reading about Pippi, I asked to have my own reddish-brown hair braided into two pigtails, and Mommy would occasionally oblige me, giving me braids not for school but for tennis lessons, or to fold up inside my swim cap. As for keeping a horse on the porch, as Pippi did, my mother said I could not have a horse unless I gave up the violin; there wasn't enough time for both responsibilities. This was indeed a bitter pill to swallow.

Every morning of elementary school, my mother stood behind me at the bathroom counter, both of us facing the mirror, and combed out the tangles that had found their way into my long hair while I slept. She'd had short curly hair all her life,

57

except for those few fashionable years when she had it ironed straight. Having a daughter with straight silky hair was a dream come true. She would pull the front sections back tightly, away from my face, and fasten them into an elastic loop anchored with two colorful plastic balls. It was a painful process, and I tried to stay quiet and still, so as not to make her angry. If I were stoic enough, Mommy might console me with compliments, the most common of which was "you're my little Wellesley girl."

I loathed the hairstyle and, of course, hated having to endure pain to achieve it. Other girls in my class wore their long hair parted down the center, fastened with a barrette above each temple. My hair was pulled back so tightly that it separated into bumps across the top of my head, and I imagined that I resembled Frankenstein's other monster, Herman Munster. As for what a Wellesley girl was, I only knew it was an ideal in my mother's mind. Mommy had taught dance at Wellesley before I was born, and the oh-so-beautiful Ali MacGraw had been her Queen of the May, in a dance she choreographed to celebrate a mysterious occasion called May Day.

I was so eager to please—not merely by relinquishing trivial possessions but also by taking on every challenge, striving to achieve perfect grades and top test scores, successful violin recitals, and the seat of concertmaster in every orchestra I joined. There wasn't anything I wouldn't do for praise and positive reinforcement. During my first few years of school, I managed to become the teacher's pet. But as I got older, things changed. In sixth grade, my indomitable spirit bumped right up against the regulated expectations of Mrs. Egre, my classroom teacher, who constantly stressed the importance of preparing us for the research papers we would write in high school— apparently forgetting we still had two years of junior high after completing her class.

After suffering several other slights from her regarding my academic endeavors—in which she essentially accused me of plagiarism when I produced exceptional work, and of lying when my father ate my science project the night before it was due—Mrs. Egre earned the horny toad's prize for all time when she chose the male-dominated *The Prince and the Pauper*, by Mark Twain, as our classroom play. It stung that she chose to ignore the note I'd earnestly printed on the back of my audition form, respectfully requesting that she consider gender-blind casting, so that the other girls and I might be considered for some of the featured roles. In the end, the title roles went to two friends—Michael and Tom—who would go on to have professional careers in the theater. Another friend of mine, also named Michael and also a future thespian, was cast as the whipping boy, paid to receive punishment for the Prince's transgressions. Ellen and I were cast as sisters, and my one spoken line was: "That's our cake, you're ruining it!"

While I know there are no small roles...only small actors... it burned me that none of us girls were given the chance to do more. By the time I arrived at performing arts camp that summer, I had lost sight of my potential as an actor and divided all my creative time between playing violin in pit orchestras and learning how to paint the sets.

Eventually, I would tire of shrinking myself. I would reach my breaking point, find my courage, stand in my power, raise my voice, step out of my comfort zone, take risks, and discover my purpose. But it would take quite some time. The shrinking and silencing of me had not yet been sufficiently effected.

Junior High: The Shrinking and Silencing Continues

In junior high, my wardrobe expanded somewhat; I was allowed to wear culottes and even some pants to school, just not jeans. Meanwhile, the challenge of conforming to teacher expectations increased. My seventh-grade math teacher, Mr. Kamoosi, would become frustrated with me for not following the proper steps when solving an equation. Though I arrived at a solution—more often than not obtaining the correct answer—I didn't receive credit because I hadn't followed all the steps. Math was so intuitive for me that I couldn't break down what my mind was doing to fully describe my mental process on paper, and my teacher refused to give credit merely for a correct answer.

At home, my mother raged, accusing Mr. Kamoosi of not being as smart as I was, of feeling too threatened to give me proper credit. As a result, I was unrepentant, and the math class situation went from bad to worse. Mr. Kamoosi warned me that I was at risk of receiving a failing grade. If I didn't pass the final exam, I would have to spend the summer taking seventh grade math all over again. The exam seemed fine when I was taking it, but afterward, I worried I hadn't shown enough steps and that he would fail me. On the last day of school, I walked into the building to collect my report card, terrified that plans for my first summer of sleepaway camp would be ruined. Exiting the building minutes later, I was relieved to show my mother the big round D interrupting the column of angular As.

When we got home, I was jubilant—performing a series of pirouettes and leaps across the backyard while my father trimmed the hedges, until finally my joints became so fatigued that, after a great leap through the air, I landed badly and sprained my ankle. My father thought he heard a bone break. He dropped his hedge trimmer, picked me up, carried me to the driveway, threaded me into the backseat of his candy-apple-red Lincoln Continental, set a Ziploc bag of ice on my ankle (secured with a bungee cord), and drove me to his medical office for an X-ray. When he saw no bones were broken, Daddy wrapped my sprained ankle in a plaster cast, from the base of my toes all the way up to my knee, and broke the news that I would have to wear it for three weeks.

Such tender moments, though few, were indelible—the way he took care of me whenever I fell, first stitching up my little chin (twice!) when I split it open as a very young girl, then wrapping my ankle in that great big cast. I can still recall being filled with pride when my tall, handsome father showed up in the doorway of Little Flower Montessori, looking positively heroic in his surgical scrubs, ready to whisk me off to the hospital and extract the counting bead I'd managed to stick up my nose. Receiving intense doses of my father's protection and care when I was injured vaguely resembled what I craved, something akin to love and affection.

So, no sleepaway camp for me—at least, not that week. First, I would have to learn how to use crutches, then spend the next three weeks trailing after my mother—her lumbering, lurching shadow—as she played in tennis tournaments, fetched groceries, and ran errands. While I was recovering from my injury, she kept me with her all day, every day. Spending this much time with Mommy was rare. And even though I was stooped over on crutches, it became clear to her during those three weeks that I was gaining on her in height; she was growing increasingly concerned.

My first three weeks away from home, soon after the cast came off, were a bit bewildering. The camp sorted us into cabins by age, not by grade, so I was with kids my own age for the first time in six years. Even so, I was both taller and more childish in shape than anyone else in my bunk, and I was too self-conscious to take a shower. When I walked in and saw the eight or ten shower heads mounted on tiled walls surrounding a single open space, I turned around, exited the concrete block of a building, and walked back to the cabin. I changed into my bathing suit in one of the toilet stalls and went to dunk myself in the lake instead. I'm not sure I took more than one proper shower during all three weeks I was at camp. I would sneak away from a social dance on a Saturday night, while everyone else was having a good time, to soap up my body in privacy.

Back home after camp, I got busy studying for my *bat mitzvah*. On the verge of twelve, I was acutely aware that I would be the last of our social group to mark this auspicious occasion. My classmates had already turned thirteen, and I had attended at least a dozen of their celebrations. Mommy drove us to a North Shore boutique, many miles from Massapequa, where I took one look at the racks of floor-length gowns and quickly sidled up to her, pleading in a desperate whisper to let us leave the shop and go elsewhere, to find a Gunne Sax floral prairie dress, like the ones several of my friends had worn, or perhaps a sheer floral top over a jumpsuit, like Suzy's, but to no avail. Mommy was quietly enraged. As I slunk into the dressing room, I heard her call me a brat under her breath. On the drive home, she scolded me for failing to appreciate how fortunate I was.

"I found a shop full of beautiful dresses fit for a princess, and you would rather dress like a street urchin, an orphan, a beggar! That's not attractive, it's pathetic! Why in the world would you want to try to look like those girls?"

I sat quietly in the back of the car on the drive home—tears falling down my cheeks from Mommy's refusal to consider my feelings, her lack of sympathy for my wanting to fit in—but my sulking accomplished nothing. I was measured for alterations to a crimson velvet gown, its long skirt perforated by wide peek-a-boo bands of ecru lace, and a matching bolero jacket. I stood on a block of wood and turned ever so slowly as the seamstress pinned the gown. I was five foot eight and a half inches, and in the middle of a massive growth spurt when I climbed up onto the *bimah* in my taupe suede peep-toe wedge-heel sandals.

Before long, I had surpassed my mother's own evidently troublesome height of five foot nine and three-quarter inches. But even Mommy was swayed when, at age thirteen, standing five foot ten in stockinged feet, I was spotted in the dressing room at Saks Fifth Avenue and invited to model for the store. Excited to take advantage of the employee discount, Mommy agreed I should accept the job.

Around the same time, she took me to see a growth doctor to learn what could be done about this latest facet of the too-muchness of me. She explained, unable to conceal her alarm, that I was now on track to potentially reach an unmarriageable height. She said I was lucky they were able to offer a remedy: *growth-stunting pills*. Developed to treat obesity in England, the medication inadvertently turned obese children into short, stout adults. This was after the doctor had peered into my eyes with a light and magnifying glass, then poked me (hard!) in the stomach to make sure I was standing up straight to be measured and explained that the special X-rays he took of my leg bones showed I still had a substantial bit of growing left to do.

"She has a mild form of gigantism," he said, as if I were not in the room, as if I had no feelings. The doctor said he was hesitant to prescribe the pills, which would more than decimate my appetite, observing, "She is already quite thin."

"Oh, that's only because she's in the middle of this latest growth spurt," my mother responded, equal parts dismissive and disdainful. "This one likes to eat, whether she's hungry or not." The doctor shrugged, sighed, and agreed to write the prescription.

With a daily pill, my appetite was banished for the duration of high school. I began a four-year period of popping a prescription appetite suppressant every day until I was delivered to college, having remained flat chested and slim-hipped, and having grown only a fraction of an inch taller in all that time.

Around the same time I was hauled off to the growth doctor, I was also hauled into the guidance office, where I found my mother in a huddle with my counselor. I was about to be informed of my IQ score, they said, because there was a problem: it was the highest in the school (except for Liz Alpert, a senior who had just been admitted Early Action to Harvard), and yet here I was—not even on track to be inducted into the National Honor Society! When I didn't appear appropriately horrified by the news, I was admonished to get my grades up to reflect my true abilities.

Back at home, Mommy explained the reason for her concern: I simply must get into Harvard or Wellesley if I'd have any hope of finding a Jewish man who was tall enough, smart enough, and secure enough to marry me. When my father arrived home from work, he found me crying on the guest room couch and asked me what was wrong. I told him: I know I am lucky not to be deaf or blind, but why, why do I have to be so tall?

What did my father do, you may ask, with this opportunity to assure his beautiful, eldest daughter that she is lovely and persuade her not to think of her height as a disability? Did he tell me I would receive more attention than the shorter girls, that I'd look better in clothes, have less need for a tailor, and get to ride shotgun? No, he blamed my mother. "While I am taller than your mother," he said, "my height is closer to the average for a man, whereas hers is significantly above the mean for a woman."

Of course, reader, you know I got my grades up, never got less than an A in high school again, and my GPA gradually crept up to an acceptable level.

The pills I had been prescribed were stimulants, so they helped me conform to both my mother's and my teachers' expectations in more ways than we had anticipated. They suppressed my appetite, kept me thin, slowed my growth, delayed my menses, *and* helped with my undiagnosed ADHD. For the first time in my life, I was able to manage my belongings, brought home the materials I needed to complete my work, carried the appropriate notebook to each class, and didn't misplace my assignments after I finished them. I stopped blurting things out in class without raising my hand first, and my handwriting improved. It was a miracle.

At thirteen, I spent each Saturday afternoon attempting to perform my new job—strutting around the sales floor of our upscale local department store, talking to people about the clothes I was wearing. At least, that was the idea. It's possible my mother thought the job would give me more poise and confidence, like the Barbizon modeling school—whose commercial promised that students could "be a model, or just look like one"—but without the annoying training or tuition. Whatever her intention, she didn't anticipate or care that it would prove a demoralizing exercise in self-examination and comparison, and would only bring attention to the parts of me that weren't pretty enough (my nose) or small enough (my *tokhes*). More likely, she was grateful to have the modeling director join her in encouraging my continued thinness.

The director observed one day—in front of everyone—that I needed to wear clothing one size larger than all the other girls—a 5/6 instead of a 3/4—a fact that scarcely needed pointing out, as we shared a single dressing room all day long. I suppose, as a practical matter, it would have been convenient if we all wore the same size, but I heard it as criticism and probably blushed as deeply as I felt ashamed. She also mentioned privately that if I ever wanted to do print modeling, I would probably have to shave down the bump that was developing on my nose—that it would likely become more prominent over the next couple of years—but that I shouldn't do anything about it until I turned sixteen.

There was also an element of secret shame. Mommy told me in no uncertain terms that I was not to let *anyone* know about or see my high-heeled "streetwalker" sandals or the face full of professionally applied makeup, especially my father. My shoes were to be kept in the box they came in, which Mommy hid inside an opaque plastic bag emblazoned with the logo of my grandparents' country club, fastened with a drawstring closure, and locked in the trunk of her car—my stilettos thus disguised as golf shoes. The problem was that, without practicing walking in high heels at home, I had no hope of becoming competent at performing my job. I could barely stand, much less walk, in the heels I had to wear. I felt like Bambi his first time stepping onto the ice. I clung to the carpeted sections of the sales floor as much as possible, just as I used to grip the wall of the ice rink. Terrified of falling and spraining my ankle again, I desperately avoided the polished terrazzo. But that was where I was expected to spend my time—strutting, posing, and chatting with shoppers.

So there were several factors contributing to my decision, one Saturday morning, to accept the modeling director's invitation for one of us to wear a Miss Piggy costume. I wanted to spend my time in the children's department downstairs because it was carpeted—but even better, I was given comfy ballet slippers to wear under the floor-length Muppet costume. Hidden inside the plush body and latex mask, I couldn't be judged for my emerging facial features or my developing figure. I could remain silent and wave at the children, or attempt an impersonation of the famous Muppet, engaging with the youngest shoppers. It was by far the best day I ever spent at the store. When I removed the costume, my hair was wet and matted, my face was flushed, and I was perspiring from head to toe. But this was my first experience bringing joy to young children, and it was a powerful discovery.

When my mother picked me up, I gushed about playing Miss Piggy and how I had become so sweaty.

"I didn't drive to Garden City twice on a Saturday so you could dress up as a pig!"

And she never took me back to Saks again.

I was quietly delighted to have my Saturdays back. In the fall, I auditioned for the Manhattan School of Music preparatory program and began carpooling to the city with kids I'd met at the All State and All County Orchestras. Now, we spent our Saturdays together each week, blissfully immersed in a community of like-minded peers—being by turns silly, serious, musical, and goofy—playing chamber music in the morning, lunching on Cokes and french fries in the cafeteria, and performing major symphonic repertoire in the afternoon. It was the best day of my week, by far.

First Spirit Messenger | Vermont, 1982

When I was fifteen, I spent the summer in Manchester, Vermont—the youngest participant in an international chamber music program where my first teacher, Patty, was on the violin faculty. One day, I was sitting at a picnic table with some adult friends when a visitor I didn't recognize—a beautiful, raven-haired gypsy woman in a white blouse and red headscarf—approached us, looking as if she had stepped out of a picture book. She walked straight up to me, took my hand in hers, studied it for a moment, then looked into my eyes and told me that in five years I would have my choice of husbands. I would have to choose between an American and a foreigner, she said, but I *would* marry one of them.

I was still a child, a virgin who could vividly remember having been ten, so the concept of marriage seemed absurd. An older friend that summer compared me to the lily of the valley—presumably because of what he perceived as my purity, innocence, and sweetness. I felt sure the gypsy had mistaken me for someone older—this happened to me often because of my height. I was a skeptic anyway, but I never forgot her prophecy, even as I pushed it out of my thoughts.

Naked in Front of My Yale Interviewer

Based on my violin performance in the Saturday pre-college program at the Manhattan School of Music, I was awarded a scholarship to the University of Akron, bundled together with a $40,000-a-year job playing in the Akron Symphony. I was forbidden by my parents to even consider it, but two of my friends—Phil and Alicia—snapped up the generous offer (the equivalent of a six-figure salary today) and went on to launch their music careers. I was happy and excited for my friends but utterly lost as to what I was going to do with myself.

That fall, as I was turning sixteen, I applied to the half dozen colleges my parents approved of. Though I loved making art and reading books, I had no aspiration in my life other than playing the violin, so my first choice was Yale, where I could major in music performance. As fate would have it, our pediatrician, Edward Underwood, was assigned to be my alumni interviewer for Yale. (I should mention that my younger sister and I privately called him Dr. Underpants, because that is typically all we were wearing while interacting with him, a fact that made us increasingly uncomfortable as we got older.)

My little sister thought it was hysterically funny, but I was mortified to have Dr. Underpants assigned to interview me for my first-choice college. I still hadn't recovered from an incident a year or so earlier, when my left nipple had grown a little bit puffy, while my right nipple, still perfectly flat, had become surrounded with a constellation of red dots. At my mother's request, Dr. Underwood examined me and said that it was normal for one breast to begin to develop before the other. Over my protestations, he declared that the red spots were undoubtedly from my pinching and pulling at my right side, to try to get it to catch up with the left.

Reader, I don't know what to say about this. I was speechless—full of outrage and embarrassment. What he said was not true, but I had no credibility to challenge his authority about what girls do to cause such an effect as the one evidenced on my chest. On the way home, I told my mother that I had definitely not been pinching my breast to make it grow, but I wasn't sure she believed me.

Okay, she didn't believe me for a second. Not on her life would Priscilla take my word if it contradicted something uttered by a white man, especially an Ivy league-educated doctor. Never going to happen.

As it turned out, Dr. Underpants advised the admissions committee that, in his professional opinion, I was still too immature to go to college—I should be given an additional year to make my application.

While my parents had followed all of Dr. Underwood's recommendations regarding my nutrition, vaccinations, and medications, they had no intention of honoring his recommendation to let me stay home and reapply to college a year later. My mother had started college at sixteen, with satisfactory results. I wondered what she thought of his breast assessment now.

On a practical level, my mother's haste to send me to college meant I would not be able to major in violin performance. Neither Harvard nor Wellesley offered it as an option. When Mommy and I visited Boston to check out the five-year dual degree program at Tufts/New England Conservatory, she decided it would be too challenging for me to manage logistically, because of my as-yet-undiagnosed but obvious ADHD, which was termed my "difficulties." Tufts by itself was deemed to be beneath me, and a conservatory education on its own was out of the question. Years later, when my own children were applying to college and asked their Gramma Priscilla what she thought of Tufts, she would answer: "It served its purpose—I met Poppa."

In our high school graduating class, I was known as the tall girl with the violin, because even though it was fully insured, I wouldn't stash my violin in the unlocked band room; I brought it with me everywhere. Yes, I got lots of "what's that you got there, a machine gun?" And when people (mostly my friends' parents) asked why I didn't have a boyfriend, my violin was typically right there in my arms for me to indicate as I replied, "because *this* is my boyfriend." Repeatedly, classmates and underclassmen alike inscribed the margins of my yearbook with requests to remember them for a ticket when I made my debut someday at Carnegie Hall. Most of my Massapequa friends had no idea I was about to surrender my professional music aspirations, and I didn't have the heart to tell them as we prepared to part ways that my concert violinist dream had been squashed.

When I did eventually perform at Carnegie Hall—during law school, with my summer camp's alumni orchestra for their fiftieth anniversary—I didn't invite anyone from high school, because it wasn't what any of us had in mind back in 1983. My classmates' one chance to see me as a soloist on a New York area stage came at roughly the same time our yearbooks were distributed, when I performed the Vitali Chaconne in G minor as a soloist with the Massapequa High School orchestra. While other girls were shopping together at the mall for prom gowns, I went to Loehmann's with my mother and found a floor-length, polka-dotted, blue-and-white dress with a hoop skirt that helped me claim a place next to the conductor equally as large as the spotlight they shone upon me.

The only person brave enough to ask me to prom was the other sixteen-year-old on track to graduate with our class. Holden was in several of our AP classes, but he was a social pariah who wore thick, yellow-tinted eyeglasses and played Pac Man during lunch. I was trying hard to keep my brainiac status on the down-low, and thus averse to being associated with Holden as I struggled to fit in with more popular kids. I told him I was in love with a Russian immigrant violinist who was at Aspen music festival for the summer, and I didn't want to go to prom with anyone else. (This was not untrue; I merely neglected to mention that Sergei had a girlfriend, and it wasn't me.) So while my friends danced to Culture Club, drank from flasks, and posed for keepsake photos at prom, I drove into the city for my consolation dinner with my sister, parents, and grand-parents at Tavern on the Green, dressed in my favorite Michael Vollbracht jumpsuit, boldly colorful abstract art printed on a black silk background, found in Loehmann's Back Room.

I would take to the stage one last time in high school, at our senior awards ceremony, to receive the feminist award from the local chapter of the American Association of University Wom-en. Feminism was not cool at that time, and there were audible snickers as I rose from my seat and ascended the stage to claim this dubious honor. As an eight-year-old feminist, I had been loud and proud, dressing up as a suffragist for Halloween and carrying a big sign that read "Good Enough to Raise Your Sons, Good Enough to Vote!" But now, eight years later, I had shrunk myself down to a secret feminist—one who longed to be loud and proud again.

There was a fierce, hidden strength within me, a deep well of self-respect, but I didn't know how to let it reemerge. I couldn't have articulated it at the time, but feminism was connected to my latent rebelliousness, to my secret hope that I could someday be loved for who I was inside—my true self—instead of how appealing I could make myself appear to a future husband. That hope was linked to some remarkable future achievement I knew I was capable of—but in what field, I had no idea.

My final appearance in Massapequa was on graduation day. I thought I was clever, because while many boys were wearing suits and ties and other girls wore dressy gowns beneath their zippered white ones, I had dressed to stay cool in the sweltering heat. As usual, I had not thought ahead. It never occurred to me that after I returned my rented cap and gown to the yearbook office on the third floor, I would have to walk through the building, cross the sunny parking lot, and get into my parents' car wearing nothing but a bright-blue bathing suit and white, low-heeled sandals. Who was feeling clever now?

My parents wanted me to "get over" my musical aspirations, renounce my musician friends as too bohemian, and get back on track prepping to marry a Harvard man. Initially, this goal was considered feasible for me to achieve as a student at either Wellesley or Harvard. When my parents were in college, a Harvard man was more likely to choose a bride at Wellesley than from among his classmates in Cambridge. There was an adage still circulating in the 1980s: "Lesley to bed, Wellesley to wed, and Radcliffe to talk to," with the understanding that Harvard men were afraid of powerful women and looking for someone from a nearby school whom they perceived as weaker and intellectually inferior.

I tried not to fixate on what Harvard men might want and to focus instead on imagining my own future as a college student. I preferred to envision myself flourishing within a bastion of liberated womanhood, rather than trying to negotiate four years in the macho culture of the Ivy League, and my guidance counselor (who nominated me for the feminist award) agreed that Wellesley was a good match. When the head of Harvard's Long Island Schools Committee called to congratulate me on my acceptance to the college, I thanked her politely, then explained I'd just accepted Wellesley's invitation to attend a special weekend program for admitted students. She laughed, but when she realized I was serious, she advised me to take the bus from Wellesley to Harvard, where I could stay with her daughter Emily, at Eliot House.

The weekend at Wellesley was enlightening. We were told that many women had chosen the secluded college just to be able to shut men out of their lives, if only for a few years. They wanted female role models, they wanted mentors—they didn't want to be overlooked by professors who focused on male students. In an attempt to verify this, I used the PA system in the Wellesley dorms to ask if anyone who had turned down an offer from either Harvard or Yale would be kind enough to meet me and discuss their decision. No one materialized.

In their bedrooms, several Wellesley students had a Harvard freshman register (a.k.a. Facebook) on their bookshelves, with the faces, names, and hometowns of everyone in the Harvard freshman class. I was told that this book was useful to have, but no one explained why.

On Sunday, I took a bus to Harvard with a young woman on her way to visit her brother at Kirkland House. She confessed to feeling devastated not to have been admitted to Harvard and said she hoped to transfer after her freshman year at Wellesley; she begged me to accept Harvard's offer and said she'd come and look me up after she transferred.

When I met up with Emily at Eliot House, she invited me to eat in the dining hall with her friends. It may have been the laughter of the Harvard men at the table that most strongly persuaded me to change my mind. When they heard I planned to attend Wellesley, they guffawed and said, "then you're going to want our phone numbers." At the time, I didn't get the joke, but I knew I didn't want to be the butt of it. And so, before returning home, I'd made the decision to go to Harvard; their laughter would never be at my expense.

"Indelible in the hippocampus is the laughter." Referring to the part of the brain that processes emotion and memory, Christine Blasey Ford—the psychology professor who testified about now-Supreme Court Justice Brett Kavanaugh's attempt to rape her when she was a teenager—spoke of the ultimate humiliation being that of Kavanaugh and his friend united in raucous laughter as they fumbled with her clothing.

Two years later, during my exile, I learned about life on the Wellesley campus from my closest friend from summer camp. Rather than reveling in their freedom to become all they could be—*sans* men—many Wellesley women were preoccupied with getting themselves invited to exclusive parties at Harvard's all-male final clubs, then comparing notes over coffee and cigarettes in the dining hall the next morning.

Back at home, sharing the details of my two campus visits with my parents, they informed me that they had discussed my situation while I was away, and the choice was clear. Now that Harvard had become fully coeducational, they realized that Wellesley—as wonderful as it once was—was now obsolete. I would go to Harvard.

I didn't bother to endorse their edict with my own decision.

Chapter 3
THE IVY LEAGUE RUB

Harvard might have caused Wellesley to appear obsolete for those fortunate enough to choose between the two, but its culture hadn't evolved to keep pace with its changing demographics. Women were now full-fledged Harvard students, but there were very few women on the faculty. Moreover, several of the elite male-only final clubs perpetuated the tradition of inviting only Wellesley women to attend their parties, thereby snubbing their female classmates. As a young woman on campus sent there primarily to find a husband, it was disheartening to watch dozens of women in little black dresses disembarking from buses parked outside the clubs, which lined Mount Auburn Street. Notorious bastions of sexual assault and predation, women nonetheless wanted to be invited as much as men wanted to join.

Freshman year, a letter intended to be read exclusively by the members of a final club accidentally made its way into a female student's mailbox, upsetting her so much that she reported it. The letter, subsequently published in the campus newspaper, attempted to woo club members to an upcoming party with the promise of a "bevy of slobbering bovines fresh for the slaughter," suggesting that all in attendance will have the chance to "slice into one of those meaty but grateful heifers." The letter briefly caused a firestorm, but it was defended as parody and the controversy soon died back down to a whisper. For the most part, many women returned to silently accepting that we shared a campus with men who found rape humor socially acceptable, and to secretly hoping for an invitation to these exclusive parties. Years later, when I learned that nearly half the women at Harvard who participated in final club life reported experiencing non-consensual sexual contact within their gilded walls, I still wondered why I had been excluded.

The first time I went into Boston alone, it was to get my legs waxed on Newbury Street. As she applied the hot wax, the esthetician told me she was friendly with several members of the Harvard football team, whom she had met at campus parties, saying they were "wicked nice guys." She asked if I knew this one or that one, and I confessed that I had not yet met anyone on the team. I called my father afterward to process this conversation, feeling perplexed that this woman—who had not attended any college—had been invited to campus parties while I hadn't. He sighed, chuckled a little, and said, "Oh c'mon, Nancy, can you really be so naïve?" I was still just sixteen years old.

I started keeping a journal during the second month of college, which has helped preserve my memories. In my first entry, I took some time to look back and record details of my first month at university, beginning with my traumatic first night on campus. My most sophisticated freshman roommate was in the process of disentangling herself from an affair with the assistant headmaster at her Connecticut boarding school. She started hooking up with guys the first day of freshman week. Because I had been exhausted from the stress of moving into my dorm and went to bed early that first night, I was treated to the sound of her drunken arrival in our common room, the door slamming shut, a male voice asking, "So, how are your roommates?" and her laughing response, "Ugh, I think they're a bunch of virgins." I wondered, mortified, how she could tell. Was it that obvious?

As freshmen, we had no adults looking out for us in any meaningful way. There certainly was no place to process what it meant to belong to the female minority at a school whose fight song begins with the lyric "Ten Thousand Men," an institution that had been a bastion of white male privilege for most of its 347 years. Instead of mentors (defined as trusted experts who train and counsel), we had proctors (a title based on a disciplinary function).

Two flights below the suite I shared with three other women, on the ground floor of Wigglesworth Hall, Entry A, a pair of married graduate students earned their keep by "proctoring" the thirty freshmen assigned to live in Wigg A and B. Vicki and Dave held appointments to review our class registration cards, ensuring that we were fulfilling our foreign language and quantitative reasoning requirements and checking that we had included a course from the core curriculum. Vicki advised me not to take the math class I placed into, as it was a pre-med class, promising me it would be a horrible hazing experience designed to get people to drop pre-med. Later, she would dispense equally valuable diet tips, like the time I realized in horror that my appetite's reawakening had caused me to gain seven pounds and I was sure I needed a flat tummy in time for a black-tie dance at the Hasty Pudding Club. Vicki supplied an emergency regimen which, when I followed it for a single day, caused me to lose four of those seven pounds.

I had become chemically dependent on amphetamines over the past four years, and nobody had thought to titrate me off them or prepare me for what it would feel like when I stopped taking them, other than telling me to "take it easy at the buffet." Symptoms of amphetamine withdrawal include fatigue, increased appetite, confused thoughts, irritability and agitation, unpleasant dreams, emotional outbursts, and depression. Most of these symptoms were temporary, but once my appetite had been restored, it remained healthy and strong.

Since Montessori school, I had always managed to find a teacher or nurturing older friend to be a surrogate mother, and soon, I would again. But freshman year at Harvard, I floundered for the lack of any such person in my life. The two previous summers, I attended chamber music programs in Maine and Vermont, where I attached myself to musicians in their twenties and thirties who proved to be devoted advisers, confidants, and cheerleaders. Now, seeking the same nurturing connection, I lay in the dark of our tiny double bedroom and confided secret doubts and fears from my pillow to my roommate, Eunice, who used the fresh intel to spread rumors about me, campaigning to convince everyone who would listen that I was still a virgin because I was a lesbian.

This was before homophobia had become socially unacceptable in liberal spaces. Gay rights activism had only just arrived at Harvard a few years earlier. This was way before Ellen's historic primetime kiss, before *Will and Grace*, before same-sex marriage was even a term, and before the rise of gay-straight alliances. This was also before the internet, and thirty years before the *Crimson* (the undergraduate campus newspaper) would institute its annual survey of freshmen. One such survey would have reassured me that by being too busy to think about having a sex life before arriving at college, I was a typical Harvard freshman—in the majority among my classmates. The truth is that I *had* thought about it a great deal, but so far, my crushes had all been either gay or already spoken for. My high school girlfriends were sexually active, and I felt ashamed of my inexperience. At the same time, my low self-esteem meant that I felt most comfortable spending time with guys who expected nothing more from me than conversation.

My mother interrogated me weekly about my social life and voiced displeasure when I replied, "No, I don't have a date this weekend." She couldn't understand why my roommates and other girlfriends weren't introducing me to the men they were no longer dating, which is how she had met my father. I worked at not judging myself or my friendships by her standards. In my head, I answered her, saying, "Well, when *you* were in college, women didn't go to bed with almost everyone they dated. It… tends to change the dynamic."

I found joy my freshman year by playing violin and, on special occasions, singing with the jazz combo that covered the breaks for the Bach Society Orchestra (Bach Soc, for short) when we hired ourselves out to play at black-tie waltzes hosted by some of the undergraduate houses. When I first arrived at college, I was not aware of how often I sang out loud, but self-knowledge is one of the things freshmen roommates are so helpful with. One of mine startled me one morning by asking me, as we were walking to the dining hall, "Nancy, do you ever stop singing?"

So maybe she wasn't a morning person. But the truth is I greatly love to sing, and always had. I can retrace my entire childhood by the songs I sang. I had gone from singing along with Fred Rogers's records to harmonizing with the original cast recordings of classic Broadway shows, to choreographing movements for the songs on my mother's collection of vintage Barbra Streisand records. And once I became an artist-entrepreneur in junior high and started earning money—by selling classmates custom bookmarks with their name written in calligraphy, addressing invitations to *bar mitzvahs* for my mother's friends, and painting flowers on matching sets of crew neck sweatshirts and drawstring sweatpants, also for my mother's friends—I was able to buy myself new records and cassette tapes: the Bee Gees, Barry Manilow, Billy Joel, Elton John, Stevie Wonder, Linda Ronstadt, the Jackson Five, then Michael and eventually Janet Jackson, as well as recordings from Broadway shows I'd seen with my family, like *Annie*, *42nd Street*, *Cats*, *Barnum*, *A Chorus Line*, and *Fame*. I knew a bit of Cole Porter from when we put on "Anything Goes" in our high school drama club, and I was thrilled when a college friend introduced me to recordings by Ella Fitzgerald and Billie Holiday. I borrowed some tapes from her and quickly added some of their songs to my repertoire.

As my seventeenth birthday approached, I knew what gift I most wanted to give myself: I would audition for the women's a cappella group, the Radcliffe Pitches, and see if I could improve my life by joining their ranks. I had attended several of the Pitches' performances and determined that my membership in this group of confident, witty, talented women would help me more than anything else on campus to connect with joy. I prepared George Gershwin's "I've Got a Crush on You" as a solo, wrote and prepared a lame but original joke, and got up on stage and delivered them both to the array of sophisticated women assembled to assess us. I was thrilled to be called back for the next round of auditions, and then the next. When I told the Bach Society Orchestra conductor, Sam Wong—a senior who also sang in the men's a cappella group, the Din and Tonics—that I'd made it to the final round of auditions for the Pitches, he offered to meet me in the music building the next day and give me a coaching session. I was too embarrassed to tell him it was my birthday, much less my seventeenth, so I accepted his kindness as a birthday gift from the Universe and—in lieu of eating dinner—headed into the auditions, my confidence buoyed by Sam's coaching, praise, and encouragement.

Heading into the final hour of my seventeenth year, I was dancing in the Wigg A31 common room at a surprise party thrown for me by my roommate's cousin Emily, when our suite's shared black rotary phone rang. Somebody answered it and called my name. My heart pounding, I put the receiver to my ear and was devastated to learn that I would not be invited to join the Pitches. Sam had told me earlier that making it this far was an impressive accomplishment for someone who had never had a voice lesson. The woman who called to break the news had actually advocated for me, and she began crying as she told me they decided to choose someone else. So in that final hour of being sixteen, I found myself consoling her rather than allowing myself to feel my own sadness. She made me promise I would audition again when they had another opening in the group, and I responded bravely that I would.

In truth, dear reader, I was crushed. As yet unaccustomed to failure, I was gutted by the rejection, believing that joining the Pitches would have fulfilled my desire for a sense of acceptance and belonging, and inspired in me a sense of joy—a sense of *being* and *becoming*. They seemed to me a tight-knit group of musically gifted women with significant social capital. They embodied everything I wanted to be, and the year before me began with feelings of deep loneliness and disappointment.

As for the connections I already had, by the time I realized that my roommate Eunice was a fake friend, she had already accepted my invitation to spend spring break in St. Croix with my father and me. At first, I thought she might keep to herself while Daddy and I spent the week playing tennis, snorkeling, and enjoying each other's company, but before I knew it, Daddy had volunteered me and my pianist roommate to give a recital together at Club One North, the premier nightclub on the island. From that point on, Eunice and I busied ourselves with practicing, rehearsing, and performing, and then—strange as it seems—we never spoke to one another again. As soon as I returned to campus, an old friend of Eunice's from Tanglewood told me she had been spreading rumors about me to everyone who would listen. After keeping silent for months, he had decided I deserved to know. So I packed up my things and spent the remainder of the academic year sleeping on a spare mattress on the floor of my friend Rosa's room in Hollis Hall, on the opposite corner of Harvard Yard.

Second semester of freshman year, I took a government course called The Politics of Women's Liberation, with Ethel Klein—a beloved professor whose overt feminism got her contract canceled by the Government Department; she would disappear from the campus when classes ended in May. In addition to being a woman, she dared to teach about what it meant to be a woman, in a school hostile to feminism and Women's Studies. Harvard's Government Department had only one tenured female professor. Klein's ouster was the latest in a long and distinguished line of scholars refused tenure due to their gender or their feminism, but it set off a firestorm of anger and dismay on campus.

Klein's lectures were standing room only, in a hall dominated by the campus's few radical feminists. I felt self-conscious as the only person wearing a dress, pantyhose, jewelry, and makeup, but that was who I was at seventeen. The course inspired me to question so many assumptions from my childhood. It also inspired me to stand outside Boston's state house with a pad of paper, one decade after *Roe v. Wade*, interviewing passersby about the right of a woman to choose whether to continue her pregnancy.

After everything my first year of college threw at me, including the toxic environment of my freshman suite, I was excited by the prospect of spreading my wings, having a big adventure, becoming fluent in French over the summer, and hopefully, finding romance. I had applied and been accepted on full scholarship to play the violin at a French chamber music program. I was elated, until I learned my mother wouldn't allow me to go. The program was in France, and she had not worked this hard for all these years to groom me for a Harvard marriage only to have me cross the ocean and lose my virginity to a Catholic.

The Quality of Mercy

The first weekend of Harvard summer school, I met a boy. I approached him at a party, thinking he was another boy altogether, with whom I had been exchanging breezy, flirtatious greetings for many weeks as we passed each other on the paths that crisscross Harvard Yard, ever since being introduced by my friend Rosa, who was doing the costumes and makeup for a film he was directing. So when I saw him across the Lowell House dining room the first weekend of summer school and sidled up to him, smiling as I smoothed my hair behind my ear, he told me I was mistaking him for his twin brother. Embarrassed, I denied my mistake, continued flirting, and before I knew it, found myself falling for him. How ironic that even after my mother foiled my plans for adventure and I ended up by default at Harvard summer school—where she had met my father—I would manage to realize her greatest fear and fall in love with a Catholic, right there at Daddy's alma mater.

I didn't lose my virginity to Pedro, because he told me right off the bat that he had a girlfriend on campus who had gone home for the summer; he had to figure things out with her before becoming serious with me. So we kept our clothes on but had long make-out sessions in his bed until I would decide I had to leave. I'd be dizzy on my way to the door, with Pedro kissing my neck and begging me to stay, but that "control" training I got from Daddy over a decade earlier came in handy. He would take me to his final club, where we would play pool, sit at the piano together and sing, or take a walk to Central Square to see old movies with his best friend, Paul. On the Fourth of July, we also went to hear Ella Fitzgerald perform with Oscar Peterson, outside at Boston Common. She was already weakened by diabetes, so her voice wasn't as voluptuous as the one I knew from her records, but Ella's personality was palpable from hundreds of yards away and her scat game was stronger than anything I had ever heard.

During this brief relationship, I discovered several things about myself: I found great joy in feeding someone I love, felt tremendous empathy when someone I care about is hurting or injured, and I was insecure about my appearance. Oh…did I just use the L-word? Okay, well…it wasn't love exactly, but it was a powerful crush. I adored our long kissing sessions, but I was sexually repressed and terrified of being found out as a virgin by someone who considered me worldly and sophisticated.

At the end of the summer, my parents came up to take

me home until it was time for the fall semester to begin. We stopped to visit friends and neighbors of ours from our vacation home in St. Croix, the Kimballs—a Jewish state senator from Massachusetts and his wife, who summered in New London, Connecticut. Relaxing on their sailboat, enjoying sunshine and friendly conversation as Mr. Kimball and my father took turns steering the boat, Mrs. Kimball inquired whether I had found a boyfriend at Harvard. My mother interrupted my answer, saying, "He's a nice boy, Nancy, but if you get serious about him, you and I are—*Boom!*" She dropped her forearm on the table between us, miming a karate chop: "Like *that*."

The previous evening, my parents had taken Pedro and me to a nice dinner in Cambridge. He was pre-med at Harvard, as my father had been, and Daddy may have enjoyed talking to him, but Pedro was *not* acceptable boyfriend material because he was not Jewish. After we disembarked the Kimballs' boat, Daddy assured me that while he would always be my father, he couldn't vouch for my mother because she had different views.

Back at campus that autumn, I told Pedro what my mother had said. Unlike Shakespeare's Romeo Montague, or Tony in *West Side Story*, he was not only offended, he was also done. Pedro had been in Spain while I was in Connecticut and New York, receiving an equally negative reaction from his family to the news of his dating me. His grandmother suggested he might do well to marry his third cousin. Then he shared the revelation that I was descended from idolators; Jews, he had been informed in Spain, had spent time worshiping a golden calf. While this was slightly less offensive than the more familiar anti-Semitic canard that Jews murdered Jesus, it was still alarming. I was hurt to realize he wouldn't fight for me—as literary heroes were wont to do—overlooking the fact that neither of our families would tolerate the match, and that neither *Romeo and Juliet* nor *West Side Story* have happy endings. Somehow, I managed to internalize our breakup as being based on my personal shortcomings.

After we split up at the start of the fall semester, I became preoccupied with finding someone else to date, eager to quell my heart-pounding pangs of rejection and longing whenever I saw Pedro or anticipated seeing him. My bulimia raged out of control, my schedule filled with parties, and I began drinking to excess, blacking out a couple of times to wake up face down on the colorful rag rug of my single room. My insecurity about not dating was briefly quelled after I spotted a tabloid at the corner store with my celebrity doppelgänger, Brooke Shields, on the cover. In the article, her mother, Terri, who was still her manager at the time, revealed that Brooke (who at age eighteen, was eighteen months older than I) was still a virgin, and that nobody had asked *her* out through all of high school either. Now that she was at Princeton, Terri said, Brooke was still not being asked out on dates, but she hoped Brooke would hold out and choose to date someone at Princeton rather than a white-trash commoner, such as Woody Harrelson, whom she might meet on set.

My insecurity also began to affect my academic work. As I gradually realized I had nothing of value to say about my chosen topic of essay for my Shakespeare class—the Bard's use of music in his plays—I wondered how I would get myself out of this predicament and procrastinated until I went home for Thanksgiving break.

Fear of failure and a complete lack of understanding of what was expected of me led me to submit a pastiche of erudite academic writing as my own. Repeating a move that had not worked to my favor when used previously—hoping to impress Mrs. Egre in the sixth grade—I once again took the train into New York City to find some fresh material that would wow my teacher. I visited the Juilliard library, located a few scholarly books about Elizabethan instrumentation and song, took copious notes, and when I returned to my dorm, rearranged these scribbled sentences into an essay of the requisite length. Even though it was not meant to be a research paper, I attached a complete bibliography, so it was easy for the teaching assistant (TA) to call a librarian at Juilliard, obtain the original sources, and prove to Harvard's administrative board (ad board) that I had cheated.

My memories of what happened next are well documented in my journal. The TA, Elizabeth Goodenough, began the process of pausing my college career by summoning me to her office for a chat. She had collected writing samples from all her students at the beginning of the semester, in the form of a brief personal essay about what else we were studying at Harvard and what we hoped to do after graduation, so she knew immediately that my essay contained many sentences generated someplace other than my mind. She also suspected I was severely delusional about the long, steep path that lay ahead before I would achieve my stated career goal of using my Harvard degree in fine arts to become the President of Christie's or Sotheby's.

She began our meeting by asking me about my recent visit to Juilliard. Nervously, I explained that several of my closest friends were students there, and one of them had invited me to use the library while I was home for Thanksgiving. Then she told me she was surprised I thought I needed to do any research; I was supposed to have done a thematic close reading of one or two of the plays, and the paper was to have consisted of my own thoughts and observations. I confessed that I wasn't able to generate enough of my own thoughts to fill the requisite number of pages and to having felt curious what other people, specifically Elizabethan music scholars, had to say on the topic. She paused, then asked if I—having begun college at such a young age—had considered taking a semester abroad, perhaps to study art history at Villa I Tatti, the Harvard Center for Italian Renaissance Studies, in Florence, Italy. When she offered to call my parents and suggest it, I crossed my arms in front of my chest, crossed my legs and told her, "Well, my parents are not open to that idea."

"Is that so?"

"Yes. I mean, no. They don't want me to miss any of my time at Harvard," I said, "and they don't want me to take time off before graduating, either, in case I don't come back."

"I see," she replied, pursing her lips. "Well, I can see from your body language that problem-solving with your parents is probably not an option. In which case, I am afraid the matter will be taken out of your hands. Nancy, your paper is full of plagiarism. I have shown it to Professor Kaiser, and he agrees that what you submitted is wholly unacceptable. Therefore, you are receiving a failing grade on the assignment and I am going to bring the matter before the administrative board, recommending that you be required to take some time away from Harvard, to do some much-needed growing up, so that you don't squander the rest of your time here. You can still pass the class, if you get an A on the final, so I suggest you get to work, but you should also prepare to be off campus for at least the next twelve months."

As Elizabeth Goodenough prepared her case against me, I had to study for and take my final exams for all my sophomore fall courses. I was a Fine Arts major at the time, and I would settle for Bs in all my other classes in order to devote most of my time and energy to preparing to crush the Shakespeare final. Deep down, part of me hoped that by acing the exam, I would show that I was a good student of Shakespeare and be forgiven, or rather, be shown grace (or some small quality of mercy). I was determined to be able to identify and discuss any line from all twelve plays on the syllabus. I knew from the previous year, in my art history courses, that the best way to prepare for a test heavy on memorization was to help teach it to others. To ensure that I would achieve a perfect score on this exam, I offered to lead a study group at the quad, convening a group of classmates in a room at Hilles Library. I invited them to flip through their Riverside Shakespeare, scan the lines they had highlighted during lectures, and try to stump me by calling them out. To the amazement of everyone in the room, I nailed every single one: act, scene, character, context, and significance!

Alas, despite receiving an A on my exam, the ad board

determined that my misappropriation of scholarly writing required a minimum of one year's exile from campus. The phrase "required withdrawal for academic dishonesty" would be added to my transcript, and I was given just a few days to pack up all my things, hand in any outstanding assignments, and leave.

I can't begin to tell you what a dark hole this cast me in, dear reader. During the brief interim between getting the news and the actual day of my banishment, I stayed in my pajamas, bathrobe, and slippers, processing the calamity in the dining hall. People would sit down or stop beside my table and ask why I wasn't dressed; was I feeling sick? I would respond by telling each person the truth: I was being sent home, kicked out for at least a year, because I had plagiarized a five-page homework assignment for the Shakespeare survey. Most people expressed shock. Some thanked me for the wakeup call; they'd be more careful. One guy guessed I had Goodenough as my TA: "Everybody knows she's the plagiarism exterminator," and his roommate agreed. "Yeah, that's her big thing," they added, as dubiously as if informing me that I'd been ticketed for driving too fast through a notorious speed trap.

Brent, my good friend from Wigglesworth, wanted me to appeal the decision, offering to testify on my behalf that I could not help quoting the library books in my paper because I had a photographic memory, but I stopped him, and confessed to having copied the sentences from notes I had taken at the Juilliard library, and also to having left a paper trail, in the form of a bibliography, that led my teacher directly to the source of the observations I misappropriated.

"Damn," said another guy, who sat down to listen. "I just gotta wonder if you wanted to get caught. Because I have totally done that. I mean, I've copied sentences straight out of books into my assignments—but shit, I would never put those books into a bibliography. What the hell were you thinking?"

I got up from the table, sighed, shuffled over to the three-gallon vats of ice cream, helped myself to another bowlful of cold comfort, refilled my coffee cup, then spooned some of the ice cream in, stirring it as it melted, and drank it. I repeated that trip to the ice cream station and coffee machine many times, until the clock ran out. When it was time to go, I packed up all my size-eight designer jeans, dance party jumpsuits, and taffeta cocktail dresses—the only thing I could fit into for the trip home were my sweatpants. Before I left, I stopped by Quincy House with a goodbye note for Pedro, who would graduate while I was in exile. I spotted a violist from Bach Soc in the Quincy courtyard and asked her to deliver it to him for me.

I wasn't old enough to rent a truck, so my roommate, Beth, rented a U-Haul and organized some friends to help me load it. I rigged up my blender to a 100-foot-long orange extension cord and served up Calypso daiquiris and piña coladas out of the back of the truck, parked in the middle of Radcliffe Quad, to reward everyone who carried something downstairs from my third-floor dorm room and up the ramp. I was still too young to buy alcohol, but my father had thoughtfully equipped my dormitory closet with a full array of booze "for entertaining," and I couldn't see why I needed to bring any of it home.

The next morning, Beth drove me and my belongings 250

miles to her family home on Long Island, where my father met us. He drove the truck to our house in Massapequa while I trailed closely behind him, driving his sedan very carefully—I hadn't been old enough to get a driver's license before leaving for college, but I had taken driver's ed in high school. Before embarking on the last leg of the journey home, Daddy warned me that my mother was probably going to be too angry to speak to me for a while. Silence would have been far preferable to what awaited me. To say that Mommy was disappointed by my reestablishing residence in the house would be a gross understatement. She told me in no uncertain terms that I was forbidden to tell anyone what I had done and why I was home, especially Mama and Papa (which is what I called my maternal grandparents).

To become eligible to seek readmission to Harvard at the end of the year, I would have to write essays reflecting on the reason I had to leave school, express contrition, and explain why I felt confident that I would not repeat my mistake. I would also need to get a full-time job, keep it for at least six months, and obtain a positive review from my employer. Since I didn't have a driver's license, it was decided that I would use the classified ads in *The New York Times* to find a job in the city, and my mother would drive me to the train station at seven each morning and pick me up every evening. She could have easily dropped me off or let me walk to a bus stop so I could get myself to a local business, such as the framing store at the mall, or let me walk or bike to work in one of the many retail businesses near the high school. Better yet, I could have started strong by taking my road test and getting my driver's license—especially since my parents owned three cars—but I'm pretty sure she didn't want anyone we knew to see me. She wanted me out of town and as far away from her as possible, for as many hours as possible.

I landed a job as a Gal Friday at an insurance brokerage in midtown Manhattan—nothing terribly exciting, but at least I'd be fulfilling one of the requirements for reentry to Harvard. This was thirty years before I would study about chakras and become a Reiki energy healer. But there I was—shame burning a hole in my stomach (the location of the third chakra, which represents confidence, self-esteem, personal power, a sense of purpose). I began eating almost as soon as I left the house each day, and continued until I was almost home. I would get out of my mother's car at the train station, go up the escalator, and buy a muffin and coffee from the cart that was parked on the train platform every morning during rush hour. I would eat the muffin on the Long Island Railroad, then walk through Penn Station, take the 7th Avenue train to 42nd Street, change to the crosstown shuttle, and pick up a bagel with a *shmear* and a second cup of coffee as I walked from Grand Central to my office. On the return trip, I'd buy a large cup of Weight Watchers soft-serve frozen treat in Penn Station (chocolate-vanilla swirl), and in this way, continued to massage my third chakra until I returned to Massapequa Park station each evening. I always ate very little at dinner, and if asked what I had done for lunch, I would answer truthfully that I had visited a salad bar near my office, without mentioning that this excursion was scheduled between multiple trips to the break room for additional cups of sweet coffee lightened with half-and-half and slices of Entenmann's coffee cake.

My father wanted to take me to get a thyroid test and other diagnostic bloodwork to discover the medical explanation for why I was blowing up in spite of his not seeing me eat very much food. So I had to confess that I was eating almost nonstop throughout the day while I was away from home. As I recall, he only muttered a few words in response, but I was finally granted permission to see a psychiatrist.

My doctor was somewhat older than my parents, a gentleman from whom my Aunt Phyllis had previously sought treatment. His office was in Morningside Heights, and he specialized in treating students at Columbia. He concluded that I was overeating to avoid dealing with my sexual repression—an awful conversation I did my best to dodge twice a week. But he asked enough questions to prompt me to reveal that the first time I encountered a naked, erect penis, my hand had been placed expectantly on top of said penis, whereafter I lay completely immobilized, almost petrified, balanced at the outer edge of a twin dormitory bed. Then and there, he decided this was the root of all my troubles, and he would not be swayed otherwise. Despite my embarrassment, it helped to be repeatedly told that my sexuality was not a bad thing—even if that advice was coming from an old man prone to preemptory conclusions.

Eventually, I decided to educate myself about sex—but in a safe, academic environment—and began boning up on this gap in my knowledge at the Massapequa Public Library. I rode my bicycle there, locked it up outside, found an out-of-the-way place to study, and systematically consumed every title listed in section 613.951 of the Dewey decimal system, from microfiche copies of Nancy Friday articles to the Kinsey and Hite Reports, to every word ever published by Helen Gurley Brown and Erica Jong. It never occurred to me to look in 306.7, the Dewey decimal location for Romance...but never mind that. Between my childhood fairy tales, Judy Blume books, and Victorian novels, I'd had quite enough of literary romance.

On weekends, I would eat anything in sight, beginning as soon as Mommy left the house. My sister and I had never been allowed in the kitchen without our mother's express permission, which was not an issue in the years before college, partially because I had virtually no appetite, but also because I was accustomed to the rules. I happened to capture a chilling recording of myself as an almost five-year-old, happily reading from a Pippi Longstocking book into my tape recorder, when I was suddenly interrupted by my mother, screaming like a banshee upon having discovered that someone had stolen a bowl of grapes out of the refrigerator, threatening that we would be spanked (later, by our father) if either of us girls had taken it upstairs into our bedrooms.

Nowadays, my hunger had very little to do with appetite or enjoyment, and everything to do with attempting to soothe my own pain. Whenever I found myself alone in the house, I would guilefully tour the kitchen—opening the pantry, refrigerator, and freezer—aware that I needed to be strategic and stealthy, both in what I helped myself to and the way I ate it. If my food consumption were obvious, it would set off a firestorm upon Mommy's return home.

On one Saturday morning, after I had gained a substantial amount of weight, my mother came into the kitchen and found me sitting at the table, a recently used plate and my journal both in front of me. I had just written out several pages of my thoughts after reading *The Women's Room*, a 1977 novel by Marilyn French set in 1950, that investigates young women's relationships with their sexuality through the character of Mira Ward, a "conventional and submissive young woman in a traditional marriage, who experiences a gradual feminist awakening while in grad school at Harvard." I had turned to a new page in my journal, upon which I was wistfully describing the 1950s as a time when "young women weren't ashamed of being virgins," when my mother walked in. In real time, I scrawled the details of our encounter on the blank page before me:

"Mommy just broke my concentration, train of thought, and mood by coming into the kitchen, noting what I had eaten, and lecturing me on being:

Disgusting	Infantile
A balloon	Sick
A slob	A sneak
A pig	Sickening

"Nobody wants to read the writing of anyone as disgusting and messed up as I am. She's really sick of it. Why don't I stop—I **must** see what I look like.

"I'm not eating until my Monday morning muffin—I **swear** it. It's true—I really feel it's true. She makes me so angry."

After that episode, I became a bit more stealthy. I learned to forage downstairs in the laundry room, where two more vaults of provisions were located. On the left side of the room, by the maid's closet, was a refrigerator full of beer and soda; the small freezer above held nothing but trays of ice. This fridge served as a cold annex to the wet bar in the den, the cozy room that lay just beyond, its cabinets filled with wine, every imaginable variety of booze, and individual-sized glass bottles of Schweppes' Bitter Lemon. Opposite the fridge stood a six-foot-tall freezer full of party leftovers: cardboard trays of small savory mushroom appetizers, triangles of spinach wrapped in phyllo dough, aluminum pans filled with stacked layers of brownies, cookies and rugelach, and plastic tubs of Tofutti, then the only commercially available nondairy frozen dessert, which meant it could be served at the end of a kosher meat meal. So as not to be detected, I would eat this food while standing in the laundry room, gnawing at it while it was still frozen. It hurt my stomach, it hurt my jaw, and it tasted like…well, mostly like nothing, but it filled me up and somehow, calmed me down. I guess you could say it numbed me, for a little while.

Soon, in her battle for control—over both my body and her party food inventory—Mommy would install a magnetic lock on the downstairs freezer, and she swore my father and sister to secrecy. When I asked each of them separately why I couldn't open the downstairs freezer door, they denied having any knowledge about why that might be. I would waste quite a bit more time trying to wrestle the door open, but eventually I gave up and found food elsewhere, buying it—cookies, mostly—in Manhattan supermarkets, then stashing the contraband under my bed, zipped into a bubble-gum pink duffel bag I had bought in a moment of wild optimism at the Danskin store by Carnegie Hall, to carry my change of clothes to and from after-work dance classes I would never actually take.

It quickly became impossible to fasten the buttons and zippers on the size-ten skirts, dresses, and slacks I wore to work, and soon after, it was no longer feasible to conceal the gaps by covering them with cardigans or sweater vests. So I took myself shopping, acquiring a size-twelve wardrobe of modest women's office attire from a Lubavitcher-owned discount shop on the Lower East Side, where I had once shopped for holiday clothes as a child. Then, when those clothes eventually became too tight to breathe or sit in, and the humiliation of returning to the same shop in search of clothes in yet a size larger was too painful to contemplate, I resorted to making impulse purchases of size-fourteen pants and blouses at the Rainbow shops inside the train stations I passed through during my daily commute.

Desperate to get away from home, I invented an invitation from a camp friend and took myself on a solo getaway to Washington, DC for the long Fourth of July weekend. I rode the LIRR to Penn Station, took Amtrak to Union Station, then boarded a metro and checked into a hotel in Arlington, Virginia. My plans centered around going to hear Leonard Bernstein conduct the National Symphony Orchestra on the lawn of the Capitol, and I would figure out the rest. I was lonely, but it felt much better than being at home.

Upon my return to Massapequa, I scoured the classified ads in *The New York Times*, found a few real estate listings I thought I could afford, and pitched the idea of my moving to an efficiency in Bensonhurst, Brooklyn. This plan would save my parents the trouble of dealing with me and my commute every day, shave a significant amount off the household grocery bills, and save me $108 a month in train fare. I showed them the ads where it said I would only need $350 a month to rent my own one-room walkup, and the subway from Brooklyn to Manhattan would cost the same as what I was currently paying to ride back and forth across midtown. My mother was probably disappointed when Daddy refused to give me permission to move out. Yes, technically, I was old enough to make my own decisions if I wanted to—I was free to leave—but he said he knew I wouldn't do it because I didn't have a death wish, and surely, I knew that if I tried to live alone in any place I could afford on my Gal Friday's salary, I would probably wind up dead, or worse.

So I continued to live in shame until I became so miserable, so full of despair—over the heaviness of my body, the shame of keeping secrets from my grandparents, and the pain of the scathing comments directed at me—I finally turned to a third set of ads. I flipped through the Yellow Pages and found an ad for an eating disorders clinic on the campus of Columbia University. I called them from my bedroom and left a message. They called me the next day at work; whispering into the phone, I made myself an appointment.

I met only once with the pair of doctors at this clinic. Mainly what they did to help me was to ask questions, then listen attentively, without judgment. As soon as I told my story to these caring, compassionate people, my shame evaporated—and with it, the compulsion to eat an excess of food. That small, simple shred of acceptance and understanding was a miracle. The recently acquired pounds of fat began to melt from my body. By the fall, I was fitting back into, if not my size-eight college party clothes, at least my size-ten work dresses; I was even able to resume belting them at the waist. This recalibration happened not a moment too soon, and not just because it had grown too cold to wear the larger-size clothes I had bought in the train station shops.

The Bearded Lady

In November, two weeks before my nineteenth birthday, after I had been in exile for the better part of a year and had ingested every available piece of literature on the topic of sex at our local public library, I met Barry, a Harvard classmate, when our mutual friend Brent came to stay with him for the weekend.

Barry, who was also taking time off to live with his parents on Long Island, to work and reflect as he pivoted from pre-med to business, reached out to me, and we drove to LaGuardia together to meet Brent's arriving flight. It was a tremendous comfort and diversion to have another friend from Harvard during this period of isolation. To help one another stay fluent in French, Barry proposed that we sign up for an evening class at the Alliance Française. We went to see French films, ate at French restaurants, and, while speaking to one another exclusively in the language of love, we became very close.

After a few weeks of exchanging French kisses and more on the Long Island Railroad, I made myself vulnerable in a letter to Barry, confessing my virginity and inviting him to deflower me. Barry accepted my invitation, but then—once we had scheduled a tryst, lied to our parents, gone to a Times Square hotel room and gotten naked together—he abandoned the deed before it was done, then dodged all my attempts to communicate until it was time for me to return to Cambridge and resume my sophomore year of college.

I wanted us to get together a second time and actually have intercourse—particularly since I'd now read tomes about it—but I thought perhaps Barry was too embarrassed. People say that the first time is always awkward, but after all the planning and subterfuge, we accomplished nothing more than an incomplete blow job and the even more awkward, painful, and bloody rupture of my hymen. I also thought perhaps Barry was appropriately mortified because after he hailed us a taxi outside the hotel to deposit me at Penn Station for a midnight trip back to Massapequa, a handful of coins slid out of his pants pocket as he scooted across the back seat, and he looked down at them and said, "Oh gosh, you're worth much more than that!"—as if the coins were my payment as a hooker. How do you apologize for saying such a stupid thing?

As we stood there in the hotel room, me wearing nothing but white silk panties, embracing him, Barry had to flip through the TV channels and ogle Baryshnikov in tights over my bare shoulder to get hard. I suppose it isn't fair to say I saw it and chose to ignore it. Hindsight is 20:20. I believed what he told me, and bless his heart, he could not tell me the truth. Not yet.

The Ivy League Rub

I returned to Harvard exactly one year after being kicked out, on the day the Space Shuttle Challenger blew up. I switched my major from Fine Arts to English Literature, the department in which I had disgraced myself, and resumed my studies with a determination I had previously lacked—the determination to redeem myself in Harvard's esteem. I fell in love with Victorian novels—which, on an emotional level, seemed to affirm my sexually stifled, archaic worldview much more comfortably than the books I had read during my year off.

Before retreating into Victoriana, though, I hunted Pedro down at the medical school and propositioned him. Months earlier, I had sent him a letter from Massapequa congratulating him on his graduation from the college, and confessing that I had been a virgin when we were together, but no longer was. Now that we were both in Boston, Pedro made it clear that he still had no interest in pursuing a serious relationship with me, but he said his friends told him he would be crazy not to accept my offer of having sex without any obligation to date. I was thrilled to finally feel free to express the affection and attraction I felt for this man after having been frozen stiff when we were dating. Sadly, our one night together in my dorm room resulted in this chilling utterance from Pedro: "So you were a virgin then, and now you're an animal!" I do not think he meant to hurt me; he seemed genuinely surprised by the transformation

107

in me. Maybe repressed Nancy was more attractive than liberated Nancy, or less threatening.

I had now gotten naked with two men, and they both disappeared directly afterward. Evidently, I was not getting this sexuality thing right at all; I would have to dial it down. Who was better suited to help me fold myself back into the closet of sexual repression than my good old buddy, Barry?

When Barry returned to campus, I hunted him down, too, which was easy because even though he was still not returning any of my calls, he was rooming with our good friend Brent for the summer. After one awkward conversation, in which Barry set some new ground rules for our relationship, he and I became inseparable, "dating" platonically. He asked if we could just be friends because he wasn't ready for a serious relationship and didn't want to hurt me; rather than lose him, I agreed. A serious relationship wasn't what Barry was avoiding, however; unbeknownst to me at the time, Barry was gradually, secretly getting in touch with his sexuality but was not yet ready to come out.

Valuing me as an entertaining and doting companion who appeared to be his girlfriend, Barry went to great lengths to keep me by his side and keep all others away, especially at Harvard Hillel, where I played the beard in a semester-long "dinner class" with the rabbi on Marriage and Jewish Law. We would load up our plates with the kosher meal being served downstairs, where all our friends were eating dinner, and balance them on trays as we climbed up a flight of stairs to the rabbi's study to eat at a large round table as we learned. Every other couple in the class was engaged. My mother was delighted by this report and encouraged me to be patient; she was sure Barry was simply waiting for the perfect moment to propose. This belief seemed to echo what Barry had told me lately, when I wanted a goodnight kiss at the end of an evening spent together out at the theater or ballet in Boston: "patience is a virtue."

We also enrolled in secular classes together—courses I would not otherwise have considered taking, including one on the Crusades and another on Genocide and the Holocaust, taught by a holocaust survivor. One winter's day in early 1987, Nelson, a guy I had recently met, came into the classroom in Harvard Hall, right before our Genocide lecture was to begin. He knelt on the floor beside where I sat—in the front row next to Barry—and asked me to get lunch with him after class at Lowell, his and Barry's dorm. I squirmed in my seat between the two of them at the dining table, especially since Barry was spouting sexual innuendo throughout the meal, implying that we were a couple into BDSM. When Nelson called me afterward, he invited me to a coffeehouse in the Lowell common room, where he would be playing the piano and singing. I brought Barry and sat next to him, my head tilting to rest on his shoulder during the most romantic song.

When Nelson asked me on a real date, we met at Shays Pub & Wine Bar on JFK Street one Monday evening after my weekly orchestra rehearsal. Once I was noticeably tipsy, he walked me around the corner to his final club, on Mount Auburn Street, where he sat at the piano and sang, then played a long series of suspended chords while asking me a series of personal questions. I confessed to him that first night that Barry and I had a brief romantic history but assured him we were now just friends and nothing more.

Beau Dearest

When Nelson and I first began dating, he asked for the passcode to my answering machine, so we could leave each other little messages of endearment throughout the day. I was so flattered and delighted by his desire for daily intimacy that I was completely duped into sacrificing my privacy and autonomy. It took me a bit too long to figure out that when Nelson heard a message from Barry, he would delete it. He evidently considered the frequent messages to be evidence of a threat to our relationship and soon demanded that I stop spending time with Barry outside of class. This meant giving up dinners at Hillel, discontinuing Wednesday night trips to MIT for Israeli folk dancing, and foregoing members-only open bar on Thursday nights at the Hasty Pudding Club. I also stopped attending Shabbat services on Friday nights in favor of attending ice hockey games with Nelson.

Soon, I even quit my beloved orchestra because Nelson wanted to spend more time with me. What was the point of performing, if not to feel connected to something greater than yourself? With Nelson, I believed I had found that; and I never thought twice when he told me how lucky I was to have found in him someone who could appreciate and accept me. In my steady diet of Victorian novels, I found robust confirmation that it was normal and good to make sacrifices when one is fortunate enough to find love. The fact that these stories were written in a different century was a detail I chose to overlook.

I knew that Nelson's demands were a bit extreme, but I felt compassion for him because I knew he'd been scarred by betrayal in past relationships. His most recent ex, Jean Neubauer, had even entertained the idea of marrying Nelson and hyphenating her last name to become known (rather hilariously) as Jean Neubauer-Bauer, but then she dumped him in favor of her Norwegian TA at the law school, after having denied anything was going on between them. Before Jean, Nelson said he dated a "sexy Puerto Rican" from Currier House who would upset him by dancing provocatively with her friends in her dorm's basement nightclub, then denying any flirtatious intentions, until Nelson finally found her *in flagrante delicto* with her neighbor. If these past betrayals meant I had to go the extra mile to prove Nelson could trust me, so be it.

Compassion can be my Achilles' heel, especially when I extend it to narcissists. From a young age, I was taught to put others' needs ahead of my own. My spirit guides continually help me identify my own needs and to make some demands for my own benefit. It's been a long road, but I am getting there. Over and over, I am learning to see the wisdom of that emergency landing survival script and the importance of dealing with one's own metaphorical oxygen mask before fastening that of others. And I've learned that when you practice radical self-care, there are no limits to what you can do.

Oxford | Summer 1987

I took a second sojourn away from Harvard the summer I was twenty. My grandparents sent me to Oxford University for a summer session in English Literature for Americans and Canadians, where I was able to take a Shakespeare survey class that would replace (but not erase) the one in which I had disgraced myself, while also studying critical literary theory. The trip was inspired by my desire to see a collection of letters written between Virginia Woolf and the novelist known as George Eliot; I was hoping to find in their correspondence a topic for my senior thesis. When I arrived, I discovered that the section of the Bodleian Library that houses the women's letters, the Radcliffe Camera, would be inaccessible, due to renovations, for the entirety of my time there. I would need to find a new thesis topic, and as it turned out, a much more deeply personal one.

At Oxford, I read some assigned excerpts from Bruno Bettelheim's book about classic fairy tales and realized my psyche had been warped by the messages I'd absorbed from these stories as a child. Desperate to liberate myself from my lockstep march toward the *chuppah*, I decided to devote my thesis work to examining the failure of feminists to produce satisfying revisions of traditional fairy tales—more specifically, their utter failure to offer girls like me an attractive alternative to the conventional marriage ending. My submission generated controversy among the English department faculty. It was subversive enough to require the assignment of a second set of readers, but not enough to prevent me from graduating with honors.

Neither did my thesis prove radical enough to disrupt me from continuing toward the unsatisfactory fairy-tale ending of conventional marriage. Evidently, there was nothing in the world that could throw me off that course—not even a cathartic kiss from a real-life prince.

My first day visiting London—about fifty miles from Oxford and a bit over an hour by coach—I met a man while shopping at Harrods. When we first caught sight of one another, we both thought we recognized the other from some previous meeting, but upon introducing ourselves, neither Marcus nor I could think of where such a meeting might have taken place. When he first approached me, I was looking down into a glass case of earrings, and he pointed to a particular pair, and said he could picture me wearing them while "standing on a sand dune, the wind blowing my dress and hair." I interpreted the words of this fully grown adult male as a sales pitch, and we both laughed after realizing I had mistaken him for an employee of the legendary store.

Marcus bowed slightly, introduced himself, and offered me his card, sliding it from a golden case he kept in the breast pocket of his three-piece beige linen suit. We got to talking, there beside the display case, and I learned he was a friend of the dean of students at Harvard but hadn't visited the campus in years, as he was busy dividing his time between London, Paris, and his "boat," which he kept in the South of France. I declined Marcus's invitation to share a meal with him that evening, as I was already committed to dining with ninety fellow students on the Thames.

The Prince and the Plagiarist

Our relationship began about an hour later, when Marcus appeared at our table and invited himself to take high tea with me and my girlfriends upstairs at Harrods. Then, realizing we young ladies had lost track of time and were at risk of missing our dinner cruise, Marcus jumped up from the table, apologized, and added our bill to his tab with a wave of his hand—explaining, as he guided us to the escalator, that he frequented Harrods often because the owner was one of his closest friends. Escorting us through the food halls, past a pair of swinging doors into the kitchen, he led us through the store's back door. We piled ourselves swiftly into a taxi, at which point Marcus pressed a hundred-pound note into my hand and sent us off to the pier to catch our boat. He was dumbstruck, later that week, when he received a Winnie-the-Pooh greeting card containing a handwritten thank-you note for a memorable first afternoon in London and a money order for the change I had received from our taxi driver.

The economic disparity between our situations was comical, or I suppose I made it so with my response to it. Marcus kept a fleet of collectible cars in the garage of an upscale London hotel, so conveniently located that he sometimes would run off and "change cars" mid-evening, as casually as somebody else dining near their flat might run upstairs to grab a sweater. He found it adorable that I could sit in the passenger seat of his white Rolls Royce Corniche convertible, or his golden gullwing Mercedes, and present an argument for my needing to treat him to pizza the next time we got together. He also loved to say I was a born princess—always insisting, when I bristled, that it was high praise. Sometimes we would just be sitting and chatting over a slice of pizza at a café, admiring the cars going by, and Marcus would comment on my regal bearing, or chuckle at what he called the imperial way I commanded my friends to do my bidding.

I had to breathe through my discomfort that I was never going to be permitted to pay for anything, and accept it as my role to be delighted by the marvelous meals and experiences Marcus arranged, such as the chance to sing my favorite jazz standards with piano accompaniment at a private underground club. When I handed the microphone back to the pianist and walked over to reclaim my seat beside him, Marcus beamed with pride and delight, as if he'd vicariously experienced my joy in performing—but multiplied. "That was splendid! You are positively marvelous!" he exclaimed. I beamed back at him, all aglow.

Can you say daddy issues? The age disparity may have been less glaring than the economic one…perhaps…but it was significant, nonetheless. It was smaller than the gap between the Macrons' ages, or the Trumps' for that matter, but at the tender age of twenty, I was literally half Marcus's age. The fact is that it was pretty glaring, yet socially acceptable—or at least it seemed to be—wherever we went. Or maybe you're just treated really well when you are very rich.

As I looked into Marcus's smiling face, it struck me that I had never seen anything quite like it, with the possible exception of my beloved grandfather, who truly adored me, and had also loved spending money on me. Besides Papa (as I called him), everyone who had ever attended one of my childhood performances had done so either out of a sense of obligation or with a touch of envy, resentment, or impatience; I often got the feeling that, to some degree, they would rather be elsewhere. My father never once complimented me on a performance, and quite often his beeper would go off mid-concert and he would head to the emergency room before the applause. Once, I found him standing in the lobby right after a youth orchestra concert and asked if I might have a dollar to buy a cookie, and—rather than showering me with congratulations or praise—he scolded me for not first having thanked him for attending my concert.

It was no wonder I sometimes had a hard time accepting such effusive compliments as the ones I got from Marcus. The experience of being with him was so unfamiliar as to be disorienting; in my mind, as ridiculous as it feels to confess it, I turned him into a fictional character, based on Mr. Rourke from Fantasy Island—a mysteriously powerful man who made people's dreams come true. I even described him as such in a postcard to Nelson, who saw right through my naïve delusion and called my parents in a panic.

Even at twenty, I was still quite sheltered. I had spent three years on a campus surrounded by mostly straight young men who appeared not to notice me, and closeted gay men who were friendly enough but indifferent to my charms—interrupted by a year during which I'd become invisible, ironically, by outgrowing my clothes by three sizes. During that time, I had grown another inch and a half taller, finally reaching my full adult height of six feet. I hadn't been out in the world long enough to learn that most straight men would find me attractive, but only those with an above-average level of confidence would act on that attraction. Evidently, it takes guts to approach a six-foot-tall woman, especially a good-looking one. In any case, I was never approached by men within a decade of my age. Not at summer camp, not on the Harvard campus, not out dancing in Boston, not on vacation in the Caribbean, not even while working a wedding on a catering crew.

With all three young men I'd dated—Barry, Pedro, and Nelson—and all six of the guys I'd kissed, I had been the one to initiate contact. When it came to meeting Nelson, we had been in class together—The History of Jazz—all semester long, and we had friends in common, most notably Roy. But in all that time, Nelson had never once spoken to me, smiled at me, or even made eye contact, until we both showed up super early for the final exam. Nelson was there because he realized he'd already memorized the entire syllabus, and I was there because, when I went to the room in Boylston Hall where all the jazz recordings were kept, I realized I had left all my course notes at the quad and I just didn't care enough to go all the way back up Garden Street to retrieve them.

Instead, I entered the spacious vestibule and crossed the room to introduce myself to Nelson, breaking a rule of final club etiquette I didn't know about—boldly mentioning that I'd spotted him going into the Phoenix Club several times and that I was familiar with the club because years ago, I had dated another of its members. When Pedro called me the next day and said, "guess who's been asking questions about you?" I laughed and guessed it was Nelson. In dropping Pedro's name, I hadn't imagined he would describe me as a classic New York neurotic, but that's what Nelson claimed Pedro had said about me. I will never know if Pedro also shared his observation that I had gone from virgin to voracious in the span of my nineteenth year. Probably.

In any case, I was in denial about Marcus's attraction to me, but I began to suspect something was up when he started making awkward references to our age difference, or struggled to keep his thinning hair in place by wearing a cap while driving one of his convertibles, becoming flustered if it flew off in the breeze. My girlfriends teased me for always bringing one or more of them to London as my chaperones; they were delighted to share in the adventure, but it was clear—at least to them—that Marcus would have preferred I show up alone.

Nelson and I had been dating for three months before we embarked on our respective summer adventures, and we'd parted ways with the mutual expectation that we would miss each other terribly and resume our relationship when we were both back stateside. He was backpacking all over Western Europe with his friend Jamie, sending me postcards full of horny reminiscence. If I were dating Marcus, it would mean I was cheating on Nelson.

When Marcus and I eventually kissed, it was like no kiss I had ever experienced, either before or since. Unlike a movie kiss, where the room spins slowly around you, this kiss simulated a black hole in obliterating my awareness of anything in the universe other than our connection. I did not so much melt as disappear into it; my heart felt as if it were shattering into a billion bits of stardust. My entire being, all of my energy, wanted only to merge with his. When the thinking part of my brain reset itself and my thoughts reactivated, I pulled away, sat up, swung my legs over the side of the bed, and crossed my arms. Marcus apologized, said "well, we were not expecting *that*!" along with a few other awkward utterances, then rang his driver, as he did at the end of all our evenings in London, asking him to return me to Oxford.

I didn't know what to think. I had felt compelled to spend time with this man, but only after we had kissed—no, more than kissed, rolled around in bed, pressed our bodies urgently against one another—did I realize how powerfully attracted to him I was. How had I suppressed such strong feelings all these weeks? I tried hard to silence a moan as I squirmed in the back seat of the limousine. I could feel my heart pounding in my chest, and the tugging in my groin intensified as my mind and body replayed the final minutes of our visit. I knew I had never experienced this degree of chemistry with anyone—not with Pedro or Barry, and certainly not with Nelson—and the strength of my feelings frightened me, and made me feel out of control.

I considered that it was probably wiser to stick with someone who didn't have this deranging effect on me. Now that we'd acknowledged the passion between us, I realized there was no way we could get together another time without tearing each other's clothes off. I decided it would be best not to see Marcus ever again.

When you are taught to prize self-control above all else, anything that threatens it is simply terrifying.

Second Spirit Messenger | Oxford, 1987

Marcus had a car phone, but we students had no phones in the dormitory. A stack of pink paper messages piled up for me at the gate porter's lodge over the next few days.

The night after the kiss, I dreamed about Marcus and awoke startled, exhausted, and confused. Using my immersion heater (which I kept for just such an emergency) and a mug of water from the bathroom faucet, I gulped down a strong cup of instant coffee in my room, then marched off to the Bodleian Library to sleuth out Marcus's true identity, searching for his face in historic portraits of certain royal Arab families, employing hints he'd dropped like so many bread crumbs along the way—his having been educated at Sandhurst Academy, then at Christ Church, Oxford, from which he graduated as the Six-Day War broke out; he had witnessed his father's death as a young boy, and his widowed mother—who now did charity work—would never remarry because his father had been too great a man.

Even without finding a photo to validate my dream, I realized that Marcus had deliberately concealed his identity as an Arab from me. The name he used in London and Paris, Marcus Alexander Rothschild, was an oddly chosen alias—presumably inspired by the gentleman to whom the Earl of Balfour had famously addressed his 1917 proposal regarding the establishment of a Jewish state, which would become the diplomatic foundation for the eventual establishment of the State of Israel. I read that Jordan's King Abdullah had been assassinated in 1951, a year during which "Marcus" had been a small boy, causing me to wonder if perhaps he was a prince of Jordan. But then I saw that many other Arab royal families sent their sons to be educated at Sandhurst and Oxford. At our high tea together, on the top floor of his Egyptian friend's store, Marcus guessed that I was Jewish; when I inquired about his nationality, he'd replied that he was European. I considered wryly that his family, no matter who they were, would most likely disapprove of me even more strongly than Pedro's had.

I broke from my sleuthing because I was trembling, and even felt a bit dizzy. Part of me wanted to continue digging through volumes on Arab royals in London, but I also needed to get back to the dining hall before breakfast was over. As I walked through the gate, back into the courtyard of Trinity College, I must have been visibly shaken, because a statuesque woman approached me and—just as I was about to offer her directions—startled me by offering *her* assistance. "You're very upset," she said, matter-of-factly but with great kindness, "and I'd love to help you." I was dumbstruck.

As it turned out, Anna was a psychic I had heard about around campus, who'd been invited to speak with all the North American students attending our summer session at Trinity. As Anna introduced herself, I felt she could see into my soul and found myself hoping she wasn't gifted enough to know I'd been mocking the don of the college for having invited her. I was an intellectual snob at the time, still afraid to believe in the great mystery, and I had loudly expressed my disappointment in Oxford University for lending credence to such psychic nonsense. But I could not deny that I sensed pure love from Anna at first sight, as I looked into her sparkling blue eyes and heard myself accept her offer without hesitation.

Her event began that very evening. My deeply ingrained skepticism prevailed upon me to skip the presentation, and I showed up just in time to catch the tail end. I saw my fellow students standing in a circle onstage, wiping tears from their eyes, as one of them wrapped up a story about something her father had said to her. I stood in the wings, wrestling with my disbelief. It was a rare moment in which my desire for help was stronger than my skepticism.

When the other students dispersed, I found Anna backstage, and she offered me a seat. As soon as I settled myself on the tall, padded stool, Anna led me into a past-life regression, which revealed that Marcus and I had been friends many years before and he had betrayed and killed me as we stood face to face on a sand dune. I reported feeling shocked to see him brandish his sword; the next thing I knew, I witnessed him slicing my body open with its curved and gleaming blade. I realized that he had killed me, yet I was strangely calm.

At the end of the regression, I knew with clarity that Marcus and I had met again in this lifetime to create peace, but I didn't know what this new revelation required of me. Back in present-day, late-twentieth-century London—with nary a sand dune in sight—I had watched Marcus morph, over the course of six weeks, from ebullient and jovial to quiet and melancholy.

Anna assured me he'd been having thoughts, feelings, and dreams similar to what I'd been experiencing. She spoke of him with sympathy and tenderness, describing the torment he was surely suffering. I couldn't begin to imagine what it must be like for Marcus to sense that he was spending time with someone he had betrayed in a past life. Someone he had killed. Someone who had been a friend.

Anna offered to host us at her country home, with the assurance that, if we would come for the weekend, we would wind up in one another's arms. Then she introduced me to her lover, Rob, who shared that they had gotten together a few years ago, after they both realized that he had been her page, back when she had been a knight. "Rob used to kneel at my feet and buckle me into my armor," she told me, laughing gently. "And now, I am her devoted servant," Rob said, "just in a different way."

This was all very interesting, but as a young Jewish-American student, I was not prepared to throw away the future my parents envisioned for me in favor of exploring an alternative path with Marcus. The vision of him brandishing his sword, slicing me open with one violent stroke, was vivid and frightening, and it haunted me; for a while, I was too shaken to return Marcus's calls.

When I finally did call Marcus back, I was still reluctant (terrified) to see him again and made excuses. He offered me a vacant apartment in New York that I might use as a *pied-à-terre* during senior year, while I interviewed for jobs, then make it my home after graduation. He wanted me to be free to take any position I liked after graduating from Harvard, without concern about the salary. He was disappointed but not surprised when I refused his offer. Of course, I would have loved to roam around a sunlit, prewar apartment with a view of Central Park rather than sharing a small, cookie-cutter space in a new building across from a construction site on Third Avenue.

It was tempting, but I didn't aspire to be a kept woman. Without addressing the heart of the matter, I assured Marcus that my parents lived close enough to New York City for me to stay with them while interviewing. I insisted I could find a first job that enabled me to split the rent for an apartment I would share with a girlfriend.

I also rebuffed Marcus's invitation to spend a week or two with him and his friends—who included Nastassja Kinski, an actress I'd loved since I saw her in *Tess*, and her husband—on his yacht in the South of France. When I expressed admiration for Nastassja's beauty, Marcus said he had dated his fill of models and actresses, and that I possessed a portfolio of special qualities none of them had; he assured me that Nastassja would find me fascinating. Despite feeling deeply flattered, I declined, explaining that I'd promised to spend the last weeks of summer working at my father's medical office, right up until classes resumed. Marcus was intent on having me spend time on his boat; he asked if he might call my father and ask his permission to "borrow" me. He wanted so badly to sweep me off my feet, but I would not be swayed.

I don't have to tell you that by now, dear reader, this did not feel like a casual flirtation. Given our dramatic past-life history and the ferocity of my attraction to him, my connection with

Marcus seemed not only powerful but deadly serious. I knew of several Americans who had married foreign nobility—from Grace Kelly to Lisa Halaby—and I was terrified of joining their ranks, imagining that if I became engaged to Marcus, we might both be assassinated.

I didn't realize it then, but the raven-haired gypsy's prophecy—which had seemed so absurd five years earlier when I was a fifteen-year-old music student in Vermont—was now unfolding into reality, precisely on time. That strange, beautiful woman told me that I would choose between two men I would meet five years hence to be my husband. I now found myself pulled between two suitors, precisely as she had described: one, a Jewish-American college classmate; the other, a foreigner I'd met in London.

I used to blame myself for having been too cowardly to go with Marcus—at least for a weekend at Anna's country cottage—to discover whether we could weave our lives together. It would be many years before I understood that Marcus and I had completed our healing work in the short time we spent together. When I read several books by Brian Weiss, MD, I would come to understand: in healing past-life trauma, it can be sufficient to be loving toward someone for even a moment.

Marcus and I experienced a bit more than that, but in the end...it was enough.

Chapter 4

WORKING GIRL | NYC

About eight months after leaving England, I would submit and defend my honors thesis on fairy tales. Despite the controversy my topic evoked among the English department faculty, I enjoyed success as a student of literature and managed to graduate with honors from the department that had been instrumental in kicking me out three and a half years earlier. In my quest to redeem myself in Harvard's eyes, I rediscovered my great love of books and decided I'd like to stick around and study for a few more years, and maybe even teach.

Despite my academic prowess, my thesis advisor surprised me by refusing to write a recommendation for me to pursue graduate studies in literature. Together with her equally brilliant and charming husband, she insisted that I must not choose the ivory tower until I had first tried living in the real world. Graduate school isn't nearly as glamorous as college, she cautioned—moreover, there is no instant gratification to be found in academia. She knew from working with me for a year how much I craved positive feedback, and she was concerned I would be miserable as a lonely, neglected academic. Together we devised a new plan: I would stay in the Boston area and find a job in publishing, and we would reassess my desire to pursue graduate studies at a later date. I wanted to defend myself against the observation that I needed regular doses of glamor, positive feedback, and instant gratification, but I found myself mute with shame. Her description of me felt like character assassination, but it was absolutely true.

This decision came after I eschewed several weeks of on-campus recruiting that had inspired so many of my classmates—including some English majors—to come to breakfast wearing pinstriped suits and dresses from Ann Taylor. Thus, I was spared a foray into the mysterious world of investment banking or the even-murkier realm known as consulting. As fate would have it, I was also spared the tasks of making coffee and photocopies for the lovely people working in publishing.

Just as I was about to print and mail my letters to all the publishing houses in Boston, I began experiencing a mysterious vaginal pain that demanded medical attention. As the doctor at University Health services examined me, she wondered aloud whether my boyfriend had been with any other sexual partners lately, and suggested I ask him directly. This seemed ridiculous, but so did the pain between my legs, so I dutifully agreed to ask him, which is how I found out that Nelson had been cheating on me with a law school classmate.

After he confessed, Nelson declared that it was impossible for me to understand him the way his law school classmates did. He also said that he was so miserable in law school that he was unable to be as nice to me as I deserved. In response, I broke up with him, discarded all the letters I had written seeking local employment, and decided I would revert to Plan A and live in Manhattan after graduation. Having turned down Marcus's offer of a free apartment (for there is no such thing as free), I agreed to become my friend Amy's new roommate, taking the place vacated by another friend who was moving to San Francisco.

I had taken a grueling job at Macy's after an interview arranged for me by Barry's parents—who were as deluded as I was—on the presumption I might soon be joining their family clothing manufacturing business. To learn the ins and outs of the industry and be an asset to them, they wanted me to enroll in the executive training program at the venerable department store, which at the time was called the Harvard of Retail.

While strolling to class with a friend one day, I learned that we were both planning to work at Macy's after graduation, except that I was starting right away and he would be in another cohort later in the summer, after traveling for a few weeks with some friends. I also learned the $22,000 salary they had offered me was about 18 percent lower than the $26,000 salary offered him—my Black male classmate, an economics major who confessed to having had zero retail experience and grades substantially lower than mine. He was as surprised by the discrepancy as I was, and suggested I call and ask why my salary was lower than his.

I was so naïve that after being upset all morning, I called Human Resources at Macy's later that day to ask if there could have been a mistake. Would she please explain the disparity in our starting salaries? Had I performed poorly during my evaluation? The human resources officer explained to me that my starting salary was calculated based on Macy's estimation of my value in the greater job market. She also confirmed that all my raises would be a percentage of my starting salary, then validated my observation that if my friend and I were to perform equally well in the job, the disparity in our wages would only increase over time.

Disabused of any expectation of fairness, I was resentful of the company even before I began working there. And I felt the pain of my low salary right away. My parents provided me a wardrobe of suits, blouses, pantyhose, and pumps for my new job, but I soon found myself forking over more than half my take-home pay to sleep on a sofa bed in the living room of a one-bedroom apartment in a new residential tower on Third Avenue colloquially known as "the dorm." I also had to pay my share of the electricity bill, my long-distance calls to Nelson at law school (he had won me back with a dozen roses and a lame apology) and to other friends scattered across the country, as well as an extra fee to use the gym upstairs. Even doing laundry down the hall cost money. Clearly, I would need to skimp on food and entertainment.

In the morning, I made myself coffee in the apartment's galley kitchen and stood there drinking it from a big mug while simultaneously inhaling a mug of instant oatmeal. Lunch was the culinary highlight of the day, composed at a salad bar close to the store. Dinner was either half a box of spaghetti, or if I felt too tired to boil water, I'd stop off during my walk home and buy a sweet frozen supper—either a jumbo cup of oat-based Skimpy Treat, another fake low-calorie ice cream substitute called Tasti D-Lite, or on weekends, a pint of Ben and Jerry's, which I would eat on the couch in front of the television I'd taken from my parents' basement.

At Macy's, my mentor was an assistant coat buyer—a thin, pale, plain-looking woman who had graduated from Cornell three years earlier. Her primary advice was that tall, beautiful women with Harvard degrees are seen as threatening; I had to understand that some people were predisposed to dislike me and if I wanted to get ahead, I would have to make an extra effort to get along with others. Especially when it came to our male colleagues and superiors, I needed to be twice as nice, and ask frequently and politely for help and advice. Other golden nuggets dispensed from the same fount of wisdom included: everyone in retail drinks Diet Coke, white coats sell best in New Jersey, and Nordstrom ranks as the pinnacle in customer service.

As a department manager, I learned I was great at helping customers and really bad at carrying out solitary tasks I found boring, such as organizing my stockroom and taking inventory. I also learned that stockboys do not have the strongest work ethic, will not come to work for One Day Sales if their department's merchandise has been featured on the cover of the Sunday circular, and that their manager is expected to do their work when they don't come in. I learned this last lesson the hard way, carrying microwave ovens from the stockroom to the register on a busy fourteen-hour day, and throwing my back into a week-long spasm. My convalescence gave me time to think, the consequence of which was that I quit the Macy's job right before the Christmas season, which no one should have to suffer through unless they are fully committed.

After a brief respite in the Caribbean, being scolded by my parents, getting sunburned, and drinking way too many daiquiris with my sister, I returned to New York and began pounding the pavement, looking for my next job. That next job, working for a man named Norman, would turn out to be a series of crazy escapades, including, most notably, two solo trips to the Soviet Union. Ostensibly sent to learn how American companies were arranging to do business with the Soviets during perestroika, I arrived in Moscow with my luggage stuffed full of contraband intended for refuseniks—Soviet Jews who had been denied permission to emigrate to Israel—material that was immediately confiscated, along with the rest of my luggage. The trips were eye opening, resulting in a heightened awareness of how privileged and sheltered my life was, and seeded the germ of an idea of how noble it would be to fight on behalf of people who were born less fortunate than I.

My boss Norman was a diverter; he did commerce in a lucrative zone, outside the purview of anti-trust laws, commonly known as the gray market. Besides giving me the opportunity to travel internationally and learn a great deal about myself, how people live elsewhere, and how business is done in the real world (while receiving a much higher salary than I had at Macy's), my duties required that I constantly skirt the edge of legality. As a budding lawyer, Nelson expressed concern about my working for Norman. It was difficult enough to do my job without listening to his criticism, but my parents had told me I couldn't quit for quite some time because I had left my last job after only six months. So I simply stopped talking about work when I was with Nelson; we talked about him instead, which was easy enough to manage.

Engagement

While visiting Nelson's family in Cincinnati at the start of the summer, I forgot to pack my diaphragm and ended up using an over-the-counter contraceptive sponge, which we learned about by reading the packaging in a drugstore while shopping for condoms. Thanks to my ADHD, much of our busy summer in New York City went by before I realized I hadn't had my period for quite some time. How long, I wasn't sure; I had a lot going on.

My best-ever roommate, Amy, had moved out to live with her fiancé as their wedding date approached, and Nelson was now living with me in the apartment I had shared with her, commuting downtown to his summer job at a law firm on Wall Street. I can't remember how it first dawned on me to consider why I might have been gaining weight lately, especially in my breasts—so much so, that I could no longer sleep comfortably on my stomach—or why the coffee at work started tasting so bad, and why I had been craving egg-and-ketchup sandwiches from the diner downstairs.

I called my oldest friend, Melanie, at her summer job up in Boston. She was employed at an obstetrical gynecologist's office between her first and second years of medical school. I asked Melanie how I could tell if I was pregnant. She told me to put my fingers up inside my vagina and feel my cervix. If I was not pregnant, she said, it would feel firm, like the end of my nose, but if I were pregnant it would feel soft and mushy, more like my lips. She reminded me that I had felt it many times before, whenever I would insert or remove my diaphragm. I put the phone receiver down, washed my hands as directed, then reached in and poked at my cervix. Feeling suddenly nauseated, I picked up the phone again and said, "Mel, it's soft and mushy. It doesn't feel at all like the end of my nose."

"All right," she said. "Go get a pregnancy test and call me right back." I hung up the phone, walked across the street to the drug store, and brought home a pregnancy test. I called Melanie again as I opened the package, and she stayed on the line while I stood over the toilet and peed on the plastic stick. I was still on the phone with her when the pink line appeared, confirming what we had already figured out. Melanie asked me when I thought this might have happened, and I told her about the sponge incident at during my visit to Cincinnati.

"Shit…no, yeah—that's not at all effective on its own, as you now know."

But Melanie told me not to worry; she would arrange everything with her boss, who would perform a D&C in the office; how soon could I come to Boston?

We were already planning to be in Boston that weekend, for Amy's wedding. "Good," Melanie said, "because it sounds like you're pretty far along. It will be easier if you're still in your first trimester. Come up a day earlier than you were planning, and I'll get you on the schedule first thing the next morning. Be at the office at eight o'clock sharp."

I did just as Melanie instructed. As calmly as possible, I called Nelson and explained the situation. I believe that all I asked of him was that he accompany me to the medical office where Melanie worked, wait for me during the procedure, and bring me back to his apartment afterward. I will spare you the details. The roughest part was probably my reaction to the valium, which made me vomit.

At Amy's wedding, two days after my abortion, I couldn't tell her that I wasn't dancing the *hora* because I was bleeding too heavily and cramping. Anyone who noticed how hard I cried during the ceremony or how emotional I was all throughout the reception would have thought I was terribly sentimental, but I was simply a hormonal wreck.

After the wedding, we returned to Nelson's apartment for a brief nap; then it was time to change our clothes and go into Boston for dinner at a fancy restaurant. I wasn't really in the mood to go out, much less get back onto the T all dressed up, but I had gotten a tip that tonight was important, so I knew what I had to do. While I was still resting in bed, and evidently mistaken for being asleep, my sister called Nelson's apartment, which was unusual. I heard him say, "Oh, hi, Sissy!" Then I heard her ask Nelson if he had proposed yet. He had no idea that I was awake, much less that I was able to hear my sister's voice through the receiver, but he played it safe, dodging the question and informing her in a cheerful voice that we were just resting after Amy's wedding and would soon be getting ready to go to a very special restaurant, Maison Robert, in Boston's Old City Hall, where he'd made reservations several weeks earlier.

So I pretty much knew what was coming next. Though I desperately wanted to stay in bed, I showered, reapplied my makeup, and dressed to the nines—taking a brand-new pair of off-black control-top pantyhose out of their package, positioning the last of the jumbo maxi pads Melanie had given me securely between my thighs, and slipping my stockinged feet into a punishing pair of high-heeled purple-and-black pumps. As I leaned in toward the dirty bathroom mirror to apply my lip liner, lipstick and lip gloss, eyeliner, eyebrow pencil, several shades of eyeshadow and mascara, I considered the fact that Nelson had planned this evening weeks ago, discussed it with my sister, yet had never breathed a word to me.

I wondered why Nelson didn't let me know that he wanted to marry me as I went through the trauma of an unwanted pregnancy and abortion. Was it to avoid being involved in wedding planning? To avoid discussing having a baby before he was ready to have one? Probably both. But even as he sat beside me during Amy's ceremony and reception, mere hours before his planned proposal, he never let me enjoy a moment of comfort or reassurance. Had we been in a movie or a novel, we would have exchanged a loving look during the vows; at the very least, he would have made a cute, cryptic remark that hinted at his intention that we might soon partake in the same sort of joy.

As I moved on to the contour powder, blush, highlighter, and bronzer, I tried to brush any confusing thoughts from my mind. This was long before smart phones and Instagram, but I was accustomed to special moments being photographed, and in any case, I wanted ours to be picture perfect. I was expecting a scene to unfold like one of the cinematic proposals I had seen throughout my life, on screens of all sizes.

All through the long, multi-course dinner, I stayed on high alert while feigning nonchalance, waiting for the big moment. When the entrée was cleared without incident, I agreed to order dessert, even though I was quite full, certain that at any minute, a diamond ring would appear at the bottom of a champagne glass or hidden inside a piece of cake. When Nelson asked for the check, I was overstuffed and confused. Was it my fault he hadn't proposed at the table? Was it because I never gave him a min-ute alone, never left to go and powder my nose and reapply my lipstick? While Nelson waited for his credit card to be returned, I excused myself and went to the ladies' room. I looked at my reflection, combed my hair, touched up my makeup, and asked the mirror "what the hell?" before heading back to the table to find Nelson offering me a mint and gesturing toward the exit.

It was quite dark as we stepped outside. Perhaps now, in the lamplight, Nelson would take me in his arms and declare his un-dying love. Instead, he suggested we take a walk to help us digest the heavy meal. I was having difficulty negotiating the cobble-stones in my high heels, so I let Nelson take me by the hand and lead me through a maze of streets until finally we entered the relative darkness of Boston Commons. Reaching a park bench, he promptly sat down and asked, "would you happen to have a tissue?" I sat next to him, grateful to take the weight off my feet.

I opened my little beaded pocketbook, dug past the compact, lipstick, lip pencil, lip gloss and comb, and proffered the tissue, which he accepted from me as he said, "you really like taking care of me, don't you?" When I agreed, he asked if I were willing to continue doing so for the rest of my life.

Ugh—not a cinematic moment at all, and not a bit romantic either. Was there nothing else he could summon to say…or do? How about getting down on one knee? As I consented to take care of Nelson for the rest of my life, I realized in horror that this query constituted his long-planned, much-awaited marriage proposal. The question Nelson most cared about had been asked and answered.

As my head stopped spinning and I realized what was happening, Nelson reached into his jacket pocket and took out a small box, containing a ring—which he explained, as he opened it, his grandmother had given him during our last visit to Cincinnati (the same trip, I thought to myself, my mind racing, during which we had become pregnant). I took a beat to consider the now incontrovertible fact that he'd been planning this proposal all summer long but hadn't given me any hint that it was coming. In fact, he'd done the opposite. Once, at a crowded, noisy bar with other summer associates from the law firm, a colleague leaned over toward Nelson and—gesturing at me with his beer bottle—asked, "So, when are you two getting married?" Without missing a beat, Nelson replied, "Fuck you very much!" Looking back, I realize Nelson was pissed that the guy was going to blow his secret plan. But at the time, I was too stricken to let on I'd heard.

In the darkness, peering at the ring in its box, I couldn't quite tell what I was looking at, but I could barely breathe. My stomach was churning, still overly full; I hadn't yet begun to digest the elaborate dinner, and now I felt it threatening to come back up. I took a moment to concentrate on restoring my breath.

"What do you think of the ring?" Nelson wanted to know. "It isn't like anything else you've seen, right?"

What did I think? The stone didn't sparkle at all in the dim light of the streetlamp, so I guessed aloud—trying hard to sound cheerful—that it was my birthstone, topaz. Nelson laughed and said no, it was a large emerald ring his grandmother had received as an anniversary present. In fact, she sat to have her portrait painted while wearing it, and it was extra special because it signified her approval of me as his wife. Then he stood and asked me to get up, and led me over to a pay phone, right nearby, which I realized was why he had chosen this bench.

Nelson called his parents collect and I heard his mother accept the call cheerfully, as if she'd been anticipating it. He told them how he'd given me the ring in the dark and that I thought perhaps it was topaz. His father laughed at how funny that was, and his mother said "congratulations, darlings!" and gushed about how happy they were to have me join the family. Then we called my parents collect, too, and I honestly don't remember a single detail of that phone call, but I am sure it was quite stilted. My parents were not delighted—neither with Nelson nor with what their private investigator had reported on the Bauers, and they were terrible at pretending.

I felt ashamed for being disappointed in receiving a regifted ring, but in truth, that was the smallest part of my hidden pain. I wouldn't be able to tell the truth about our engagement weekend to a soul—least of all, my parents, who cared more than anything about my marrying well. So I resigned myself to the fact that I wouldn't have a cute proposal story to trot out and tell my friends or future children. I accepted Nelson's paltry, pitiful, self-centered REQUEST THAT I TAKE CARE OF HIM, even though there was no promise of love or support attached to it, because it made me feel a bit less badly about killing the potential life in my uterus, which—without my intervention—would presumably have become a baby boy, my firstborn son. Yes, the doctor told me the gender of the fetus, and no, I have no idea why. But by marrying the lost baby's father, I could tell myself I was merely delaying his birth until a more auspicious time arrived. I also felt less fearful about my future because Nelson would presumably take care of me, even though he hadn't made any such promise. These were just a few more secrets I was too ashamed to share with anyone.

Reader, that is how I accomplished the task my mother set out for me ten years earlier, as a high school freshman. Fourteen months after graduating from Harvard, I was engaged to marry a Harvard classmate who was tall, male, Phi Beta Kappa, summa cum laude, reasonably good looking, musically talented, confident to the point of arrogance, affluent, and Jewish. Nelson— with his Harvard Law School degree and high-paying associate position at a white-shoe law firm on Wall Street—embodied everything I had been sent to college to achieve in a fiancé.

The rub—perhaps the one (almost) satisfying detail—was that my parents didn't approve of him. Okay, it was *truly* satisfying; in fact, it was more than a bit thrilling. You see, Nelson was "not like us" and therefore inferior; Nelson was an atheist, a Reform Jew, a Midwesterner, and—according to the private investigator Daddy hired—the brother of a drug addict and the youngest child of *swingers*. Nelson's parents were reportedly both alcoholics, an exhibitionistic former model and a depressive poet who had inherited a great deal of money made during World War II, and seemed to be primarily engaged in pissing it away.

Aside from his abject narcissism and the scandalous history of his family, there was another, more intimate drawback about Nelson I could never discuss, least of all with my mother. He shared an opinion of me that Mommy had ingrained in me since before I could remember, frequently affirming that I was difficult to love, and that I was lucky to have found someone willing to put up with me. In my deepest, most secret place, I'd always hoped to find a partner who felt differently, but since I didn't love or accept myself, I guess I didn't know how.

Dear reader, the evening of my engagement to a man who did not honor, cherish, or respect me, I *may* have felt lucky, even relieved—but I didn't feel happy, not one little bit.

My friendship with Barry had always been complicated by his deep fear of revealing his sexuality to me. He suffered from an internalized homophobia and had deliberately given me false hope that we would marry before Nelson came along and laid claim to me during our college days. After graduation, Barry was often in Asia for his family's business, but he would see me when he was in New York—while Nelson was at law school in Boston. He'd ask whether I thought I would marry Nelson, and if so, if we'd move to Cincinnati. I sensed that Barry wanted to dissuade me but knew his efforts would be ineffective so long as he stopped short of claiming me for himself—which only sharpened my gratitude for Nelson's desire to take me as his bride, for the other man I loved clearly had no interest in spending his life with me.

Third Spirit Messenger | Summer 1990 | NYC

One evening not long after our engagement, while walking home from work, I made eye contact with a beautiful woman on the sidewalk of Third Avenue, and she beckoned to me. I found myself drawn to her, riveted as she described her ability to see the hidden truths about a person, dead or alive, just by handling their possessions.

Within the hour, I had reached my apartment and turned right around, returning to her with some objects of Nelson's: the well-worn softball glove he used to play with other lawyers in Central Park and a greeting card he'd given me some months earlier. First, she held the items in her hands with her eyes closed, then opened her eyes and studied them; when she spoke again, it was to advise me—or rather, urge me—to postpone the marriage. She warned me that Nelson was terribly insecure, loved his mother much more than he loved me, and would try to control me, gradually stripping away my independence and making me increasingly unhappy.

On some level, I knew every word she said was true, and I

also realized Nelson had been chipping away at my autonomy ever since we met. I called up my newly married girlfriend and asked for her support in acting on the stranger's advice. But she saw my situation through the lens of her own happy newlywed life, and she told me this was crazy—I had found myself a wonderful husband and I should not postpone anything.

Reader, I married him. And as things went south, I never forgot the beautiful stranger's foreboding insight and dire predictions. As her words bore truth and became increasingly more evident, I knew with certainty that I had made a terrible mistake.

The morning of the wedding, I woke up in my childhood home, trembling, and could not seem to stop. I also had terrible stomach pain. My parents attributed these symptoms to my sensitivity to the Persian Gulf War, which had begun two weeks earlier and dominated the headlines of *The New York Times*. But as troubled as I was about the violence overseas, I knew better. I was terrified. I passed the long, slow Saturday at my parents' house, where my mother tried to reassure me that it was normal to feel nervous. The wedding would not begin until 9:30 at night because the sun sets so late on Long Island in August, and nothing could be set up at the temple until after *havdalah* (the service performed at the close of the sabbath).

I stood beside Dennis, the family hairdresser, waiting for my cue to walk down the hallway toward the sanctuary, then down the aisle. Balanced on kitten heels, my legs shook inside my floor-length Carolina Herrera Alençon lace gown, and he noticed. Dennis was divorced, gay, and cynical—a year older than my mother. He had been providing cuts, color, and his own special brand of family therapy to my grandmother, mother, aunt, sister, and me for several years—along with many celebrity clients—out of his one-room salon in the West Village. He told me to take a deep breath and lighten up. "It's your first marriage, hon," he said, in a soothing voice. "It's a rite of passage. Before long, you'll be moving on and trading up. Keep practicing your French, and I guarantee: you are going to make a fabulous trophy wife in a few years!" I snort-laughed, shook my exquisitely coiffed head, and began walking toward my parents.

And that is how, at age twenty-three, I found myself standing under an elaborate *chuppah* made of birch trees, being kissed so aggressively in front of all my family, friends, and two of my ex-beaus that it felt more like an assault than a public display of affection. Afterward, Nelson explained that he had kissed me "that way" to show the rabbi who was boss—how dare he tell us that in order to have a Jewish home, we had to keep kosher! But I knew there was more to it. Nelson had insisted both Barry and Pedro be present at our wedding so they could "see with their own eyes" that he had won—that I had chosen him. That dominating, full-body kiss demonstrated once and for all that he was my master; I belonged to him.

Following the ceremony, guests enjoyed an elaborate cocktail hour while the wedding party posed for formal portraits—after which Nelson abruptly abandoned me to spend time with his siblings, parents, and grandparents. He and I are featured together in precisely none of the candid photos from the reception; even in pictures of me doing the *hora*, I'm not holding Nelson's hand. I danced with my friends for hours, and Barry stayed by my side so constantly that as the band packed up their instruments, the leader stepped down onto the dance floor, came over to us, slapped Barry on the back, and congratulated him. The moment was too mortifying for either of us to utter a word.

Chapter 5

JOYLESS NELSON | 1990 TO 1994

Nelson had promised me loyalty and financial security—compensation, he said, for his not being particularly romantic, brilliant, or interesting. There were other dead ringers at the outset as well. While he considered himself funny, he knew I didn't appreciate his penchant for puns—especially after hearing them the umpteenth time. He was horrible at choosing gifts for me, and I can't recall him ever making a romantic gesture, other than the roses he gave me after I broke up with him in 1988. But up until we moved from New York to his hometown of Cincinnati, he made good on his promises.

Nelson didn't care much about having a career as a lawyer; his family saw his legal education as a savvy investment that would pay them back in spades when Nelson restructured his grandparents' estate so his family would inherit more of their fortune and less would be taken by the government.

As newlyweds, we lived at 30 Lincoln Plaza, a luxury building directly across from Lincoln Center, upstairs from Lincoln Plaza Cinemas—a wonderful theater that showed foreign and independent films. No longer employed with Norman, thanks to Nelson's edict that I quit, I was free to explore other avenues of income as an artist-entrepreneur. On weekends, when Nelson was watching football, I would sit on the sidewalk outside the vacant lot just south of our building, talking to tourists and selling them wooden picture frames I had embellished with dried roses, seashells, braided tall grasses, and moss—inspired by merchandise offered in shops downtown—made from little treasures I'd collected at the beach. It was there that I saw a flyer for a community opera company and joined the orchestra just in time for a production of *La Bohème*. Following the run, Nelson asked me not to play in another production; there were too many evenings I was absent when he returned from work, leaving him to figure out dinner for himself.

During those first four years of marriage, we took frequent vacations together: deluxe accommodations at exclusive hotels and resorts in Mexico, Israel, Egypt, Spain, Italy, Hong Kong, and Thailand—costly trips funded entirely by dividends from Nelson's trust. The existence of the trust was the only thing I ever knew about Nelson's finances; he never shared any other details with me—either before, during, or after our marriage. Despite being luxurious, our holidays were rarely enjoyable. Our itineraries were never collaborative, and Nelson was a rigid, ambitious, over-scheduled traveler. When I asked, during our drive from Rome to Positano, whether we could stop and see the legendary ruins at Pompei, he refused. I pleaded with him: the well-preserved murals in this ancient place had inspired me to become a decorative painter. The driver overheard us and said it was on our way. Nelson conceded, but insisted it was too hot to walk around outside—he and the driver would wait in the car while I ran and saw what I needed to see. It was a lonely way to travel, yet I was able to visit places I had read about as a child, seen in the Metropolitan Museum of Art and on slides in my college classes.

It was during these four years that I also began to see the writing on the wall. Before we were engaged, Nelson had been kind and solicitous—taking the train from Boston to New York every other weekend, working as the train sped between the two cities so he could focus on courting me while he was in town. We went to the theater, attended concerts at Lincoln Center, even stood in line to see Woody Allen movies the day they opened and walked hand in hand through Central Park. During football season, we made weekend trips to Cincinnati. These visits involved my shopping for designer clothes with his mother, dressing up for dinner at expensive restaurants, attending repertory theater performances, and going to listen to live music until the bars closed. Then we'd walk down the street to his parents' new house to retire for the night.

I would be the only one awake the next morning. I'd drink coffee, go for a run, shower, eat breakfast, flip through the local newspaper, and putter around the silent house overlooking the Ohio River. Nelson and his parents would all sleep until it was time to go see the Bengals play. After the game, we would fly back to LaGuardia—Nelson with tears in his eyes as our plane took off from the airport in Northern Kentucky.

Between the excessive alcohol, rich food, and lack of sleep, and the stress of playing a role—not doing anything in front of

Nelson's parents that he found distasteful, and not letting on how strange I found the people, places, and food in Cincinnati—every first morning back in New York, I woke up sick, with a painful sore throat, and it would take me all week to recover.

We initially rented a tiny studio apartment on the twenty-second floor. Our building more than made up for the small living space by being directly across the street from one of the preeminent cultural hubs of New York City. The building featured a liveried staff, rooftop pool, lushly landscaped private backyard, state-of-the-art gym, and every imaginable service and amenity. The apartments were originally intended as *pieds-à-terre*, so the kitchens were tiny and windowless—just big enough to stash a fridge, range, and toaster, with a countertop perfectly sized for unpacking a bag of Szechuan takeout.

Even when Nelson got a raise and felt inspired to move us up to a one-bedroom on the thirtieth floor, our kitchen remained miniscule. I did the best I could to make our little space in the sky above Manhattan feel like a proper home. When one of my decorative painting clients on Park Avenue was throwing away a corner cabinet she had ripped out of her dining room, I hauled it home in a taxi, painted it to match our wedding china, and had the building's handyman install triangular glass shelves above it in the corner of our living room so I could retrieve our wedding gifts from my parents' basement and display them in our apartment. We rarely used our beautiful new dishes. When Nelson and I ate meals together, it was either at a restaurant, at a friend's apartment, or on the couch in front of the television.

Nelson had insisted I give my notice to Norman a month

before our wedding. As the newest lawyer at the firm, it would not reflect well on him to be connected to a company conducting business at the margins of legality. So as soon as we returned from our honeymoon in Asia (imagine season one of *White Lotus*, set in Asia in 1990, without a visit from anyone's mother-in-law), I enrolled in a decorative painting program at Parsons School of Design, where I'd taken art classes since moving to New York after college. Before long, I was working as an apprentice to my faux-finishes professor and taking commissions, making my living as a decorative painter.

The following year, I partnered with Lori, the sister of a woman Nelson and I met on vacation in Mexico. Having me as her creative partner gave Lori the confidence to put herself out there as part of a professional team, and she got us gigs with clients she met through her furniture refinishing job in Soho. We started glazing walls in living rooms and dining rooms, not only in Soho but also on Fifth Avenue, Park Avenue, and Central Park South. It was fun, and the money was good—much better than what Norman paid me, so much better than working at Macy's. Plus, it was loads of fun, and I got to wear paint-spattered denim overalls to work.

Once we were man and wife, Nelson worked long hours at a job he seemed to despise, spending all his free time drinking, watching sports, or doing both at the same time. He had very little to say to me, other than criticism for my seemingly endless transgressions—like leaving an object on the surface of a piece of furniture, or a towel on the bathroom floor, forgetting to make the bed, not keeping the sections of the Sunday newspaper in their proper order—or, inexplicably, using traditional Hebrew phrases such as *Shana Tovah* when I wished members of his family Happy New Year. He wasn't interested in making any plans that might conflict with his sports-watching schedule, had no interest in sex, and no longer showed me any affection unless we were on vacation. If he wasn't at the office, all he wanted to do was sit on the couch, cocktail in one hand and remote in the other, waiting to be fed.

Of course, dear reader, I wondered what could account for the dramatic change in Nelson's behavior toward me since our wedding day. He'd become domineering, dismissive, negative, and critical—I couldn't even imagine broaching the subject with him. Things were so bad that by the time I took the train out to Massapequa to collect my china—even thinner than I'd been at my wedding, overdressed in designer silk clothes and ruby earrings acquired on our honeymoon—my mother easily intuited that I was miserable.

We sat in her car waiting for my train back to the city, and she asked me why Nelson hadn't come out to the island with me. I don't remember what I said, but I recall that she responded by saying that we could nullify the marriage and return the gifts—no questions asked. And that I shouldn't feel guilty about the cost of our 200-guest, black-tie wedding. "Daddy and I did all that, spent all that money for ourselves, and for our friends," she said, in a rare moment of honesty and graciousness. "You are not at all responsible." I took that in for a long moment, wiped my tears, then shook my head: no, this was something I'd have to figure out and fix on my own.

It was a stunning conversation for me to process on the train back to the city. I had no idea at the time that my parents had been wishing for months that I would call off the wedding— they had both been waiting for me to confess how unhappy I was. Ironically, my mother observed that I seemed to be shrinking myself to fit into my relationship with Nelson. Sadly, she couldn't see the parallel to our mother-daughter relationship in my subjugation of my very self to suit the whims of the person who should have loved me the most, just for who I was.

Months earlier, when I developed an aggressive ear infection that spread into my mastoid bone, the ENT specialist suggested I stay with my parents to receive the antibiotic injections I needed rather than be hospitalized or come to his medical office twice a day. One night that week, at the dinner table, my father shared that he'd looked in on me that morning, just before leaving for work, and saw my sleeping face resting on the pillow (in my extra-long, extra-narrow childhood bed) and thought to himself, "she can't get married, she's still a baby!", but he took it no further.

My parents agonized about whether to share their observations or voice their concerns to me, but they were both too afraid that Nelson and I would react to their disapproval by eloping (or worse, marrying in Ohio) and cutting them out of our lives. I had been determined to marry Nelson, and now— despite my mother pointing out the emergency exit—I was determined to stay married.

I had to think up a way I could make our marriage better. Over the past few years, I noticed that I would have great ideas during my early morning runs in Central Park. A few weeks after collecting our china—following a particularly egregious episode with Nelson at his sister's house that rendered me speechless—I decided to go for a run and to keep running until the elusive solution to my misery popped into my head. I tore out his sister's front door and into the woods outside Westport, Connecticut, my feet pounding the dirt as I ran down the country road, waiting for clarity to catch up with me. But I was out of stamina before I could think what to do. Collapsing onto a stranger's lawn to rest, I lay on my back, stared up at the trees, and waited for an answer.

I could only conclude that this bossy, unbearable new attitude had taken hold because Nelson obtained a Harvard Law School degree and was employed as a lawyer, whereas I had only graduated from college. The idea wasn't that farfetched— he *had* tried to excuse the affair with his law school classmate by saying that she understood the intensity of the experience he was going through, whereas I was a mere college student, incapable of imagining how much harder and more stressful law school was.

In my sad, confused state, it seemed only logical that I should enroll in law school so I could understand my husband better, and earn back his respect.

I switched gears from artist-entrepreneur mode to pre-law. My new weekday routine included visiting the local branch of Stanley Kaplan on my way to work every morning, stopping in for an hour or two to take part or all of a practice LSAT so I could ace the exam and get into NYU or Columbia Law

School. Despite my perfect LSAT score, honors degree in English, and a glowing recommendation from a former employer, Harvard Law was not an option—the commute from New York was too long, and Nelson wouldn't hear of me staying in Boston with a girlfriend four days a week. And while the Harvard Law tutor assured me that Harvard Law School wouldn't hold my required withdrawal for academic dishonesty against me, it was a blemish on my transcript that caused most other law schools to look askance. So I threw myself on the mercy of the Jesuits, and they responded generously, offering me a place in the incoming class at Fordham Law.

On my early morning runs, I noticed a store getting ready to open on the Upper West Side, right by the Natural History Museum; one day, they pasted a big "ARTIST WANTED" sign in the window, and I went home, showered, printed out my résumé, and returned to apply for the job. The owners were confused as to why I wanted to work in this low-wage, zero-growth position, but they decided to give me a shot. And that is how I became the in-house artist for Uncle Futz, a boutique catering to celebrities, other wealthy people, and especially their kids. I decorated the windows with poster paint and used paint pens to customize merchandise, from mylar wallets to wooden toy chests.

Despite the fact that Nelson had demanded I quit my job with Norman, he responded to my plan to attend law school by insisting that without my full-time income, we would need to move from our glamorous apartment building into a more modest place with a lower rent—which meant saying goodbye to the rooftop gym, with its lap pool above Manhattan, Stair-masters with a view, and my beloved aerobics classes. My paltry salary from Uncle Futz was laughable in Nelson's eyes, and once I started law school, I'd have no income at all.

The move infuriated my father, because when he offered us three years of financial assistance, his offer was rebuffed—so he understood (correctly) that Nelson wanted to punish me for enrolling in law school. But I was unfazed. I loved the spacious sublet I found for us on West 73rd Street, with its high ceilings, built-in bookshelves, and big sunny kitchen on the fourth floor overlooking Amsterdam Avenue.

My parents were thrilled by my acceptance to law school. They'd been critical of my wearing overalls to work, climbing ladders to do my job, and always seeming to have traces of paint on my elbows, knees, hair, or cuticles. Now, they demonstrated their enthusiasm by offering to pay my tuition, even though I was married, probably because they sensed Nelson was less than thrilled. This wasn't the first time during our marriage they had picked up the slack—though Nelson's parents were far wealthier. As a first anniversary present, after learning we had no paid help, they gifted us a year's worth of weekly visits by my aunt's housekeeper.

At our new address, we were a little bit farther from an entrance to Central Park, but actually closer to the reservoir, where I spent most of my daily running time, and so much closer to my beloved Fairway Market, where I could now buy myself a scone for breakfast on the way home, popping it in the oven to heat to perfection while I showered. Because it was a smaller building with a smaller staff, our new environs felt more neighborly, more *haimish*; the move backfired as a punishment because I was so happy in this new place.

The night before my classes at Fordham began, my parents took my grandparents, Nelson, and me out to a fancy dinner. When I confessed to not feeling excited about starting law school the next day, my grandfather exclaimed, "Then, don't go!" He knew me so well and must have suspected I wasn't born to be a lawyer. By admitting a lack of enthusiasm for the prospect of becoming one, Papa felt I had given him an opening to save me from whatever pressure I was feeling. But I couldn't tell him the truth; I was too ashamed.

All my life, I had been taught that my misfortunes were my fault, and the lesson was an isolating one. The repeated message throughout my childhood—that nobody wanted to hear from me—Daddy's "Hand" training, his frequent bribes to remain quiet in the backseat during road trips, the expectation that my sister and I would keep silent during dinner unless spoken to, Mommy's scathing condemnation during my shameful isolation as an exiled eighteen-year-old—all of this made me reluctant to share what I was going through now, in my marriage.

The great surprise of law school was that I enjoyed it more than I had expected. My peers feared my exam scores were wrecking the curve, and I won an award for writing the best brief in the annual Moot Court competition. Winning the Mulligan was a feather in my cap that would have helped me land a job at a top New York City law firm. Nelson wasn't happy about it at all. He warned me that divorce rates were higher in two-lawyer marriages than among the rest of society. I countered that statistics are misleading, though this one might be true because of the types of people who become lawyers, rather than being a result of their chosen profession.

Nelson's plan for sabotaging my law career was to get me pregnant and then—at just the right moment—announce we were moving to Cincinnati. But knocking me up would prove more difficult than the first time. My body was responding to the stress I was under, throwing itself into a hormonal imbalance incompatible with producing or sustaining new life.

I bought a fertility thermometer and took my temperature as soon as I woke up every morning, graphing it on a chart taped to the wall behind our bed. I presented the data describing my physical dysfunction to my doctor, and she gave me a pill to counteract the chaos my body was signaling. The body never lies, but we can sometimes override its protective wisdom with medicine, and that is precisely what we did. As a result of the prescribed medicine, I experienced severe mood swings and abdominal bloating; nonetheless, we would increase the dosage—and the side effects—twice. By following the data points on my temperature graph for just over a year, and dutifully having sex each month as soon as a spike on the graph indicated I was ovulating, we managed to conceive…Clomid twins, which reportedly occurs in five to 12 percent of the pregnancies abetted by the medication.

Nelson and I would learn at our first ultrasound appointment that one of our twin fetuses had developed with "multiple severe fetal anomalies incompatible with life." Almost halfway through the pregnancy, I had a terrible new crisis to deal with. We agreed that we wanted to reduce the risk of preterm birth, to optimize the outcome for the viable life inside me, that of Twin A. We learned about a procedure called selective termination, whereby ultrasound imaging is used to guide a needle to the fetal heart to inject potassium chloride, causing the heart to stop and the fetus to die. Generally, when performed during the first trimester, the fetal material is reabsorbed. We were already well beyond the first trimester though, and the clock was ticking, because the longer we waited, the more likely it was that the procedure would result in a miscarriage. We needed to make a decision right away.

Nelson and I took a trip out to Massapequa to visit with my parents and discuss the situation. The four of us sat on lawn chairs in the sunny backyard, overlooking the canal, holding cold bottles of beer and glasses of lemonade, admiring the garden as it came back into bloom, listening to the water lapping at the bulkhead as the tide came in from Great South Bay. Nelson and I took turns explaining what we had recently learned about the pregnancy, and what we were thinking of doing about it.

First of all, there were two fetuses growing in my uterus—which explained what my parents had recently judged, during the Passover seders, as my exaggerated exhaustion and excessive appetite. But more important, one of the twins was severely deformed. This twin would never be able to live outside the neonatal intensive care unit, and if he managed to be born alive, his life would cause great trauma and expense with essentially no upside. And so, following the medical advice, with the goal of

159

saving the life of Twin A, we planned to pursue selective termination, so as to allocate all available space and nourishment in
my womb to support his continued development and maximize
the length of gestation. The procedure had been practiced for
almost a decade, and we'd researched and met with various local
doctors who performed it.

"Stop right there," my father said.

"Why?" I asked.

"Because medically, there is no need for you to go through
all of this."

"What did you say?" said Nelson, leaning forward in his
lawn chair, clearly bristling.

"This is unnecessary," my father repeated. "You guys are
young and healthy, you haven't been trying for that long…"

"Thirteen months!" I interjected.

"That's not very long at all. You can start again, with a clean
slate, and that is absolutely what you should do. Just have an
abortion, Nancy, and try again, because I will tell you something
else. You may not be able to see it yet, on an ultrasound, but the
other twin is also deformed, I can just about guarantee it."

"What!?"

"Take it easy, take it easy…and let me explain. As you know,
early in my career, I worked with crippled children at Shriners
Hospital in Boston. Every time there was a deformity in one
twin, there would also be a deformity in the other. Not the same
kind, necessarily, or to the same degree, but in every case, with
twins, there was always something off with the other kid. There
is no reason you should have to deal with that. You're fortunate

to know this in advance, instead of after the child is born and you're stuck having to deal with a crippled kid. It's a rough road, and I can tell you, you do not want to go down it."

I looked down and poked my straw at the ice cubes melting in the bottom of my glass. Daddy had dedicated years of his professional life to supporting disabled athletes, matching them with the best prosthetic devices, traveling the world to help them compete in the Paralympic games. These athletes inspired millions, with the ability to achieve greatness in spite of blindness, limb deficiency, and more. They were loved and admired around the world, bringing hope and inspiration to people struggling with all sorts of adversity. Now Daddy seemed to be saying it would be better, at least for their parents, if none of those people had been born.

On the way back to our apartment, Nelson might have encouraged me to process my hurt feelings from the visit with my parents, but he was too consumed by his own indignation. Over dinner at Szechuan Garden that evening, he announced we would be moving to Cincinnati—and soon, before the baby arrived. He was so miserable, he couldn't imagine being a parent in New York for a single minute. We had to get far away from my family, who clearly did not see us as adults able to make our own decisions.

By "our" decisions, of course, he meant his. He was scared and anxious, so he was taking over. Nelson was really saying, "I need you to get really mad at your parents, because I don't want them calling the shots in our lives." He knew I loved New York City and never intended to move farther than a county away. He also knew I dreaded living in Cincinnati—but now that this pregnancy had me all hormonal and traumatized, he was taking advantage of my vulnerability. What I could not see was that this move was going to help me grow up and find my strongest, fiercest, most loving self—in ways I could not even imagine from this vantage point. Do you know the old saying, "It's always darkest before the dawn?" Wait and see.

Unbeknownst to me, Nelson had already received several job offers "back home," and his parents had been house-hunting for us; they'd already visited over a dozen potential "starter homes"—and we needed to get to Cincinnati as soon as possible to select the home we both loved best.

I have blocked from my memory most of that Cincinnati visit, minus the distinct impression that my presence was ancillary: if I had skipped it, we still would have moved into the very same house. Touring the house his mother preferred, I plopped myself down in the primary bedroom, positioned just below one of the neighbor's decks, and said, "there is just no way I could live here." But Jackie explained to me why it was the best location for us, we wrote an offer, it was accepted, and the matter of our "starter home" was settled.

Back in New York, I told Nelson I needed him by my side during the selective termination. He said he was unable to: he had to return to Ohio the day of the procedure to attend our real estate closing; for various reasons, it could not be rescheduled. So after my classes that day, I called the bank in Cincinnati and spoke with the vice president, explaining the medical crisis we were dealing with. He immediately agreed to reschedule the closing. When I called Nelson with the good news, he reacted with anger and hung up on me.

The day of the selective termination, I left class, Nelson left his office, and we met up at New York Hospital, where they reviewed the procedure with us: they would hook me up to the ultrasound machine, insert a needle through my skin, deep into my belly, penetrating the wall of my uterus and piercing the heart of Twin B, and inject the potassium chloride, which would stop the heart from beating. In the procedure room, I was instructed to lie down on my side and stay as still as possible. The technician spread cold gel across my belly, then scanned my uterus with the transducer. After a moment, the doctor sighed and said, "Okay, I'm going to press my hand pretty hard against your belly for just a moment." As he did this, he explained, "I'm trying to see if I can adjust the position of Twin A. The way they're positioned currently, I'm unable to access Twin B. Just, ah, remain still, um— take some slow, deep breaths—and, ah, we'll see if we can't get Twin A to move out of the way a little bit. All right? Okay."

I stared at the cinderblock wall in front of me, covered with faded green paint, concentrated on breathing, praying, waiting, hoping.

The doctor failed to persuade Twin A to move. "Wow, he isn't budging. Let's have you come back in a couple of days and we'll try again, all right?"

What popped into my mind was that he was protecting his brother. Please God, don't let me think like that.

Nelson said he was sorry, but he would not be able to come to any more of these appointments. I would have to (1) figure out how to pass my current classes and stay healthy and pregnant while undergoing multiple attempts at selective termination of the deformed fetus, (2) figure out how to complete my Fordham degree as a visiting student at the University of Cincinnati law school, (3) find a new doctor in Ohio willing to take on a high-risk-pregnancy patient, then (4) manage to deliver a healthy baby from this complicated, stressful pregnancy. Like my secret plan for saving our marriage, I would have to do it all on my own.

Nelson accepted a job on the partnership track at a law firm in Cincinnati, one block from his father's office in the heart of downtown. Once we moved to Ohio, Nelson and I ate out every weekend, alternating between his parents' country club and the most expensive restaurants in town. Our first summer there, while I was pregnant and Nelson was studying for the Ohio bar, his favorite joke as he ordered a bottle of wine with dinner was, "I'm drinking for two." He would become so intoxicated by the end of the meal, he'd have trouble getting up from the table, and I had to steady him as we exited the restaurant. By the time we reached the car, he would refuse to let me—the new driver—drive us home. It was frightening to be in a car driven by a drunk, but it was a fear I was well accustomed to from childhood and adolescence, just intensified now because I was in the passenger seat (not the back seat), and I had a delicate, precious passenger within me.

Max's Dramatic Debut | 1994—Cincinnati

My parents flew to Cincinnati Monday night, September 20, 1994, as I was admitted to the hospital. They arrived at the delivery room early Tuesday morning, ready to support me as I delivered two babies—one alive and one dead—into the world. Monday morning's weekly ultrasound had revealed that Max's placenta was calcifying; the medical team was concerned he could no longer receive sufficient nutrition in the womb.

Nelson cried a puddle of tears onto the shoulder of my mother's blouse as he witnessed me moaning through a Pitocin-induced contraction. Defensive, I protested that I had only moaned because they taught us in childbirth classes that it would help, and I was happy to do many more hours of this work, if necessary. Nelson exclaimed that he couldn't bear for me to be in pain and begged me to agree to an epidural until I relented. The risk of paralysis was more frightening to me than any pain—but even while I was laboring to deliver his child into the world, Nelson's needs trumped mine.

Seeing that he had a camera hanging from his neck, the obstetrician invited my father to step closer and take photos of the birth, and Daddy did, capturing incredible images of Max emerging into the world.

After I delivered Max's placenta, the nurse told me it was time to push again. Because the selective termination had been performed in my second trimester, the expired fetus had remained intact. I had to deliver Twin B and his placenta as well. I pushed until she told me to stop, hearing the thump of the dead baby as they dropped its little body into a metal bowl. When they asked if I wanted to see it, I declined—but saw my father turn away from me and look down into the bowl. I only wanted to see Max, and soon enough, I did. He was all I wanted to care about. Nursing my baby, holding my baby, staring at my baby's perfect sleeping face in the hospital bed beside me, I told myself I had everything I needed. Max was here. All was well.

Fourth Spirit Messenger | 1994—Study the Moon

The pregnancy had been a triumph. From day one, I had been following the dietary guidelines in *What to Expect When You're Expecting*, but once I knew the pregnancy was at risk, I doubled down, following every suggestion to the letter. As the weeks ticked by, I employed a combination of fervent prayer, meticulous diet, cautious behavior, and close medical supervision. Not only did I give up my beloved coffee, but when I ordered a scoop of vanilla ice cream during our vacation in Spain and it showed up laced with tiny shavings of chocolate, I ate around it, leaving most of the delicious dessert untouched; that was how fiercely I committed to avoiding even a trace amount of caffeine. Still, it seemed nothing short of a miracle that my uterus had remained stable and occupied for a full trimester beyond the selective termination of Max's fraternal twin; I hadn't needed to be induced until well into the fortieth week.

Back when we were in the process of deciding what to do and selecting a surgeon, Nelson and I pored over statistical graphs showing the likelihood of the pregnancy extending any number of weeks beyond the procedure. To my great relief and amazement, Max stayed in my womb beyond every medically predicted date. So here I was, at home with my miraculous baby, grateful while awake—but once asleep, haunted by dreams of forgetting to feed or neglecting to care in some other way for Max's twin, subconsciously blaming myself for failing him, yet forbidden to grieve lest my husband accuse me of being "willfully depressive."

Then one day, out of the blue, I received a call from a woman at University Hospital, where I'd given birth. She proceeded to read the notes of the dead twin's autopsy—which I had consented to have performed for the sake of science—but never expected, nor was I prepared, to hear. I listened anyway, in horror. Reflexively, after hanging up the phone, I called my father—the only person I knew who had seen the dead baby. I asked Daddy if I might read aloud to him the gruesome, detailed description of the defects they had cataloged and shared with me. I told him the baby's heart had been outside its chest and asked him how that was even possible. I know Daddy meant well, but he could not have been less comforting. He said, "I know all about it, Nancy. I saw it, and you have to understand something: it was not a baby, it was a monster."

How could that have possibly helped me? I still don't have the answer.

A new friend I'd met in Cincinnati—another young mother who'd endured a similar loss—slipped me the phone number of a gifted seer and told me to call. The woman who answered said she could see a gray-haired, bespectacled great-grandmother who wore her hair fastened in a bun—an ancestor whom I had never met but who nonetheless loves me and watches over me.

I was instructed to study the moon and learn the significance of its phases, and to remember that the powerful celestial body is out there, doing its thing—whether we can see it or not—and to take a lesson from that. She also said my unborn twin was a soul who loves me deeply and had chosen to come into my womb and die there in order to wake me up to the miracle of my life, to jolt me out of complacency. She also reminded me not to devalue or underestimate the pure joy I find in dressing up, or in dressing baby Max.

I am processing the message about Max's twin to this very day. I digested the message and clung to it, wanting to believe every word. Though I knew of no great-grandmother who fit the seer's description, I tried to dismiss this niggling thought. It wasn't until after I began writing this book that I would learn which great-grandmother sent the message: it is Helen, my father's father's mother, who loves me and watches over me. For more than twenty-five years before her identity was revealed, I carried her comforting message in my heart, despite a faint shadow of skepticism. Thanks to my newly discovered cousins, I know who she is and what she looked like, both as a grandmother and as a little girl. Not only does her appearance as a mature woman match the seer's description, but I can see that I resemble her today, just as I also did as a young child. Now that I know who she is, and can look at her picture, I can easily believe that she has loved me forever. I know that her spirit is around me.

What I have learned about the moon is that it's most powerful when it is not visible to us. That's right: the new moon exerts a greater force upon earthly tides than the full moon does. We would be fools to continue to believe in only what is visible to our human eyes. Consider viruses, for example, and bacteria—both invisible to the naked human eye. We cannot see the wind…only observe its effects. Ditto for love. There is so much more to this existence than what we can see.

The more I thought about the content of this mystical phone call, the more I realized I had allowed myself to be cut off from joy. I had tamped down the promptings of my spirit in order to continue being what I thought of as strong, responsible, brave, and loving. I had hoped Nelson would become a more pleasant companion if I were more careful not to offend or upset him. I strove to satisfy all his needs and demands: I dropped off his dry cleaning and picked it up on time. I had dinner ready and handed him a cocktail when he returned home from work. I made reservations at his favorite restaurants on the weekends. I had lunch with his mother. I tried very hard to put everything away where it belonged and keep surfaces free of stray objects. And I toiled to transform our rather nondescript shoebox of a house into a home he could feel proud of, working with a contractor to renovate the kitchen and all three bathrooms. I kept fresh flowers on the dining room table and planted bulbs in the yard.

But it was all to no avail. Nelson was unhappy in our marriage; he complained to our mutual friend and former next-door neighbor from Lincoln Plaza, Carl, that I was too devoted and attached to the baby. Horrified by this warped perspective, and by how much alcohol he saw Nelson consume during his brief visit to our new home, Carl urged me to get Nelson to an

AA meeting, to get him to a shrink, and that we both get to a good marriage counselor, right away.

Had it not been for my precious babe—whose smiles I now lived for, whose life I had fought for—my own life would have been dark and empty. I was imprisoned in my lonely and unhappy marriage to Nelson, paralyzed by a neurotic thought spiral, a lack of faith in myself that prevented me from leaving. Ultimately, it was my love for my child that saved me. I felt ashamed at the thought of this dear little person growing up and seeing how I cowered, how I made myself small. I recoiled at the idea of my child knowing me as the disappointed, unhappy person I had become. I knew Max wouldn't respect me if I didn't find a way to respect myself. I wanted to be a role model—to show Max how a loving, joyful life could be lived.

I struggled under that inspiration until a talented stranger, Miriam Spears, showed up and persuaded me that if I could be brave, I could still experience joy in my life—lots and lots of it.

Fifth Spirit Messenger | Spring 1996—Batavia

When I was still pregnant with Max, an interior designer named Beverly heard about me through Marti—the seamstress I hired to make curtains for Max's nursery—who'd called her with a hot tip: she had discovered a talented, professionally trained decorative artist, newly arrived from New York.

Even though I was young, my credentials were a rarity in Cincinnati at the time, and Beverly was ready to cash in on them. She began touting me to her interior design clients as her favored resource for high-end decorative painting. She invited me to join her in the Laura Ashley Décor booth at the upcoming Home Expo, told me to bring a portfolio of my work and lots of business cards, and promised she would promote me. At the expo, Beverly strutted across the aisle, went up to the top decorative painter in town, shook her mane of flaming red hair, and declared in her fabulous British accent: "There's a new painter in town, from New York, and she's gonna give you a run for your money."

In a short span of time, Beverly and I became close and—as my older, wiser, been-there-done-that, divorced friend—she could see that my spirit was shriveling within the confines of my marriage. With the most loving of intentions, Beverly tricked me into seeing her spiritual advisor. She said she was making plans to pack up and move back to England in response to a reading she'd received from Miriam, a psychic out in rural Batavia, Ohio. Naturally, I didn't want my most cherished new friend to leave the country; Beverly was one of the only people I knew in Cincinnati not connected to my husband. I also felt concerned that someone I cared about would disrupt their entire life based on the advice of a fortuneteller living out in the middle of some cornfields.

Beverly duped me into seeing Miriam by flattering my intelligence—inviting me to experience a reading myself so I could explain to her how Miriam managed to manipulate people into thinking she was channeling wisdom and guidance from a divine source.

My day of surprises began with my first impression. Miriam was a sweet-faced, tiny older woman—a devout Christian, poor as a church mouse—who hugged each visitor as they arrived at her door, the threshold to a type of home I hadn't even known existed: a dark, cramped, one-bedroom basement apartment in rural Ohio, twenty-five miles east of Cincinnati, cluttered with statues and framed pictures of Jesus and his mother, Mary.

"I see you standing in a dark tunnel," she said, after Beverly's session ended and Miriam and I went into her bedroom and sat down, knee to knee, in two rickety wooden chairs. She had taken my hands in hers and closed her eyes. "You are in a dark tunnel," she repeated, "and they're saying you don't realize the door at the end of the tunnel is so easy to open. They are telling me you are to go to the door and open it, and you will step through it, walk out of there, step into the light. And when you do this, you will be amazed at how light, how happy, how free you will feel. Great joy awaits you."

"Does that make sense?" She opened her eyes and looked up into mine, which were full of tears. "Oh yeah, heh-heh, I guess it does," she said, and shook her head, clucking to herself. "I only know what they show me; you're the one who's got to make sense of it. So, I hope it was helpful."

What Miriam said to me may not seem profound or earth-shattering, but the levy broke when I heard her words. I am not too proud to admit she changed my life, almost immediately. In that instant, and again as I hugged her goodbye, I knew with certainty and clarity I had to leave my marriage, as swiftly as possible. Suddenly, I believed it would be easier than I had been telling myself it would; I believed I could do it, and everything would be okay.

My therapist, Bruce Levine, heard about the session and my reaction a few days later and threw up his hands, laughing. "I don't know what to tell ya, Nance," he said, "except look—you've been coming here twice a week, for what, six months?, and you keep saying you don't know what you want to do, and then you pay a woman what, fifteen bucks and you have this breakthrough? I may not believe in this stuff, but if I were you, I would keep going back and seeing her." He laughed again.

Miriam was the right person at the right time, and I couldn't argue with the truth of what she said, or dismiss her point of view, because she knew absolutely nothing about me. She was merely channeling Spirit because it is her gift, and it is what I paid her fifteen dollars to share with me on the first day of our acquaintance.

At age twenty-nine, while dwelling in secret depths of despair, I drew powerful inspiration from Miriam's utterances. Even though I had scoffed when Beverly invited me to visit her, I would return to see her many times. Miriam's first session was my fifth experience receiving spirit messaging out loud from another human being and, as before, her words struck an undeniable chord of truth. During previous experiences, I had known in my heart the truth of what I heard, yet I lacked the courage to act upon the insight and clarity the messages conveyed.

I had not been ready to receive spirit wisdom until that moment. I hadn't hit rock bottom yet. I still thought I was supposed to figure everything out myself. Until my twin pregnancy went off the rails—like a runaway train, dragging me to a place where I needed to connect more deeply with my faith—I had believed I was in control of my life. Rock bottom is the place where we are shattered; it is where a closed mind is forced to open. It is most decidedly not a place in which to dwell, but one to scramble up and crawl out of.

Chapter 6

PREPARING TO LAUNCH | 1996— CINCINNATI

Max was not yet two—still nursing for comfort and as part of his bedtime routine—when I packed up to leave the home we shared with his father. I split up the matching four-poster beds I'd painted for Max's future big-kid room, gifted to us by our friends Jamie and Heather, taking one of them to our new apartment so Max would have an identical bed in both homes. The nursery was the hardest room to leave behind. Max wasn't ready to graduate to a bed, so I claimed the Italian, white-lacquered crib I had sold some of my stocks to buy. I left the dresser-cum-changing table that matched the crib, and the custom upholstered glider where it sat—beneath its matching window curtains—and said goodbye to the cheerful farm-animal mural I painted while Max was growing in my belly.

I had been like a train set on a track heading straight toward this marriage—a track laid on the lessons I'd absorbed all my life long, about myself and my future. My first thirty years were lived to please my parents and conform to societal expectations so I could win a husband, as if that were life's grand prize.

The train had derailed.

Other than the fact that I was a ten-hour drive from "home" with a toddler to raise on my own—and couldn't take the child out of Hamilton County without Nelson's permission—I was free. My life was finally mine, to live on my own terms.

Security and Abundance

Every year of my childhood, my maternal grandparents transferred shares of blue-chip stock into my name on my birthday, creating a nest egg they hoped would give me confidence when I grew up and launched myself into the real world. They had confided their fear to my unmarried aunt, Phyllis, that I would be in a great hurry to marry—and that in my haste, I would choose poorly. Their fears were realized, and they lived to see my life unfold as they had predicted. What they didn't anticipate was that in Nelson's desire to control me, he would attempt to drain away the financial security they worked so hard to build for me over the course of twenty-one years.

In New York, Nelson and I never discussed living on a budget—although he had insisted we move to a cheaper place when I enrolled in law school, mainly as a way of expressing his displeasure. But once we moved to his hometown and I was occupied with our newborn, I was put on a monthly "allowance"—a smidge below the $250 a week we were paying Samantha, the young woman who babysat part-time while I finished my law degree. Nelson said we could manage to forgo my contributing a salary to our household, but he could not afford for me to be a financial drain. Feeling ashamed for not bringing enough value to the marriage and guilty for extravagances like developing photos of our baby nearly every day, buying photo albums, and making frequent trips to Baby Gap to dress our little model, I wrote checks to Nelson from my investment account, reimbursing him each month for the amount I spent in excess of $1,000.

Meanwhile, his mother had hired an expensive baby nurse who bossed me around from the minute we got home from the hospital, instructing me to express my early, antibody-rich milk so she could feed Max from a bottle while I slept. Having this woman in the house made no sense to me, especially when she wasn't willing to do anything except take care of the baby. I was more than happy to do the work of mothering, and had no desire to outsource any of it to a stranger. So when I asked her nicely to drop off our dry cleaning and pick up the groceries on the list I'd printed, she refused. And I fired her.

Nelson was frustrated with what he saw as my excessive attachment to our son. He was impatient for the two of us to take a vacation without the baby; he would frequently remind me that as soon as I was ready to wean Max, we could take a cruise along the Amazon, as his parents had recently done. All of this helped me see two things: money was never the issue, and the last thing in the world I wanted was to leave my baby so I could be alone with Nelson.

Nelson's modification to our "home economics" turned out to be a blessing in disguise, because it made the continuation of our marriage absurd. If he wasn't willing to support his wife and son financially—if he valued my presence less than that of our part-time hired help—my self-esteem required that I leave.

177

I found the courage and strength to leave Nelson well before he cleaned me out. I may have had poor judgment—staying with him after he cheated on me with a law school classmate; marrying him in spite of his lame, lackluster proposal, a second hand ring, and loud messages from my gut the morning of the wedding; staying married despite being utterly abandoned during the ceremony, reception, honeymoon, and beyond; seeking medical intervention when my body balked at having a child with him; navigating a selective termination without his emotional support; leaving my friends, family, and the city I loved to live in a place I had always disliked—but I am not a complete idiot.

I knew our arrangement wasn't normal, and not just because it wasn't like the family I had grown up in. While Max was an infant, I took a course in family law, which turned out to be priceless. Prior to taking that class, I'd known nothing of financial abuse, so I didn't recognize the classic signs. So far as I knew, my husband treated me the way he did because I was such a disappointment as a wife. But I came to understand that this was not how marriage was designed to work, and ours was not like other people's marriages. Still, I was so ashamed, I didn't dare tell anyone.

Reader, have you ever given someone excellent advice, then failed to take it yourself?

While still a student at Fordham, I published an insightful article on the dangers of attorney-mediated divorce, in which I examined the vulnerability of wives and the tendency, especially for mothers, to fall into poverty following divorce. I described hidden pitfalls in the mediation process and urged less-powerful spouses to seek the protection of the court system, warning them how the habit of accommodating a more powerful spouse during marriage made it likely they would be manipulated to their detriment in mediation.

To be fair, I *tried* to follow my own advice. In fact, I did better than that; I took advice from a Yale Law School graduate—my friend Rick, who got me the name of Guy Hild, Cincinnati's top-rated divorce attorney at the time. I was naïve though, because I didn't consider that this so-called "super lawyer"—a member of the same country club as Nelson's parents—had more to lose by hurting the Bauers than by hurting me. Guy pointed out that dissolution would provide a swifter exit from the marriage, sympathizing with how difficult Nelson was being and empathizing with my eagerness to begin the next chapter of my life. I knew Guy was a hotshot lawyer, but I feared I would end up bankrupt if I sued Nelson for divorce without a prenuptial agreement in a town where his swinger parents had literally been in bed with a state senator and several judges. I had an inkling these family connections were the reason Nelson had been in such a rush to move us to Cincinnati before our baby was born.

Nelson was in disbelief when I told him I wanted to leave him and move back to New York with Max, but he called my bluff and agreed that I could go for a month to "try it out"—so long as we had a temporary separation agreement in place.

Max and I moved into an unfurnished sublet a mile north of Lincoln Plaza on the Upper West Side. With an air mattress, stroller, portable crib, diapers, some clothes, and very little else,

I began making strides toward supporting my baby and myself by doing work I loved. My favorite professor from Parsons had more than enough work and was happy to share the overflow with me. Massimo Ferragamo welcomed me to town warmly, promising me work in his showroom and store, and offered to connect me with his contacts at Bergdorf's and Barney's. I was filled with joy being back in New York, and seeing how Max blossomed every day in his stimulating surroundings. My belief in the laws of abundance was ringing true, as I joyfully used all my gifts and connections to create a fabulous new life for myself in Manhattan as a single mom.

It was painful to learn, after a few short weeks, that I would not have the option to stay in New York—unless I wanted to live apart from my child and merely visit him while he grew up, Nelson demanded that I return to Cincinnati and remain there for the next sixteen years.

My euphoria vanished. After tasting freedom in the creation of my own joyful, abundant life in my beloved city, I went back to Ohio, resolved to try harder at the marriage.

I moved back into our so-called starter house again, purely out of fear. I missed New York so much—more than before—and I fixated on getting back there. Nelson tried to use my longing as leverage and issued a list of conditions to be met if I wanted permission to visit New York again and see my friends and family. Certain behaviors and attitudes would likewise need to be demonstrated if I wanted to host my family in our home in Cincinnati.

Suffice it to say that Nelson's behavior, as I contemplated

leaving, became so intolerable that I agreed to take the "easy" way out, following Guy's advice rather than my own instincts.

Looking back, I believe Nelson felt unworthy of love, never believed I truly loved him, and did not trust that I'd stay with him. Those beliefs became self-fulfilling prophecies. As the seer in Manhattan who held Nelson's softball glove and urged me to postpone the wedding predicted, his attempts to isolate and control me made my life increasingly miserable.

Dissolution of the marriage meant that Nelson would keep all his precious money, and I would need to make peace with my decision and its consequences. To be free of suffering around my choice, I had to take responsibility for it—think positive thoughts about my decision and release any negative thoughts around it—and move forward in joy.

And so it was—after enduring years of emotional abuse—I found that my freedom was priceless. Once I made up my mind to reclaim it, I couldn't move fast enough. I was still learning about myself and life and love, about giving away my power, about shrinking myself. And the life-changing lesson—that the best-spent money is earned by sharing your gifts with the world—awaited me, just around the bend, as I committed to my freedom and my own worth.

Once I unshackled myself, abundance would flow to me.

Faith and Abundance

I know that I was a kind person in my early life. Being scolded for giving away my buttons didn't stop me from being generous. In grade school, I gladly shared my packed lunch—or my after-school snack—with anyone who forgot theirs. I tried to adopt the stray cats who followed me home. During thunderstorms, I sheltered our frightened dog in my bedroom, even though he was not allowed. I befriended people who, for one reason or another, were lonely and didn't fit in. I was drawn to the kids who got saddled with snarky nicknames by mean teachers. I had a natural way of connecting with people and making them feel seen and accepted. Even when dodging an invitation to prom, I never wanted to hurt anybody's feelings.

Now as then, many moons later, I believe I've become a more compassionate person, and a wiser one, because of the mistakes I've made in life and the consequences I've suffered. In leaving my marriage and gaining my freedom, I had self-respect because I took less from Nelson than I deserved, and I turned my focus forward—choosing to put my energy into creating a beautiful life for myself and our child. I became scrupulous about not taking a penny more than he wanted to give. I was so determined to prove I needed nothing from Nelson, I reimbursed him for the new bed linens for my apartment before he had the chance to spot the line item on the credit card bill.

Nelson said he appreciated all the work I had done to improve our home, and—as a testament to my effort, talent, and good taste—promised to split the profits when he sold it. When he moved with his second wife to a larger, more expensive home in another part of town so she might have an easier drive to her parents in Louisville, Kentucky, Nelson claimed he hadn't cleared a penny of profit. Much later, I would meet the new owner of the house I had once renovated and lived in, and they would tell me what a *mensch* Nelson had been—how kind and generous in negotiating the sale. Years after the fact, I understood with blinding clarity: he had chosen to enrich strangers to spite the mother of his child, even when helping me wouldn't have cost him a dime.

When I completed law school, I discovered that I wouldn't be able to take the bar exam: First, I was living in Ohio, where the laws differed in countless ways from the laws of New York I'd learned at Fordham. I also found myself in a state of extreme stress, which interferes with the brain's ability to acquire new information. In truth, I wasn't exactly devastated to realize I couldn't practice law—I never felt I was cut out for it. I had gone to law school in a desperate attempt to repair my marriage. My misery had been a private shame I was afraid to confide to anyone.

Growing up, I was taught I wouldn't be able to support myself—but now, I had to overcome my fears about poverty. Ever since that tumultuous time, I have come to trust that the rules of abundance would continue to bless me. Faith is a confidence in what we hope for and a belief in what we cannot see, and I did need to find my faith again before I could move forward on my own. In the Torah, we are told God speaks to Abram and tells him: "Go from your land...to the place which I will show you." Abram does as he is instructed and is well compensated for his unwavering faith. I didn't hear a divine command, but after six months of psychotherapy and a single session with a gifted clairvoyant named Miriam, I found the faith required to open the door and walk away from a life that had made me feel like a prisoner.

I started life over again—joyfully, from scratch, on my own terms—although I still felt like a stranger in a strange land. When Samantha, my former babysitter, first laid eyes on my new apartment, she admired its beauty and convenient location. When she learned that my rent and utilities were roughly equal to the amount I would receive each month from Max's father, she reveled in my good fortune. "If I got knocked up, I would never get anywhere near that much from Chris," she said, referring to her on-again, off-again carpenter boyfriend. Samantha's reaction gave me a welcome new perspective. I had worried about how I would support myself without alimony, and dreaded that my anticipated poverty would make me the object of others' pity. It felt good to realize my situation was, in fact, an enviable one.

Grateful for our wonderful new home, I steeled myself to become poor, then surprised myself by finding plenty of creative work I loved and receiving enough income to enjoy many of the finer things in life. I became a successful entrepreneur again the minute my first marriage ended—when I was twenty-nine and Max was one year old.

I realized, of course, that by taking nothing for myself and supporting myself as an artist (even a fully employed one), it was likely that our child would grow up going back and forth between two households with disparate economic realities. But I didn't view this as a hardship for Max—I thought it would help teach him an important lesson I had learned many times over by passing time with melancholy, dissatisfied people who had more money than they knew how to spend: Money is necessary for survival, but money alone cannot buy happiness.

The question I needed to answer was whether I could be a good enough parent for Max without access to Nelson's family wealth. To truly move on with confidence and joy, I had to dig deep and recover two things: faith in a loving presence that supports me, and my dormant opinion of my own worth, which I had previously smothered in exchange for the hope of receiving love.

Ever since college, Nelson had seen my friend Barry as a threat, and early in our marriage, demanded that I cut off communication with him. Now I reached out to Barry again, longing for contact with someone I thought had once loved me. Barry said he'd missed me terribly, that the loss of our friendship had been painful and difficult, and that he'd wanted to reach out so many times but stayed strong by consulting his volume of *Pirkei Avot*, which instructs that to be a good man, one must honor the institution of marriage.

It encouraged me to know I still had a devoted friend in Barry. He confided that he'd broken off an engagement because he continually compared his fiancée to me, and she had always come up lacking. Once again, Barry allowed me to interpret his remarks as indicating he wanted to build a life with me, as his partner. It wasn't true, but it helped me feel special and gave me hope for the future at a time when I needed all the help I could get.

Exit Interview

Just after our marriage came to an end, Nelson and I attended our first parent-teacher conference together. As we exited the preschool—feeling a bit giddy from having heard such glowing reviews of our child—I invited Nelson to sit in my car. I played a new Barbra Streisand song for him and sat watching the raindrops trickle down my window as the car filled with reassuring lyrics suggesting that what we perceive as mistakes actually contain valuable lessons. When the song ended, Nelson turned to me and told me the lesson he had learned from our marriage: he was a male chauvinist, and a selfish one, and he now realized that in order to have a happy marriage, he would need to find someone less independent. He said he felt fortunate that men are regarded as growing more attractive with age, whereas he realized he had taken my best years. I had peaked two years earlier at age twenty-seven, he observed, before becoming a mother.

Outside the Dark Tunnel | Single Motherhood

As Miriam predicted in her first session with me, my spirit suffused with joy from the moment I realized I was on my own. If I had been wearing a hat, I might have thrown it into the air, like Mary Richards in the opening credits of *The Mary Tyler Moore Show*. I was overjoyed for the opportunity to create a home on my own terms. This was the first time in my life I had the freedom and resources to do this, and it felt amazing. As a single mom in Cincinnati—the sole creator and owner of my newly reclaimed life—I realized I had an opportunity to live joyfully by connecting to the love and gratitude I felt for my child and by giving thanks daily for the source of strength that inspired me to carve out space to be myself. I know I radiated joy from every fiber of my being because the world mirrored it back to me; I attracted wonderful new friends every day with my positive energy.

I spent the first day in our new apartment alone. Max, not yet two years old, was staying overnight with Nelson for the first time, as he would soon do every Wednesday, so I could set up his bedroom. After assembling his crib, I unpacked and put away his little clothes in the closet, then lined up all of his favorite picture books against one wall—designating the back corner of the room as a space for playing games and doing puzzles—and made a mental note to find him a bookcase. Under the window, overlooking the rear garden, I set up his big-boy bed, with a denim comforter and lots of throw pillows—for now, we would use it as a bedroom couch to sit on and snuggle together during story time.

Meanwhile, Samantha, together with her brother and his friend, carried our remaining possessions upstairs to my apartment on the second floor—even my beloved and heavy Stairmaster. Feeling awash with gratitude, I took their orders for pizza, then strolled down the sloping, tree-lined block toward Clifton Avenue into downtown Clifton as the sky painted itself orange, purple, and pink. I passed a colorful trinket shop, a Mediterranean café, and a place to get Chinese noodles before ducking into a graffiti-covered pizza restaurant called Two Sisters to order myself a veggie supreme, in addition to three other pizzas for my crew. The feeling I had on the return trip that first evening—hiking back up the hill, balancing four pizza boxes as the sun slipped out of sight—was the same feeling I had when I shared a tiny apartment in Manhattan with my friend, Amy, right after college. I would walk home from the corner store, hugging a copy of *The New York Times Sunday Edition* wrapped around a pint of Ben & Jerry's ice cream, my heart full of the sweet anticipation of creating the rest of my life in a wonderful new place.

Finding our new apartment had been tricky. Apartment building managers in snooty Mount Lookout and Hyde Park, where Nelson still lived, refused to rent to me because I was divorced—a problem I hadn't anticipated. I decided to look near Max's daycare instead, and found a charming walkup on the second floor of a former Victorian mansion, right by the University of Cincinnati. It was a stately red-brick home, built for a cigar manufacturer and his family in the late nineteenth century, replete with all the old-world details our modern four-bedroom house had lacked. And we found ourselves surrounded by love and beauty.

I was in awe when I first climbed up to the spacious round front porch, grasped the intricately carved brass doorknob, and pushed open the heavy wooden door, inset with decorative leaded glass. One flight up a grand staircase, past a massive stained-glass window and behind another door, was a mint-green Rookwood tile fireplace framed by a pair of Doric columns, a delicate garland relief gracing its painted wooden mantelpiece. I swooned.

Many grand Victorian-era homes featured a basin, either inside or adjacent to the bedrooms. Our living room had originally been a bedroom, and beside it was a petite, gray-and-white marble basin with fluted edges and cabinets above and below. The upper cabinet doors were set with beveled mirrored glass panels, and the space had its own oval-shaped window. Every time I used it, whether to freshen my makeup or as a wet bar for serving cocktails, its historic beauty resonated within me and brought me joy.

My bedroom was located in a turret on the side of the mansion, so the wall around my bed was curved, which delighted me. There was a full wall of "communicating" linen cabinets between our two bathrooms, through which I would occasionally call, "go to sleep, Max!" when I heard him calling for me but lacked the energy to sing yet another lullaby.

I missed the convenience of having a garage to park in and I hated having to go downstairs, out the front door and around the back of the house to do our laundry in the basement, next to the workshop of an alcoholic sign painter who would occasionally steal my panties out of the dryer, but the positives far outweighed the negatives. Being able to walk Max to daycare was freeing, and we had a large and beautiful park, an art movie theater, a public library, an old-fashioned ice cream parlor, and many other delightful places within walking distance.

We found ourselves surrounded by intelligent, educated, friendly young women. On the third floor, in the renovated attic, was Leigh, a graduate student in psychology. Leigh was another "secret" divorcée, who had endured a trial like mine, struggling to find a landlord who would rent to her in spite of her scandalous past; like me, she realized she simply had to stop mentioning it. When Leigh would disappear to Cleveland for the weekend to visit her boyfriend, Max and I would march up the stairs to feed and play with her cats. In exchange, Max was welcome to come up and bathe in Leigh's clawfoot bathtub, as he had outgrown the large Rubbermaid bucket I used to fill with bubble bath for him.

Downstairs lived a newly minted women's history professor, Mona, whose duplex apartment included the mansion's original kitchen, complete with built-in icebox. I was happy I'd covered our long, window-lined, wainscoted hallway with a collection of small cotton rugs so Max's busy little feet didn't disturb Mona as he ran back and forth above her head. In appreciation of this and smitten by his charming personality, Mona would invite Max downstairs to bake muffins, cakes, and cookies with her. She also included Max on the otherwise adult guest list for her Beaujolais Nouveau parties, an annual gathering of friendly young academics whom Max and I both adored.

At the first of these parties, I met a young law professor who told me that the quirkiest thing about the University of Cincinnati law school was an allegorical painting hanging in the library—rumored to have been painted by a student in lieu of sitting for a final exam. I grinned from ear to ear and confessed that the student was me. I explained that I had been the mother of an infant, about to leave my marriage, and I knew I didn't want to practice law, but I did want my diploma. I arranged with the professor that I would enroll in the four-credit course in federal antitrust law if I were permitted to paint my final. Curious to see what I would paint, and impressed with my *chutzpah*, he acquiesced.

The *New Jersey Law Journal* got wind of the story and gave it front-page attention with the headline, "Law Student Masters the Fine Art of Avoiding Exams." His leniency criticized, Professor Lassiter and I got ourselves out of trouble by publishing the painting, *Naked Restraints of Trade*, along with a pair of articles we wrote about it, in Cardozo Law School's *Intellectual Property Journal*. My article, "Painting the Law," proposed a new career path for law school-educated artists, wherein creative graduates would create works of art as pedagogical tools for teaching complicated principles. This lofty goal was never realized, but I did get a solid B for completing a demanding four-credit course without doing any of the reading. (Shh.) Lassiter took joy each year in borrowing the painting from its spot in the library and using it to teach his class in federal antitrust law.

My first weekend in the new apartment, Max was with Nelson, so I could continue to unpack and settle in, but I also knew I had to go out and do something fun or I would end up renting a video and eating a pint of Ben & Jerry's on my couch. All three of my single girlfriends had other plans, so I took myself to a polo match my landlord's handsome son had told me he was playing in. It was a fundraiser put on each year by young men who had attended Saint Xavier High School to benefit the local (Catholic) children's home, and I figured it would be full of athletic, civic-minded young people.

This was two years before Google and a year before discovering I could Ask Jeeves, so I had no idea what a Jewish-American princess should wear to blend in at a polo match. I had seen *Pretty Woman*, however, and based on my memory of the film, I thought I had a clue. I put on my most preppy looking dress (a short, body hugging, blue-plaid taffeta silk sheath) and showed up alone—only to discover this was not at all what Catholic women wear to a polo match, at least not in Cincinnati. The other women were all in Lilly Pulitzer and Laura Ashley dresses and seemed less interested in meeting me than the women in *Pretty Woman* had wanted to meet Vivian Ward.

After an awkward minute, a nice-looking young man approached me, saying that we'd met at a Planned Parenthood fundraiser the year before and he'd been devastated when he heard I was married. Learning that I was now single, he expressed regret that he was moving out of town the very next day to attend Kellogg business school in Chicago. But he invited me to a garden party in Hyde Park, saying there was someone there I had to meet. This is where I was introduced to Becky Bolce, whose brother, Beau, was a sought-after interior designer. Becky listened to our mutual friend brag about my credentials and decided on the spot that her brother had to know about me right away.

Sure enough, the next day, I got a call from Beau, asking if I knew how to do subtle wall glazes. I assured him I did. Then he asked if I knew how to lighten up a dining room intended to have been a flattering pale peachy pink but glowed with an intensity evoking shrimp cocktail. I laughed and proposed tinting a white glaze with the faintest hint of pink and dabbing it on with fine-gauge dry-cleaning bags, which would leave a delicate, textured pattern in the glaze. He said, "Okay, I have a job for you."

When Beau walked into the client's house and found me hard at work in the dining room, his first words were: "Oh, thank GAHD you know what subtle means! I was afraid you were going to try to impress me and go over the top."

Because I worked hard, understood subtle beauty, and charged a fair hourly wage, I earned repeat business from Beau as well as referrals from his clients—and my schedule allowed me to remain available to Max, arriving in time to sit beside his cot every day, rubbing his back as he awoke from his afternoon nap at preschool, while also managing to earn between $45,000 and $50,000 annually—which in 1990s Ohio provided a comfortable life and the opportunity to put away a bit of savings for my future.

The second weekend I spent in the apartment without Max—about a month after I'd moved in—my sister Susan came out from New York City for my housewarming party. After the guests departed, she shared with me her impression that these seemed like people who would be my friends—which was not the case with anyone she'd met previously in Cincinnati, when I was living with Nelson. For the many years since then, I've kept a framed photo snapped of Susan and me at that party, sprawled across my couch and each other, celebrating my newfound freedom. I wore a sheer, long-sleeved black blouse, partially unbuttoned over a leopard-print satin bra, with tight black cotton-and-Lycra leggings and bare feet, signaling the new beginning I'd found the strength to manifest and the happiness that radiated from me as soon as I did.

Earlier in the evening, while showing off the sparkly jewelry adorning our newly pierced navels, Samantha and I were posing for a photo when Bert walked through the door with Beau, who'd brought him along as his date. When he introduced us, Beau explained he'd told Bert that I played the violin, had moved here from New York City, and had been married to Nelson Bauer, whom I'd met when we were at Harvard together.

"It's so nice to meet you, Bert! I've heard about you! Beau said you play the piano…"

"Yes! We'll have to play together sometime…"

"…but he neglected to tell me you were gorgeous!"

"Ha! Thanks!" Bert said sheepishly, as if he hadn't heard this all his life. "Beau says you're very talented."

I poured Bert a glass of the Veuve Clicquot he and Beau had brought, and we continued talking, quickly discovering we had similar passions, including luxury bed linens and torch songs from the 1930s.

Bert was handsome in an angelic way, with a square jaw and broad, wide-open face with high cheekbones and bright blue eyes framed by long, straight, thick blonde hair. He kept an upright piano at his apartment in Hyde Park Square, and we would get together there and make music, cavorting our way through the Cole Porter Song Book, then diving into classic Broadway musicals. Bert soon became a beloved friend and confidant. I would sometimes bring a guy I was dating over to Bert's to listen to us play, and afterward, I would listen with interest to his opinion of them, as well as judge the new suitor based on his impressions of Bert.

One day, Bert and I decided to get ourselves booked onto the event calendar at an old folks' home, performing our favorite songs from the residents' courtship days. I was amazed at how crowded the social schedule was at the senior residence, but I managed to book us between a butterfly slideshow and bingo. Bert looked dashing in his tuxedo, and I wore a floor-length, form-fitting black gown embellished with black bugle beads, sequins, and Swarovski crystals. We took turns singing classic tunes, while Bert accompanied us both on piano and I played some melodies on the violin. The audience responded by singing along; some even got up in their walkers and danced. Needless to say, it was a joyful and gratifying experience.

Nurturing the Next Generation of Musicians

It felt to me like Max was born loving to sing. Of course, I'd been singing to him every day since before he was born, and I knew he could hear my voice starting around twenty-seven to twenty-nine weeks of gestation. At that point of my pregnancy, during our first month living in Cincinnati—which was also my first month driving a car—I bought some music recorded especially for young children. I never drove anywhere without popping in a cassette tape and singing along so that Max was literally surrounded by the sound of my singing voice.

Once he was born, I sang to him even more often. Max now spent seven hours a day at the Jewish Early Learning Center (JELC), a cooperative daycare. I worked there several hours a week—changing diapers, cutting grapes in half, reading books, and playing with finger puppets. We both learned new songs at JELC we could sing together on the short walk home, or while we sat outside on the porch on Wednesdays and alternating Fridays, waiting for his father to pick him up. That's when Max began to learn to sing harmony. I didn't think it was so remarkable at the time—just a tremendous source of comfort and joy. Instead of expending enormous effort to make light, cheerful conversation while we both felt anxious about our impending separation from one another, we sang.

I wasn't allowed to paint the walls in our new apartment—similar to the rules at Nelson's house, where, despite my professional training and experience, I'd been allowed to paint only the nursery. Rather than invest in removable wallpaper, I decorated Max's new bedroom by tacking up with poster putty every one of his finger paintings, as well as the paintings he did with tempera and brush, as soon as he completed each one. He typically produced several masterpieces a day, so the high-ceilinged walls filled quickly. The room might have looked insane to a decor magazine editor, but to me it was an authentic celebration of Max's pure, strong impulse to create.

The cooperative daycare community continued to be one the greatest sources of blessing for both of us. It consisted mostly of rabbinical students and their babies and was located around the corner and just up the hill from our apartment house in the basement of Hebrew Union College, which trained and ordained rabbis. Nelson's grandparents had been founding patrons of the seminary, so our baby scored one of the few spots reserved for local parents not enrolled at the college. This was how—far from home and severed from all family but Max—I managed to find a spiritual community in Ohio, something I'd been denied access to by Nelson's refusal to join a congregation during our marriage.

The rabbinic students with babies took turns descending from their classrooms and sanctuary to the basement, where they—along with professional, trained staff and other parents—together cared for those babies. The students would sing to the children every day, in Hebrew and English. Through the daycare community, Max and I were connected to the greater Cincinnati Jewish community and to all the Jewish holidays, rituals, and practices. Max loved the performative aspects of Judaism, and relished the repetition of chanting prayers and singing blessings.

At home, if he wasn't sleeping, Max was bursting with energy and curiosity, and he kept busy in virtually every corner of the mansion. He might be visiting with any one of our housemates: baking downstairs with Mona, bathing upstairs at Leigh's or playing with her cats, tossing a ball in the backyard with the garden-floor neighbor, Wayne. If he were in our apartment, he might be finger-painting in his bedroom, working to solve a jigsaw puzzle, beating me at a game, or watching a VHS cassette of *Sesame Street* or *Arthur* from his highchair in the kitchen while I cooked.

When we went out, we could often be found cruising around downtown Clifton, the neighborhood adjacent to the University of Cincinnati. We were easy to spot because Max loved to pedal a big yellow plastic tractor, another hand-me-down from Heather and Jamie's kids. We would take the tractor across the street and roll right through downtown to the public library, park it outside, then sit on the floor—Max nestled in my lap or sitting beside me on the carpet—and we'd read books to our hearts' content until it was time to go home, whereupon we would check out two or three of our new favorite things: books recorded on cassette tape.

Sometimes, on a Saturday, we'd drive across town to Hyde Park and sit on the carpeted steps of Joseph Beth Booksellers' children's department, snuggle into an enormous stuffed version of Clifford the Big Red Dog, and read books before visiting the bookstore café for hot cocoas. As an adult, Max is now an audiobook narrator (and uses they/them pronouns), and I love how their work occasionally reminds me of some of our sweetest shared moments of their early childhood—like listening to a cassette recording of *The Tub People*, both of us cozy in pajamas, following Max's bath upstairs at Leigh's.

Small miracles surrounded us. Big Sky Bread, the bakery at the end of our street, was staffed by lovely people who knew that Max and I were on our own and were all too happy to donate their leftover bread at the end of each day. They let me know what time the collection truck came by, so Max and I could stop in beforehand to pick out a free loaf to bring home. During those early days in Clifton, Max and I would sometimes chalk a colorful sidewalk mural together outside the bakery to express our joy and gratitude, while gorging ourselves on slices of fresh pumpernickel bursting with plump raisins and chewy walnuts.

The zoo and the children's museum were a short drive from our home; both offered affordable, single-parent memberships encouraging brief, frequent visits to match our short attention span. Kings Island Amusement Park was free for kids under age three, and by purchasing a season pass for myself, I was able to treat Max to the delights of a world-class amusement park whenever we wished to go. He became a lifelong roller-coaster aficionado and, after a visit to the park, would rapturously describe every twist and turn of the day's rides as he lay in his crib, until he was too tired to speak another word.

It was a magical time, but it wasn't always sunshine and rainbows. Sometimes, Max and I had difficult conversations.

One evening, before Max outgrew the Rubbermaid bucket and began bathing upstairs at Leigh's, I was enjoying the upper-body home workout known as bath time. I knelt on a bathmat at the edge of the gray marble shower stall and spun the tub around and around as vigorously as I could, pretending I was operating a private ride at Kings Island, as Max gradually became clean in the bucket of darkening bubble bath. When I paused in between spins to catch my breath, he looked up at me from the foam and said, "Dad gave Hever a ring."

I took a beat, then realized Max was telling me Nelson had proposed to Heather, a young single mom who had moved into Nelson's house with her son, Cameron.

"Oh, that's nice, sweetie, so…they're getting married?"

"Yes," Max said, looking unhappy.

"What's the matter, sweetheart?"

"Do *you* want to marry my dad?" Max asked, taking my breath away.

"Oh honey," I said, "I *was* married to your dad…and…it wasn't good."

"Why not?" Max asked, his sad, earnest face threatening to break my heart.

"Well...your dad and I...well, we hurt each other, sweet-heart."

"How?" Max asked, his brow furrowed with worry. "With your hands?" He'd been learning about this at daycare.

"No, honey. Not that way. No, we hurt each other...with our words."

I hadn't considered that Max might have no memory of the three of us living together as a family. Or maybe he *did* re-member but didn't understand that it had been a marriage—the same thing his father and Heather were now planning.

Had they married, Max's life would have included a step-brother—Cameron, Heather's son, who was three months older than Max—but when Heather read the prenup, she moved out and moved on.

My Own Grown-up Person

Meanwhile, I was finally evolving into my own grown-up per-son.

I purchased a pair of black Doc Martens "combat boots," set up an LLC for my mural business, leased a Ford truck, and de-fied convention in so many other ways—big and small. I began coloring my own hair, stopped getting my legs waxed, placed a personal ad in the local free paper, and tried dating random guys whose voicemail responses made me laugh. I also dated Greg, a house painter I'd met on a job; Gary, the manager of a Ford dealership and a minor league baseball player, who had asked for my number just before I left the charity polo match; another Gary (secretly called "Gary deux" by my friends), a furniture salesman who picked me up at a Friday night worship service at a humanist temple; and "Greg deux," a guy who was both an electric bass player and the lead singer of an eighties cover band.

While none of them turned out to be "the one," what I managed to learn from spending time with these men was that I was not really all that difficult to love, after all. With proper care and handling, I discovered that I was not only attractive, sexy, and desirable, but also good-natured, funny, playful, and affectionate—a delightful companion. It took a few rounds of learning this lesson before I was able to believe it. I had no intention of breaking anyone's heart, but I broke up with most of these guys when I realized we didn't have enough in common to share our lives.

I also had a memorable one-night stand while vacationing alone in the Caribbean—with a bartender named Carl, who was not looking for a meaningful relationship, so ours was fated to be an ephemeral encounter that left me only with charged recollections of what was possible in a tropical rainstorm under the night sky.

For the first time in my life, I was really on my own. Answerable only to myself, and with a child who now vanished every Wednesday and for two weekends each month, I gradually became aware that I had given myself the space and time to figure out what made me happy, and the power to manifest it for myself.

When I was with Nelson, he'd discouraged me from playing the violin, which had been one of my greatest sources of joy. During college, he persuaded me to give up Monday night rehearsals with my chamber orchestra—Monday evenings were a convenient time for him to see me because his all-male social club never held events on Mondays. Once we moved to Cincinnati and Nelson took possession of his late great-aunt's baby grand piano, I was stunned when in front of guests he asked me to stop "whipping out" my violin to harmonize when he sat down to play and sing because it distracted him.

Feeling rusty after almost a decade with barely any opportunity to make music—but buoyed by my new surroundings—I took out my violin again, determined to reclaim the joy I'd once found with it. I played for kicks and tips at a local Clifton coffeehouse—making lots of new acquaintances and booking paying gigs performing at weddings and marriage proposals. I was overjoyed to have the work and counted it among the hidden blessings of being prevented from returning to New York City, where sheer competition would have made it improbable.

When Nelson took Max to Connecticut to celebrate Christmas with his sister and parents, I flew to Saint Croix with my violin and a suitcase of bathing suits and short sundresses. Accustomed once more to playing, I had the renewed confidence necessary to sit in with bands that spanned the musical spectrum from blues to alternative rock. Although I was playing for my own pleasure and the joy of connecting with audiences and other musicians, I was delighted to enjoy free meals at the bars and restaurants where I played, and shots of Grand Marnier patrons sent to the stage for me to enjoy between songs. And whenever I stepped down from the stage, I discovered new friends waiting to meet me.

Back in Cincinnati, more new friends appeared, as if out of thin air, and felt moved to help me. Due to a seemingly random but highly fortuitous series of introductions, I found work painting for some of the wealthiest families in town. Drawing upon the excellent instruction I received at Parsons School of Design and during an apprenticeship to one of my instructors there, I was able to delight my new clients, creating delicate wall glazes, *trompe l'oeil* tiles, and gilded crown molding for lawyers, doctors, and business owners who lived in ordinary homes (or ordinary mansions) but aspired to live in palaces.

Time to Shave the Beard

A few months later, Barry invited me to co-host a five-day-long Young Presidents Organization (YPO) conference with him in New York. YPO calls itself "the global leadership community of extraordinary chief executives." He had taken over his parents' failing clothing business and turned it into a success, then created a consulting agency that did the same thing for other companies.

In considering our wardrobes for the cocktail and dinner events on our schedule, Barry asked that I make us a pair of coordinated, beribboned faux-Venetian masks for a black-and-white ball he'd organized for the last night, in what he knew to be my favorite room in all of New York City: the Temple of Dendur at the Met. The ball was preceded by cocktails Wednesday night at Asprey, jeweler to the British crown; then cocktails Thursday evening at Armani, which had just doubled the size of its flagship store on Madison Avenue; then Friday night dinner at the home of the president of the Leslie Fay dress company, a lavishly painted duplex penthouse with sweeping views of Manhattan from its various balconies.

Barry explained that there was no one else he could imagine co-hosting the conference with. He admitted that he'd deliberately planned the ball in my favorite space to delight me, choosing Armani as a venue because he knew I loved the brand, selecting Asprey because no other jeweler was fit for a queen, and arranging for us to visit the Pomerantzes' penthouse because he knew I would appreciate the murals.

And so I agreed. What girl wouldn't? But it was during this conference that I finally realized, during a slow dance with him at the masked ball, that Barry was undeniably gay but too afraid to tell me, since he'd been lying to me and using me as a beard for so long, including right now. He avoided me throughout the ball, chatting furiously with everyone else, just as he'd done during the week's previous events, until finally—emboldened by champagne, intoxicated by the fragrant beauty of my favorite New York party space transformed into a wonderland, and spurred on by another gentleman who expressed bewilderment that he was lucky enough to enjoy my company for so long without any interruption from Barry—I walked up to him, tapped him on the shoulder, and demanded a dance.

Flustered, Barry excused himself from his conversation with another handsome man and led me to the dance floor, but when I felt his torso stiffen in my embrace, the way he carefully held his body at a distance from mine, I realized in a flash that he was gay. Everything that had not made sense for the past decade suddenly came into crisp, clear focus, and I found myself speechless (struck dumb? dumbstruck?). However we choose to describe it, dear reader, it was an exceedingly rare condition for me.

Sixth Spirit Messenger | November 1997—Utah Healer

Early in November 1997, I had the occasion to schedule a visit with a Utah-based healer recommended by an old friend, who was in town for a week or two. I reached out and invited her to the apartment while Max was at daycare. She'd survived a serious car accident and spent some time in a medically induced coma, from which she awoke with a new singing voice she now used as a tool in her healing practice.

As I lay face down on my bed, she lined up crystals along my spine and directed her voice at each one in turn, vocalizing a different frequency toward each point. As she sang, insights arose in her mind, and she asked me to release energy around a series of traumas. She asked me to let go of the hurt from my father abandoning me emotionally as a child, after I had chosen not to become a doctor. This was a novel thought at the time, but one I recognized as true, and I agreed to release it.

Then she asked me to release the pain from my husband abandoning me during our marriage. When I shared that my ex-husband had not left me, she clarified—she was referring again to an emotional abandonment, which had occurred during my pregnancy. As we wrapped up, she congratulated me on shifting my energy so much during a single session and assured me I would see the effects of the change immediately, because I would now be attracting a different sort of person.

This was about a year after our marriage ended. And oddly enough, it was on a recommendation from Nelson that I would soon pay a visit to a group of grandmothers at Wise Temple who offered matchmaking services to Jewish singles. And that, dear reader, was how I came to meet Paul—who was then a graduate student in psychology at the University of Cincinnati.

I chose profiles from a binder—the matchmakers required all first-time visitors to choose four people they would like to meet. Paul received a blue postcard in the mail, informing him "female #534" was interested in hearing from him. He drove to Wise Temple, presented the card, and was handed the binder of women containing my profile. He liked what he saw…until he read that I was divorced and a mother; he had no interest in parenting another man's child. The wise women listened to Paul's objections and told him to lighten up. "She also indicates she is looking for companionship," they told him. "Nobody is saying you have to marry her; go enjoy a nice meal together!"

Paul took my number and gave me a call. The phone rang on Wednesday evening, three days before my birthday, while Max was spending the night at Nelson's. Earlier that day, I had a session with Miriam, during which she envisioned me collecting broken pieces, rearranging them, and making something even more beautiful. I was still new at interpreting Miriam's messages and took this literally. I'd taken out of the closet a Ziploc bag of broken china—a casualty of Max's unbridled curiosity—and was cementing pieces of it onto the wide wooden frame of an antique mirror, making a mosaic—a textbook definition of making something beautiful from something broken.

Paul called in the middle of my project, and when he asked what I was doing, I told him all of this. He found it interesting, and different, but he wasn't frightened away. Later, after Paul and I met, dated, married, and created a loving new family from the pieces of a broken one, I would understand Miriam's vision in a new way.

Our first meeting took place on my thirty-first birthday— the starry night sky above us upstaged by a big orange moon over Madison Road as we set off on a shared adventure. I picked him up, and we drove to a cocktail party at my girlfriend's Hyde Park carriage house, then on to a champagne reception at the Contemporary Arts Center to celebrate the new Roy Lichtenstein exhibit, and concluded with a late-night supper at Carol's café in Over the Rhine. It was an evening replete with bizarre and comical events.

Less than an hour into our acquaintance, Paul learned I was wearing a wig—that my real hair didn't begin to resemble the short, straight blonde pageboy Velcroed into my hat. When I invited Paul to the exhibit opening, I neglected to mention that the invitation called for "creative dress." Paul wore jeans and a plaid shirt. During the cocktail party, he accepted my apology for the oversight—as well as my offer to wear the wig-hat, which made him look very much like Dana Carvey in *Wayne's World*.

Once at the museum, he was interrogated by my inebriated former in-laws. The hostess of the cocktail party joined us at the museum. She was one week post-abortion, and there—across the gallery—was the man who had impregnated and then ghosted her; you can imagine how quickly she became drunk. Paul and I ducked out of the madness to have a quiet dinner together down the street, where we were approached and interviewed by the local society gossip columnist. I lied and told the gentleman I was wearing a wig fashioned out of my friend Bert's hair, saved for me during his recent haircut, and Paul and I had a good laugh imagining this moment from our first date making it into the *Cincinnati Enquirer*. After dinner, we found ourselves caught in a snowstorm, and almost ended our night (and our lives) when I drove the wrong way down a one-way street, pulling over to safety and turning around after heading directly toward the grill of a blessedly slow-moving Mack truck.

Paul took it all in stride, said he preferred my real hair, and that he would be interested in a second date. I was disappointed when he didn't kiss me goodnight, but then he came back to the car and my heart skipped a beat. He opened the passenger-side door, said "it would have been bad if I forgot this and I let you drive away," and he leaned in. I leaned in too, only to see him dip his head down and retrieve his house keys out of the cup holder. Harumph!

Other men I dated had been eager to meet my son—take him to an apple orchard, go pumpkin-picking, or take him to a field to kick a ball around—but Paul was hesitant to spend time with Max. Although he did show up one evening long enough to light Hanukkah candles with us, play a bit of dreidel, sing some holiday songs, and give Max a harmonica as a gift, for a long while, Paul was strict about seeing me only when Max was with Nelson. Feeling sympathy for Max's upheaval following his parents' separation, Paul hoped to spare him unnecessary trauma if things didn't work out between us.

After about a year and a half on our own, a few months into dating Paul, I managed to score us a lifetime membership at the Powel Crosley, Jr. YMCA when I was hired to lead a team in applying a faux-granite, sponged-paint finish to the interior walls while they were closed in observance of the Martin Luther King, Jr. holiday. I negotiated to complete the entire massive paint job in a single day by agreeing to accept compensation in the form of lifetime memberships for everyone on the team, then recruited Paul and a half dozen artsy people I knew.

The Y was where Max had learned to swim. When he was small, I would stand chest-deep in the cool water and watch him travel, hand over hand, around the perimeter of the large, antique tile pool. Eventually, he found the confidence to let go and swim through the water into my waiting arms. After the pool, Max loved to stand in the hot tub, find the thermometer dangling at the end of its rope, hold it in his little hand as if it were a microphone, and imitate the ringmaster from Ringling Brothers and Barnum & Bailey Circus. One memorable evening, as we emerged from the locker room to head home, we found the local band Over the Rhine performing in the lobby. Reenergized by the live music, we danced until we were both exhausted.

Paul never shared his thoughts with me about protecting Max from being injured by our possible breakup, so when I learned that Paul hadn't invited us to a backyard barbecue he was hosting, I was hurt and confused by what felt like mixed signals. I arranged to pay another visit to Miriam. She described seeing a man setting down suitcases and taking apart a brick wall that surrounded him, one brick at a time. Next, the scene shifted, and she saw us holding hands—meaning we were connected in friendship—with rings floating over our heads, symbolizing a future marriage.

Convinced I had found a gem of a partner, I invited Paul to vacation with me at my parents' condominium in the Caribbean, treating him to snorkeling and horseback-riding excursions and the complimentary meals at restaurants where I sang and played the violin. After that trip, Paul stopped dating other people, and began hanging around with both Max and me. He says he fell in love with me while sitting alone at my kitchen table, listening to me sing lullabies to Max in his room, down at the far end of the apartment's long hallway.

All my worry about Paul avoiding my son turned into the greatest blessing as soon as his walls came down. He was wonderful with Max—kind, energetic, and endlessly patient, constantly looking for ways to support me as a mom. Max responded by becoming besotted with Paul. Now, when I was making dinner, rather than sit and chat with me, or watch one of his VHS tapes, Max would accompany Paul across the street to the park to kick a soccer ball, watch the ducks, or ride the horsey swings.

During Max's first year of preschool at Yavneh, as his friends and classmates started to become big brothers and sisters, Max told me he'd like to have a baby brother. Was this something I could do for him? He wanted to know. I told Max I could give him a baby brother or sister, but I didn't think it was a good idea to do this without having a dad in the family, as babies were a lot of work. He thought about this for a moment, then said, "maybe Paul Newman could be the dad!" I told Max I would think about it.

One evening, after celebrating *Simchat Torah* with us at a raucous, candy-fueled dance party at our synagogue, the three of us returned to the apartment, and after waiting for me to finish tucking an over-sugared boy into bed, Paul asked if I thought we should get married. Just like that. Matching his casual tone, I said yes—then, exhausted, we went to sleep. I awoke the next morning and telephoned Paul at work to make sure I hadn't dreamed the conversation. He said I hadn't. Just like that.

Though he was a poor graduate student at the time, Paul wanted to give me a gift as beautiful and precious as I was to him. He decided to sell the entire collection of baseball cards he had amassed over the course of his childhood, which—because it included some Mickey Mantles—enabled him to buy me a beautiful antique platinum brooch, set with diamonds and sapphires, my favorite precious stones. It was the sacrifice of his beloved card collection that told me how much my happiness mattered to Paul, and this made the delicate brooch so much more meaningful to me than Nelson's grandmother's four-carat emerald ring (which I subsequently learned she couldn't wear anymore, because of arthritis).

Thanks to my maternal grandfather, Sam—who had the presence of mind, as he lay dying in the hospital, to write checks to each of his daughters and granddaughters—I was able to say "no thanks" to my parents' begrudging offer to host my second wedding on Long Island. Thanks to Papa's precious gift, Paul and I enjoyed the independence of planning our own three-ring ceremony with Max—complete with a local rent-a-rabbi, an illuminated *ketubah*, a beautiful *chuppah*, a kick-ass klezmer dance band, and a catered luncheon reception at a bed-and-breakfast in Cleveland Circle.

It meant the world to me when, at breakfast before the ceremony, my grandmother presented Paul with Papa's favorite star sapphire cufflinks and studs, which Paul fastened into the buttonholes of his tuxedo shirt and wore as he stood beside me beneath the *chuppah*. Papa Sam's younger brother, Harry—with whom Papa had danced so vigorously at my first wedding—obliged me by chanting the *sheva brachot* during the ceremony. When I approached my great-uncle Harry afterward to tell him how beautiful and meaningful it was to hear him do that for us, he said, "you're welcome, and we meant it." As we embraced, I shed a few tears, feeling the powerful presence of my beloved grandfather's spirit.

Why did we marry in Cleveland? If you have never lived in Ohio, you may not realize this, but Cleveland is 240 miles up the road from Cincinnati—exactly as far as Boston is from Massapequa, not what you would call convenient. For starters, Paul and I had mixed feelings about Cincinnati at the time and wanted to marry someplace other than where Nelson and his family lived. Also, as soon as we'd announced our engagement, my parents called Paul's and invited them to meet for dinner in New York, where they wasted no time in insulting them, their absent son, and me—insinuating that he could only be marrying me to avoid having to earn an honest living, and declaring they had no intention of supporting us. (Because why else would anyone want to marry a beautiful, kind, intelligent, talented, creative, adventurous, successful entrepreneur who was also a loving parent?)

After that horrific response to the news of our engagement, Paul and I didn't want it to appear that either set of parents were hosting our wedding, so New York and Philadelphia were eliminated. When Nelson's oldest friends, Jamie and Heather, offered to help me plan the wedding in their city, it seemed a strange idea at first. But when I heard that George Burns and Gracie Allen had eloped in Cleveland, that clinched it; Paul and I accepted their offer and began planning our *simcha*.

We chose not to use the photographs taken by the professional photographer we hired, choosing instead our friends' candid shots for our wedding album. In his proofs from our wedding day, we saw that the photographer captured my parents, aunt, and grandmother standing in a huddle, removed from the celebration, their faces reflecting deep disapproval—in stark contrast to us, the bride and groom, whose faces were streaming with tears of joy.

Before taking her seat for the wedding luncheon, my mother took me into a hallway and whisper-screamed at me—furious that I had seated my uncle Harry with strangers instead of family—"why would you DO such a thing!?"—as if I had made a thoughtless mistake. I didn't think it was the appropriate time or place to explain that I had deliberately seated Harry and his wife Leah with other lovely people who approved of our marriage. I simply replied that in fact I had not made a mistake, and I returned to my celebration.

After the guests dispersed, Jamie and Heather took four-year-old Max home with them and their kids, and Paul and I had a brief but ecstatic honeymoon, spending the first night of our marriage in a beautiful hotel in downtown Cleveland, the second at a spa called Mario's a few miles away. Then, soon after we collected Max from our dear friends and headed back to Cincinnati, Paul kissed us both goodbye and left town to begin his post-doctoral fellowship, and Max began the first of six weeks of half-day summer camp while I hustled off to paint my last few local murals. I would pick Max up from camp every day after lunch, and either hand him off to Bert so I could paint some more in the afternoon, or spend the remainder of the day with him at some combination of the library, the community pool, the amusement park, or the zoo. Then I would prepare dinner for two, put Max to bed, and once he was asleep, spend the rest of the evening talking quietly to Paul or Heather on the phone, and bit by bit, packing up all our possessions.

Chapter 7

CAGE DOOR, LEFT OPEN

Entering my new marriage meant walking away from everything I had built for Max and myself in Cincinnati. I assumed—
or rather, had faith, based on my past success—that I would find
a way to build my business again after joining Paul in Detroit,
where he'd been accepted into a selective post-doctoral fellowship program. It was the closest opportunity to Cincinnati Paul
could find—but it was still 260 miles away.

Nelson wanted me to remain conveniently close to him and
offered to cover all expenses associated with my commuting to
see my new husband every other weekend during the first two
years of our marriage, plus the cost of both our long-distance
phone bills. But Paul and I found the prospect of long-distance
marriage unappealing. Rejecting Nelson's offer, we agreed to
look for a place to live in Toledo, Ohio—still in the state, which
was important to Nelson, and a challenging but manageable
sixty-mile commute to Paul's job in Detroit. We also agreed
that Max would continue to spend every other weekend in Cincinnati with his father.

While we looked for a rental home in the northwest corner

of Ohio and filled out the kindergarten application for HAT, the Hebrew Academy of Toledo, Nelson drew up a relocation agreement for the two years of Paul's fellowship, which—because of an oversight or laziness on his part—included clauses that had no relevance to our situation. My lawyer read it and phoned me right away: "They say that any man who represents himself has a fool for a client. That also goes for drafting your own legal documents. It looks like Nelson put this together himself, and he did such a thorough job that it lets you move to Michigan with Max."

I was confused and insisted that wasn't possible. Suffice to say that in Nelson's overinclusion, he'd made the intent of the agreement ambiguous, which opened the door for us to relocate to Michigan for the duration of Paul's fellowship since the law states that ambiguity must be held against the drafter.

Hmmm. I knew what Nelson had intended. As a tax lawyer, he was out of his depth and had cut-and-pasted a bit too much boilerplate language into the agreement. What spurred me to act in my own interest was my lawyer's breathtaking remark: "Girlfriend, you have been in a cage so long, you don't know what to do now that the door has been left open."

Paul and I took a collective deep breath and scrapped our Toledo plans. We discarded Max's application for the Hebrew Academy of Toledo, enrolled him instead at the much bigger and better Hillel Day School in Farmington Hills, Michigan, and rented a modest ranch home a few minutes' drive from the school. Furious at my defiance of his wishes and afraid of losing his child, Nelson demanded I put a significant portion of my remaining securities in escrow, either to ensure we would return, or to "make it painful" if we chose not to. He also reduced the already modest amount of child support he paid to reflect his anticipated expenses: additional gas, increased car maintenance, hotel rooms, restaurant meals.

As a postdoctoral fellow in neuropsychology, Paul received a $34,000 salary, before taxes, and our rental home—no bigger than my Cincinnati apartment—was $1,300 a month, or $15,600 a year, before utilities. Our share of Max's tuition (we were splitting the $14,000 annual cost with Nelson's parents) was $7,000. All of this was daunting, but we remained optimistic. After Paul left the house that first morning, depositing Max at his kindergarten class before heading to work, I climbed up onto one of the pieces of furniture that had been gifted to us and painted "*Life Is an Adventure*" in huge green script across the entire length of our living room wall. Then, when I least expected and most needed it, I was blessed with a professional referral—the result of work I had done seven years before, in Ohio.

Back when Nelson and I were newlyweds living in New York City, the first nursery mural I painted had been a gift for Nelson's childhood friend in Cleveland—who by now had become my good friend, Jamie. Jamie's sister-in-law, Dee, lived in nearby Ann Arbor and sat on the board of directors of the Hands-On Museum. During its closure for renovations, I agreed to paint a mural in the museum for free—driving almost an hour each way five days a week to paint my heart out onto the museum's basement walls, spending several weeks working without pay, as an aspiring artist so often does, grateful for the exposure.

The museum board wanted to have what they called an "educational narrative" mural, which would teach a bit of science to those who encountered it, bit by bit, as they walked along the corridor, almost like pages of a picture book. I came up with the idea to paint the various stages of the life cycle of a butterfly—accurately, but eighteen times larger than life. The mural depicts a humble white egg sitting on a leaf; then, a caterpillar; a hanging chrysalis; an emerging adult, waiting for its wings to dry; and, near the end of the hallway, a resplendent butterfly with a wingspan of about six feet. After so many days of depicting the butterfly's life cycle with scientific precision, I took artistic liberties with the outstretched wings, making them look as if they were made up of so many panes of rainbow-hued stained glass. I signed my name to the mural, entitled it *See How I Grow*, and privately dedicated it to Max, who seemed to be shooting up in height suddenly, even during the brief period of time I had been busy painting the mural. The connection to my own metamorphosis was not lost on me either.

My creative efforts paid off. The museum was so pleased with my work, I was commissioned to paint another mural on the three walls of the "water play" room, a newly constructed space on the main floor, for $7,000. Not only would my fee for this job cover our entire portion of Max's kindergarten that year, but my reward would extend far beyond the project.

As I wrapped up work on my second of two murals, the board held a black-tie reopening gala at which my *Under the Sea* mural drew enormous attention, by virtue of being chosen as the site for a table of *hors d'oeuvres*. My parents came to Ann Arbor for the occasion, and I felt like the belle of the ball—posing for my father and newspaper photographers in an evening gown I found on markdown at Nordstrom Rack (it was designed for a six-foot-tall woman and had a layer of chiffon over silk charmeuse that could not be hemmed). I never imagined the amount of praise my work would garner or publicity I would receive. The story managed to reach from Ann Arbor all the way to suburban Detroit and led to many other professional opportunities, thus effecting the successful relocation of my business in a very short time.

Joy abounded in our new life in Michigan. Hillel Day School had an engaged community of parents, and Max made new friends and enjoyed numerous playdates. One family recognized the 513 area code on the kindergarten class contact list and realized we'd followed in their footsteps. Cindy Cohen called and explained that their family had relocated from Ohio one year before us, when Cincinnati-based Proctor and Gamble decided they needed her husband to represent their interests at the Kmart headquarters in Troy. Both of the Cohens turned out to be from Long Island, like me, and we became close friends, taking turns hosting shabbat dinners at each other's homes.

We enjoyed visiting Ann Arbor too, where I had earned a family membership at the Hands-On Museum. Max loved eating at Zingerman's Delicatessen and, of course, playing in "Mommy's" water room at the museum; he never left without posing with his own wings spread wide, next to the butterfly I had painted.

Even driving together into the heart of Ohio every other

Friday became a fun adventure for Max and me. Kindergarten and first grade classwork didn't have to be made up, so in that respect, missing school every other Friday wasn't a burden. To keep things educational, we became members of COSI (now called Imagination Station) in Toledo, and we would pack a picnic lunch and stop there for an hour or two of scientific fun on our way to Wapakoneta, Ohio.

A Bris at the Old Folks' Home & Other New Beginnings

The following year, while pregnant with Sam—my second son—I received a call from the director of the Detroit Jewish Home for the Aged. They asked if I would be willing to come and paint some flowers and other bits of cheer on the hallway walls of the home and in their spa. I found I loved spending time in the home, where residents would park their wheelchairs next to me and watch me paint while they recounted their favorite stories. Soon, I came up with another idea for how we could bring joy to the residents of the home, beyond the vibrant artwork I was adding to their living environment.

The residents often attended memorial services in the social hall; I would hear announcements to that effect on the public address speakers while I was painting. It made me sad that the social life of this community seemed to revolve around the death of its members. Thinking about this one day as I worked, I decided we should ask whether we might host our son's *bris* there, which, God willing, was fast approaching. This use of the social hall would provide residents a joyful and welcome contrast to their typical gatherings.

Paul agreed and the director did too. We arranged for the in-house catering staff to provide its standard spread and informed our *mohel* of the plan. And so it came to pass that I stood on a stage, holding a microphone and being handed a disposable diaper as an emergency receptacle to catch the copious tears of joy streaming from my eyes as I tried to express to my parents, my in-laws, and a room full of new octogenarian friends what it meant to me to be naming our son Samuel and *Shimon* on the second *yahrzeit* of my beloved Papa Sam.

Sam had arrived with gusto, about two weeks ahead of schedule. It happened the night Max returned from Nelson's second wedding in Kentucky—which meant he acquired a stepmother and a brother in a single weekend. After he was born, I noticed the strangest thing about Sam. Knowing him as I have now for more than two decades, I can state with authority that Sam was fully himself from day one. The nurse cleaned him off, weighed him, did an Apgar test, and handed him to me. Sam was in a great hurry to begin what would be a very big first meal, after which he appeared calm, serene, and self-assured.

I'd had no idea newborn babies could behave this way—Max had been born full of volatile energy, squirming and flailing every time he was set down, bleating like a little lamb until he was picked up again and swaddled, and would only fall asleep while nursing. By contrast, Sam was exquisitely alert, observant, and responsive, but also…preternaturally calm. It was the first of many signs that he was an old soul.

I was awake for so much of Sam's first night of life, as I could hear nurses slamming shut filing cabinet drawers on the other side of the wall, but Sam slept for hours. When a nurse came in to check on us, she was alarmed when I told her I hadn't woken the baby to feed him. "He's nearly ten pounds," I told her, "and anyway, just look at him—he's fine." After I fed Sam again, the nurses helped us pack up all his things, and sent us home on the first snowy day of fall.

Before long, Paul's fellowship would end, and we would pack up and move back to Ohio.

We rented a townhouse and moved back to Cincinnati right before the events of 9/11, which brought a traumatic interruption to a long chapter of relative peace and prosperity. Americans' priorities and attitudes about spending money seemed to change dramatically, overnight. Homeowners in Cincinnati were feeling instability and fear, and many were willing to invest in only those home improvements that would make their homes sell faster, with maximum return on investment. To add insult to injury, Home Depot started offering classes in DIY faux finishes, and selling not only sea sponges and turkey feathers—tools of the trade for professionally trained decorative painters like me—but also an array of "adhesive wall murals" and decorative decals. Though I believe custom murals are an empowering, transformative experience for my clients—children and adults alike—my handiwork was now regarded as a luxury, even a frivolity, and my market shrunk to a select group at the top of Cincinnati's socioeconomic ladder.

It was time to reinvent myself…again.

Paul and I found ourselves in a financial Catch-22. Hoping to buy a home in Wyoming, Ohio—reputedly the most diverse and well-educated community around—we found it very expensive relative to other Cincinnati neighborhoods, because of its award-winning public schools. With scarce cash reserves for a down payment, we needed to get my stocks back and liquidate them if we were going to be able to afford buying a house. Unable to convince Nelson we had moved back to Cincinnati for good—not just to scam him and leave—he was reluctant to release my stocks from escrow, and we watched their value plummet. Rather than do battle over the frozen funds, I chose to focus on generating new income; meanwhile, time was running out on our lease.

Now that Nelson and I were living in the same county again and custody handoffs were more frequent, things between us seemed worse instead of better; we sparred over every parenting issue, displaying an utter lack of trust and respect for one another. I hired a therapist to support Max and hoped she could help; I also felt that Max's interest in theater would provide a healthy outlet for his emotional turmoil. He spent every Saturday at Cincinnati Conservatory of Music's prep division and worked hard developing his craft from the time we moved back to Ohio. By high school, Max was being hired for local professional productions, even playing the lead in Neil Simon's *Brighton Beach Memoirs*.

When it was time for Max to apply to college, we made a

trip to visit Columbia, but I was soon informed that Max would only be applying to programs that offered a BFA in theater. Paul and I believed in the importance of obtaining the best possible liberal arts education before pursuing a vocational degree. But because Nelson was paying for Max's college, we had no say. I thought about how I resented my parents for railroading me into getting the education they wanted for me. I knew that Max would be financially secure, and would have many opportunities in life to learn, grow and develop. Not wanting to alienate my gifted child, I bit my tongue and encouraged them to follow their dream. Also, with virtually everyone opining loudly that Max needed a backup plan, I felt Max deserved a mom who would be in their corner. As a high school graduation gift, I presented Max with a thick book I had spent months making, filled with all the photos I had taken of them as a performer, since the age of three, together with all the programs, tickets, floral cards, and other scraps of memorabilia I had kept in a massive file folder in my desk.

Sam, the Sage

Sam was a conversationalist from the get-go, well before he learned to speak an established language. He began making word-like sounds very early on, but they weren't recognizable language. His first preschool teacher, Betty Ann, a former speech pathologist, expressed alarm at Sam's proclivity to chatter away in his alternative language, insisting that we take him to see a specialist, but we demurred. He wasn't overdue to be fluent in English, not even close. Also, Sam's stature tended to confuse people. From the moment he was born, he'd been "off the chart"—his height and weight graphed at points beyond the color-coded percentiles of the growth chart. Although he was weaned at eighteen months, we were often the target of scathing looks from passersby who deemed him too old to still be nursing, and sympathetic looks from people who, like Betty Ann, incorrectly perceived his infantile speech as indicative of a developmental delay.

Fortunately, we could see that Sam was happy, healthy, and thriving, and he didn't seem the slightest bit frustrated by other people's inability to understand him. Because he called things by consistent names, Paul, Max, and I learned Sam's language and we were able to respond to him. I would speak to him in English (duh!), telling him the word for each item as I handed it to him, until seemingly overnight, Sam switched over to English and began speaking in full paragraphs.

I distinctly remember several conversations while I was driving not-yet-three-year-old Sam home from his morning preschool at Ohav Shalom, buckled into the car seat directly behind me in the minivan, next to baby Isaac, who was not yet one. One day, after chattering all the way down the highway, Sam announced, as we turned into our subdivision, "Mommy, I love talking to you!" and I said "Sam, I think you just love talking, sweetie!" and this evoked a happy sigh.

Another day, as we approached our neighborhood, Sam announced, "they're cutting the grass today!" As I turned the corner onto our street, I responded cheerfully, "No, not today, honey. Today is Wednesday. The men come to cut our grass on

Friday. That's in two more days." As we reached the back of the long, winding street, our house came into view, and our lawn was dotted with several men riding mowers. Wide-eyed, I lowered the window to greet them, and one of them approached the car and said, "There's heavy rain in the forecast tomorrow, so we're cutting today instead of Friday."

"How did you know?" I asked Sam, turning around to face him before driving up the hill and into our garage. Sipping fruit punch from his Capri Sun, Sam raised one eyebrow, shrugged, and beamed a sweet Sammy smile.

Weeks later, I hired a young sitter from Croatia who had been working nearby as an *au pair*. Until now, I'd been inseparable from Isaac, my youngest, for a full year. Max took a bus to attend public school, and I strapped Isaac into a car seat in the minivan to drive Sam to and from preschool at the synagogue every day. At a friend's urging, I agreed to hire a sitter to spell me twice a week in the afternoon so I could begin to step back into the world without anyone in my arms. I would leave Ivana in charge of the two little ones for their naps, snacks, and afternoon playtime twice a week, returning to the house after Max arrived home.

Sam's nickname for our sitter was Aye-aye, which sounded like the first letter of her name said twice. One day, Ivana was due to arrive soon after we returned from preschool. As we neared the house, Sam announced, "Aye-aye's not coming today." I corrected him, saying, "Actually, today is Tuesday, which is one of the days Ivana comes to visit you." I parked the minivan in the garage and followed Sam into the house, carrying

Isaac in my arms. The answering machine was blinking. I hit play, and there was Ivana's voice, explaining that she was unable to come that day. I looked down at my wise little boy. Sam had that same sweet smile on his face, and one raised eyebrow, looking up at me as if to say, "I told you so, Mommy; why didn't you believe me?" I made a note to try to reserve judgment the next time.

Another way I learned to trust Sam was by observing his excellent intuition about people. He seems to have been born with an extraordinary ability to read and assess people's energy—their sincerity and intentions. Now that Sam's an adult, we know he has many extraordinary abilities. And as much as I am impressed by his musicality, his comic timing, his intellectual and academic prowess, I am still utterly in awe of his social skills and emotional intelligence, which I estimate as being at least as far off the charts as his height and weight ever were.

Isaac, the Unicorn

When Isaac was born, many people saw my big strong baby as a future professional athlete. Strangers would peek into the stroller and ask if he had a contract with the Cincinnati Bengals. A sports agent and his wife gave us a baby gift of a fleece blanket embellished with colorful felt baseball bats, footballs, soccer- and basketballs, asking if they could represent Isaac "when the time comes." I know I was supposed to laugh it off, but the truth was I didn't appreciate the frequent, superficial judgment. I felt that Isaac would just as likely turn out to be an artist or musician, or perhaps a poet.

When I first brought newborn Isaac along with me on a visit to Miriam, she glanced down at him in the car seat and said, "Oh, look how happy he is to be reunited with you! You two have been together in a past lifetime and he chose to be with you again. You will always be very close!" What a lovely thing that was to hear.

Isaac has such a unique energy that acquaintances often don't know what to make of him. More times than I can count, people trying to describe Isaac have called him a unicorn. When he was younger, kids at school would often assume Isaac was gay, and tease and taunt him, as they also did with Max and Sam. I didn't have to say a word to him about this, because his brothers told him how foolish those kids were being and assured him it didn't matter whether he was gay or straight. After we moved out of Ohio, some adults in his new school even mistook Isaac for a girl. First, the orchestra teacher told me "*she's* quite a good cellist." Then, a custodian accused Isaac of lying and refused to let him enter the boy's bathroom when Isaac "claimed" to be a boy.

After three frustrating months in fifth grade, Isaac decided to cut off all of his gorgeous long hair. But of course, it was about more than just his hair. I've since learned that because my children were never taught to conceal their emotions, never discouraged from expressing themselves or scolded for crying or singing, dancing or leaping—they don't conform to traditional gender stereotypes, and for some people this is disorienting.

At Max's *bar mitzvah*, five-year-old Isaac, a ballet student at the time, wanted to contribute to the special occasion by doing a series of leaps and pirouettes down the temple's center aisle during the service, just as he did every time we entered the bagel shop. That sounded just fine to me and Paul, and we gave him our blessing. After the service, Matti—a young lesbian who almost a decade earlier had been my flower girl—told me how the sight of Isaac dancing so freely and joyfully down the aisle had affected her. "That was just so beautiful to see, Aunt Nancy," she said. "I had to tell you how deeply touching and heartwarming it is for me to see you giving Isaac permission to be fully himself. I don't know why people treat girls and boys so differently, I just know that they do."

Matti was right, of course. Her generation, my kids' generation, more than any other before it, is calling out all gender-based behavior restrictions as stupid and harmful, and yet they persist; we still have a lot of work to do. Over the past several years, Max has come to disidentify with their gender assigned at birth, rejecting masculinity and its societally reinforced tropes.

As for Isaac, he stopped studying ballet, but adores swing dancing. He's become a cellist, a musical theater performer, a jazz singer, an ultimate flying disc athlete, an orchestra conductor, and an award-winning composer. More than either of his siblings, Isaac is so expressive, sensitive, and over-the-top goofy and adorable that—when people behold all of this sparkly exuberance emanating from a six-foot-three-inch athlete's body—they may well look at him and say he's a unicorn, just as they did when he was five.

I don't know whether Isaac and I were siblings in a past

life—Miriam suggested something to that effect, and the dynamic between us has often seemed that way to Paul—but the details have not yet been revealed to me. I love when people say he's my mini-me, even though he's three inches taller. And I'm amused when people say Isaac tells stories the same way I do, with extensive quotes and tremendous detail. I'm bemused when they observe that he's super intense or dramatic, because he expresses himself in a way that feels natural and familiar to me. And I love seeing him excel in all the passionately creative work he is doing in the world, and often think that my life would have been more like Isaac's if I'd had the same encouragement and support when I was a child, especially if I had been born a boy. Isaac still calls me and Paul frequently, and I often observe that his joys are magnified in me, as well as his sorrows.

I am working with my therapist on creating a healthy emotional distance between myself and all my children. One of my mantras is that the goal of parenting is to produce independent, capable adults. Another is to recognize that, having poured myself into the three of them for so many years, this is my time: to take radically good care of myself and to use my energy in ways I could not allow myself to do when I was preoccupied with parenting—such as writing this book. When my intention to publish a memoir was first announced, in a 2009 article written about me in *Tri-County Press*, the journalist noted "Nancy's children and family are the center of her life." Even as I strive to shift that center toward myself, watching all three of my children grow into confident, capable, caring adults is a source of joy beyond compare. And in this era of rampant gun violence, drunk-driving, drug addiction, suicide, and so many other perils, I am deeply grateful that they are all alive and well.

Together, this little crew of mine—Paul, Isaac, Sam, and Max—inspire me to be my best every day. More than any other title I have held in this life, I am so happy and proud to be my children's mom, and always want them to feel happy and proud to claim me as such.

Blind to the Truth

It has always been…let's say, interesting to me to be told that I don't look Jewish. During college, my ethnic ambiguity had been a source of confusion and hurt. More than one person asked me out based upon an unspoken assumption that I was not Jewish—then, upon discovering their error, ceased communication with me. Others, sometimes after a few cocktails, have been bolder, insisting I am either too tall, too athletic, or too good looking to be Jewish. My father warned me that people at Harvard would also pay me this peculiar sort of "compliment" and advised me not to mistake it as anything other than what it was: pure, old-fashioned antisemitism. I wondered how Daddy explained this mistake when people made it about him. Many years would pass before I solved the mystery.

Since childhood, I've corrected people who offered their opinion that I didn't look Jewish. I remembered my mother's scornful reactions to the suggestion when I was young; evidently, this was something rude people said. Surely it was racist, antisemitic—why wouldn't I object? I had known all four of my grandparents, and I was certain that Golda and Harry Illman, and Sam and Esther Brochstein were all Ashkenazi Jews whose parents brought them into the world on land that was once part of the Russian Empire (in Shnadava, Poland, and Ukraine), then escorted them through Ellis Island into America.

Once I reached adulthood, it wasn't uncommon for a person of mixed background to recognize something familiar in me, then—seeking affirmation and connection—ask what my non-Jewish parent's ethnicity was. I would demur, defending my Jewish pedigree. My Hebrew name was *Nechama*, I had attended six years of Hebrew School, had become *bat mitzvah* at twelve at a temple whose annual fundraiser was emceed by Kal Seinfeld—whose son, Jerry, would become a famous comedian. My father had grown up in the Jewish enclave of Dorchester, Massachusetts; my mother had gone to East Midwood Jewish Center in Brooklyn (born between famous neighbors Barbra Streisand and Ruth Bader Ginsburg) before moving to Nassau County in time to attend Great Neck High School. If I had wanted to brag, I could tell people I still had the letter, received when I was an infant, informing me that my maternal grandparents had made me the youngest patron of the Jewish Theological Seminary, or that at age eight, I would be invited to stand before a large gathering of the Seminary on Long island and recite the blessing over the *challah* as future president of the United States George H. W. Bush presented my grandfather with an honor. I never mentioned either of these things to anyone, because I was embarrassed by my family's relative affluence. But growing up in Massapequa, I hadn't known anybody "more Jewish" than I was.

I have repeatedly learned, but often forgotten, that I should identify myself as Jewish when I meet people in a non-Jewish context, because nobody ever assumes it, and failing to mention it can sometimes cause awkwardness—as it does when your new neighbors invite you to a Whites-only barbecue, which happened when we first returned from Michigan. Later, it would also lead to my being invited to introduce the public screening of a film that promotes the hatred of Jews, but that is another story.

Paul and I had lived in Cincinnati long enough to know that we had to choose our neighborhood carefully if we hoped to feel accepted. We wanted to live in Wyoming, Ohio, which had a reputation for being the most diverse and well-educated community in the area, but it was too expensive to comfortably house our family of five. To avoid encroaching upon a homogeneous White enclave, we deliberately searched the Hamilton County auditor's website—which shows the names of every homeowner in the county—to identify a diverse subdivision. Both our surnames are ambiguous; especially when said aloud, they could be either German or Jewish. The presumption in Cincinnati, until proven otherwise, is that you are a Catholic, of German descent. Having previously owned a home with Nelson in a neighborhood where it took me months to notice that almost all our neighbors were blond, I was happy to have this online tool to identify a more multicultural area for our kids to grow up in.

Confident that we'd discovered just that, Paul and I purchased a 1980s colonial-style home from the original owners, named Siekmann, who were moving to Pennsylvania. When our new next-door neighbor spotted me with baby Sam balanced on my hip, supervising the unloading of our moving truck, he walked over and introduced himself. After hearing our full names and sizing us up, he invited us to a backyard barbecue that Sunday. At the party, I approached him as he stood in a circle of men, discussing a neighbor who had written a musical drama about the history of the Civil War-era farmhouse around which all the rest of our homes had been built. I asked "Is he here…the owner of the farmhouse? I would love to hear the story of his home!"

"Who, Horwitz? Here? Today? Ha! No, he's not here," the men responded, almost in unison, laughing and gesturing with their bottles of beer. As their laughter rang out and the sneers on their faces registered, I felt chills run up my spine. Until that moment, I had failed to notice that everyone around me was White. Of course, Lester Horwitz wasn't there—except for Paul and me, only White Christian homeowners had been invited to this gathering. All the Asian, Arab, and Jewish names Paul and I had seen on the website belonged to folks who had inadvertently moved into a White enclave.

We were never greeted by these formerly friendly neighbors again, nor was Max invited back to swim with their kids in their backyard pool, as he had been every day of our first week in the neighborhood. When school started in September, kids at the bus stop—who had played daily with Max that first week—snatched his lunch and played "monkey in the middle" with it, throwing the paper bag back and forth over Max's head and smashing its contents to bits in the process. When I told our other next-door neighbors, a Palestinian family with whom we had become friendly, why we had decided to sell our house and move to a different neighborhood, they thanked me for validating what they had feared was just their paranoia. Soon, they would also thank me for increasing our home's value and selling it at a much higher price point than what we'd paid two years before; this would benefit them when they sold their own home. As I'd done in the nineties, I had used my vision, professional training, and hard work to improve the value of my home. Unlike what happened when Nelson deliberately underpriced our marital home to deprive me of remuneration, this time I would see the profit of my labors. Paul and I cleared enough money flipping our house that we were now able to move our family to Wyoming.

In Wyoming, we became the second owners of a midcentury home built near a historic farmhouse. Alice Fegelman saw me on the front lawn and came across the street to introduce herself. She had lived in Cincinnati all her life, volunteered that she disliked my former in-laws, and said she was happy to welcome another Jewish family to the neighborhood. She told me that Mr. Poage, the owner of the original farmhouse, had been an avowed antisemite, and she was proud to have been the first Jew to move to the street in 1964, the year the Civil Rights Act made it illegal to refuse to do commerce with a person based on religion. She also told me, with disgust, that the private golf club just down the street still didn't admit Jews as members.

Alice had recruited her Jewish friends to become her neighbors, managing to persuade several of them to build homes on the street as well. I told her we had bought our home from the previous owner's estate, without a realtor, and that our octogenarian neighbor—named in the owner's will as the listing agent—tried to confirm that we were Christian before selling us the house. During a showing on a Sunday afternoon, she asked the infant in my arms if he was wearing such a pretty sweater because he had come straight from church. I played along, recalling that I'd been barred from renting more than one apartment after triggering Catholic prejudice toward divorcées, less than a decade earlier. Now, Alice assured me that I had not imagined the realtor's poorly hidden agenda.

Weeks after we arrived, Mr. Poage's elderly nephew, who together with his wife was raising a granddaughter close to Max's age, invited Max to play golf at the club. I advised Max he'd be a guest at a restricted club—where he and his parents would be denied membership—and was amused when he chose to wear my old Harvard Hillel tee shirt (with Harvard spelled out in five Hebrew letters) as part of his golf attire. Yep, that's my kid.

Hoping to promote my mural business, my new decorative furniture refinishing service, and paint-color selection service to potential clients in the local Jewish community—and to inspire readers to derive more joy from their living environments—I began writing an interior design column for the *American Is-*

raelite, the country's oldest English-language Jewish weekly. I offered readers practical and creative tips on interior decorating, including clever ways to economize, and even delved into color science, sharing which colors stimulate appetite (red), make you feel happy (yellow), and improve concentration (green).

Ironically, the column would make me a bit of a social pariah among other Jewish parents in Cincinnati; readers who didn't know me were embarrassed to have me enter their homes and discover their lack of interior decorating prowess. I struggled to find work and resorted to taking jobs "for exposure" again, but this time, they didn't lead to paid work.

Thankfully, Paul was doing well at his job; he was finding success as a member of the neuropsychology team at Kettering Medical Center in Dayton, about an hour from home. When a director position opened at the local rehabilitation hospital right down the street from our house, I encouraged him to apply. He hesitated, uncertain he was qualified to manage other neuropsychologists. I challenged this limiting belief and persuaded him to inquire. He eventually succumbed to my campaign of persistence and applied for the position, even after learning he was competing with his former mentor. He showed up for his interviews feeling relaxed and projecting confidence because he knew we would be okay if they didn't choose him—and he got the job!

Along with the new position came a significant increase in salary, and Paul told me I should take some time to see what else I might love to do, in the widening space between mural commissions. "With all due respect," he said, "thanks to your encouraging me to apply for this job, my salary has increased by about as much as you earn in a good year painting murals, so why don't you give yourself a break for a minute? Explore what else you might love to do."

The Gift of Time and Space

This was the game changer, the magical moment when everything shifted for me. I would be eternally grateful to have this opportunity—as a mother of three young children—to look within, more than I ever had before. It was incontrovertible proof that I had found a partner who truly saw me, celebrated me, valued my unique talents and interests, and supported my becoming everything I wished to be. It was also the start of a period of massive personal growth: I began my yoga practice, joined a civic orchestra, formed a piano trio, and obtained a number of certifications—in Reiki energy healing, plant-based nutrition, and aromatherapy. I designed and founded creative programs—first for children, then for adults—and hosted them at my home. I grew spiritually, musically, artistically, and socially, like no other time in my life. Not by chance, all of this growth happened during a period of time when I wasn't in contact with my parents, which meant I could follow my own inner promptings, explore hunches, and investigate new interests without criticism.

We joined a Reform (progressive) congregation, which my parents would have condemned for being different from the way they worshipped. I found it so much more *heimish* and lively than any other spiritual community I'd been a member of. Participating in the life of Valley Temple—first as a congregant, then as a Sunday school teacher, and one Purim as Queen Esther, eventually contributing my talents as both muralist and violinist—inspired me so much that I considered enrolling in rabbinical school. David, a rabbi friend I'd met back when we had cared for one another's babies at JELC, responded with enthusiasm to this idea and offered to mentor and counsel me through the decision-making process. Through David, I found the Hope Springs Institute, a retreat center teeming with spiritual energy, where I would have several transformative experiences.

My musical leveling up began on November 11, 2008, on the seventieth anniversary of *Kristallnacht*. After dinner, I left the kids at home with Paul and took myself to a concert at Plum Street Temple, featuring Sylvia Samis—the associate concertmaster of the Cincinnati Symphony Orchestra—playing on one of the Violins of Hope that had been rescued from concentration camps when they were liberated in 1945, then collected and restored by Amnon Weinstein. While an actress stood at a microphone and read from Sylvia's late mother's memoir of being imprisoned and orphaned at Auschwitz, Sylvia stood beside her, playing the theme from *Schindler's List* on the restored violin. The steadiness of these two talented women—one reading a firsthand account of unimaginable atrocities endured, the other playing a beautiful, poignant melody as her mother's words sliced the air—took my breath away.

I sent an enraptured email to Sylvia as soon as I returned home, in which I attempted to convey how impactful her performance had been and to express how much I admired and appreciated what she had shared that evening. I told her I'd noticed in the program notes that we both lived in Wyoming and had attended the same summer chamber music program in Blue Hill, Maine. This last detail conveyed that I was an accomplished musician, and she responded by inviting me to visit her on Saturday evening of the upcoming Thanksgiving weekend— to read some string quartets with her, her son, who was a cellist, and a violist friend from the symphony.

I couldn't believe my good fortune. After we read quartets for three hours and paused to have a bite to eat, Sylvia complimented my playing, and asked where I was playing these days. I confessed sheepishly that I was playing only on occasion, with a few other members of the Valley Temple in their Friday Night Live band. Surprised and sympathetic, Sylvia suggested I consider joining the Seven Hills Sinfonietta, a local civic orchestra that included some excellent musicians. Then we sat back down and resumed playing music until sometime after 2 a.m. The next morning, in a haze that was equal parts exhaustion and gratitude, I realized that music had to inhabit a bigger place in my life, and decided to take her advice.

I joined the Sinfonietta and before long—through sheer dedication and enthusiasm—became their concertmaster. In 2011, the Sinfonietta would honor me further by inviting me to perform as a soloist with the orchestra, and I would invite a brilliant artist, Tatiana Berman, to play the Bach Double Violin Concerto with me. I had first played the piece as a child; now, as a middle-aged woman, I returned to Sylvia's house and paid her for a series of lessons to help me polish it back to performance readiness. This was a tremendous privilege and pleasure, not least of all because my parents would travel from New York to Ohio to attend the concert. Glancing over at my mother while performing the second movement, I could see she was visibly moved; my father photographed me and Tatiana standing together backstage, an image that I treasure, partially because it reminds me that he and I managed to reconcile before it was too late.

The orchestra conductor's ex-wife, Jennifer, was an accomplished cellist. Together with her beloved piano accompanist, Melody, we would form a trio and play Mozart, Beethoven, Dvořák, and more, giving concerts throughout the Cincinnati tristate area. Jennifer proposed the Sanskrit word *Samadhi* as the name of our ensemble because our goal in playing together was to achieve moments of connection to the highest form of consciousness through the music, where we felt something akin to the divine.

Sylvia played an essential role in my return to the world of music—a world that brought me endless joy and made my heart sing in a way nothing else could. There was something extraordinary about our connection, and I wasn't surprised to discover we had several significant dates in common. Paul's birthday is the *yarzheit* of not one but both of Sylvia's dear parents, I share a birthday with Sylvia's late mother, and Sylvia shares a birthday with my mother. While Sylvia is several years younger than Priscilla, she is still sufficiently older than I, helping to fill the emotional void I carried all my life. She was so warm, encouraging, and kind; I became very fond of her as well as her dear husband, Charles, and their beautiful Samoyed, Silver. Unable to find the words, I expressed my deep gratitude to Sylvia with a small painting of a pink rose growing in a cracked old pot among some ruins.

During our three-hour-long weekly trio rehearsals in my living room, when Melody or Jennifer stopped playing due to a stiff neck, a sore shoulder, or a headache, I would set down my violin and put my hands on the location of the pain, working to ease its release. They found my touch comforting and asked whether I'd considered becoming a masseuse. I confessed that touching others in a therapeutic way brought me joy, and they spoke of many musicians they knew who suffered from musculoskeletal pain related to playing their instruments. If I would skill up, I could be a blessing to the local community.

I began to inquire what training I might obtain and repeatedly received the same answer each time: "Nancy, you seem like you'd be a good Reiki healer." The third person I asked told me she was hosting a Reiki One attunement and training the next weekend at her wellness center, and I signed up—stepping onto my path as a Reiki healer before ever having received a single treatment in the modality.

I fell in love with practicing Reiki; it felt as natural to me as painting or playing the violin. I felt abundance flowing into my life again, realizing that when I operate with a high vibrational energy—when I tap into peace and gratitude, when I spread joy and love in my community—the same quality of positive energy returns to me and improves every aspect of my life.

Once I became certified as an advanced practitioner, I leveraged online marketing companies, like Groupon and its competitor, Amazon's Living Social, to supplement the word-of-mouth buzz in the local music community, and soon had a busy healing practice in the lower level of my home.

But my forays into intertwining my gifts with the community didn't stop there. I teamed up with another artist mom whose son was a kindergarten classmate of Sam's, and together we created a summer art camp for kids at her painting studio. The following summer, I created my own version of the camp and ran it with my former flower girl, Jamie and Heather's daughter, Matti, who came down from Cleveland to stay with us. When school started up again in the fall, I spun the summer camp into an after-school program on the lanai. The program was so well loved that when the weather turned cold, my students begged for me to extend the season, so I bought a bunch of space heaters at Costco and ordered oversized sweatshirt smocks for the kids to wear that proclaimed "ART MATTERS" on the front, and "AND SO DO I!" on the back.

Through connections I made in the local yoga community, I was invited to attend a day of the World Peace Yoga Conference on a full scholarship, where I met former dairy and cattle farmers and learned enough about farming, nutrition, and veganism to feel inspired to make the leap from pescatarian to vegan. I enrolled in an online certification program in plant-based nutrition with Colin Campbell, author of *The China Study*, after which there was no looking back. More than a decade later, I have done plant-based food demos at farmers' markets, per-

sonal training studios, in Whole Foods Market and other grocery stores, as well as in my home, and recently served as the
DC chapter chair of Jewish Veg, an organization committed to
demonstrating how Jewish teachings are most consistent with
a plant-based diet.

After being hired as a violin soloist to perform Norwe-
gian-style fiddling with a high school choir, I found myself en-
amored with a group of about a dozen teenage singers. Inspired
by their curiosity about my energy and lifestyle, I created a program called Practices that Serve, and hosted them at my home
for five days. Six of the young women managed to attend, and I
began the week by inviting them to take seats in my living room.
First, I had them journal about transformative experiences that
had shaped them, and I created a safe space in which they could
share their writing with each other. Everyone received a Reiki
session in my healing studio, we practiced yoga in my backyard,
went to the produce market, prepared and ate plant-based food,
watched a jarring documentary about the food industry, painted
a still life on the lanai, and made beaded jewelry to remember
our special time together.

Magically, while I was writing this section, I received a message from one of the parents of an art camper who spent time
at my house in 2009: "Nancy, I just wanted to let you know
that you played an important role in the development of my
daughter. She attended your summer camp when she was 7 or
8 years old. Now, she is a professional makeup artist. She also
still does the sun salutation she learned from you. I am extremely grateful." Deeply touched, I shed a happy tear or two. The

following day, a grown-up former student wrote to me herself, saying: "I am forever grateful for everything you've taught me. You will always be a part of who I am now. Love you for that! I am still painting; it is my happy place! And I am still doing yoga, I just can't remember all the names, just "hello, sun" and "hello, moon." She sent a video of her recent paintings and said she wanted to gift one to me. There is truly nothing to fill one's heart with joy so much as reciprocated love and knowing you've touched another's life.

Marriage, the Second Time Around

Having given Max his first harmonica on the night they met, Paul would go on to teach Max how to kick a soccer ball, operate the horsey swings in Burnet Woods, tie a pair of shoelaces, ride a bike, hit a whiffle ball with a bat, toss a frisbee, and so much more. When we were first married, they'd go out to hit baseballs in cages and play round after round of mini golf. At home, Max would walk just in front of Paul, between Paul's arms, and help to push the lawnmower. I remember sitting on the couch in Michigan, nursing baby Sam as I looked out the window, watching the two of them together and feeling so grateful.

Paul and I have now shared a life together for over two decades, along with a deep and abiding affection for Max, Sam, and Isaac. We were parents together out of the starting gate and spent the first twenty-one years of our marriage parenting every day. We've celebrated several of our wedding anniversaries watching Max perform: as Fiyero in a children's theater workshop of *Wick-*

ed; as Speed in a high school parking lot production of *The Two Gentlemen of Verona*; and two years in a row, we celebrated at the Aronoff Center as he accepted an acting award at the Cappies.

Paul is a loving, supportive partner who sees me for the complex person I am and allows me the freedom to continue becoming my truest, best, most fully realized self. Sensitive to the fact that I'd been financially abused during my first marriage, Paul insists I manage all our finances. Aware that I'd been emotionally abused—repeatedly told I was unlovable and difficult to live with—Paul never stops reminding me how loveable I am and demonstrates his love every day.

Occasionally, we'll see a character on-screen whose mother is unkind to her. If I'm triggered by the story, the flood gates sometimes open. Paul wraps me in his arms, sometimes dropping a warm wet tear or two onto my neck, telling me how sorry he is for the ways I have been hurt, and how grateful he is that I've broken the mold. On a lighter note, he is still waiting for me to recover from the trauma of being forced, as a novice bridge player, to compete with life masters; he struggles with my aversion to card games. To me, this speck of recreational friction is a reminder that nobody is a perfect match for anyone else; we grow closer by choosing to accept one another, with all our flaws and imperfections. I am grateful for our differences, and our ability to communicate about them, because they help us continue to grow. Nothing is a better mirror for us than our most intimate adult relationships, and our marriage is no exception; it inspires me to become a better person.

Since the beginning, Paul has celebrated the fact that I challenge him in positive ways and nudge him out of his comfort zone, and he's delighted that I'm claiming ownership of my role as an instigator of joy.

Seventh Spirit Messenger | 2007—Peebles, Ohio

In 2007, as I prepared to turn forty one, I registered to attend a silent retreat at Hope Springs, and it was during a guided meditation there that I was visited by Max's twin, whose heart I had allowed—no, invited—doctors to stop with a fatal injection not once, not twice, but during multiple attempts on four separate visits to New York Hospital. For twelve years, this soul had seemed to be nothing but dead, lost to me and the world.

Aaron's spirit made his presence known during my first weekend retreat at Hope Springs, while I sat in a yurt called Spirit House. My friend David, who had volunteered to mentor me through the process of deciding whether to become a rabbi, had urged me to peruse the various offerings on the center's website. When I did, the silent retreat captured my imagination. As a gregarious and verbal person, I could hardly imagine a wordless weekend. On Friday evening, as our group prepared to enter thirty-two hours of silence, Mary, the priestess leading the retreat, said she would be guiding us in a spirit meditation Saturday evening. She advised us to consider which spirit guest we each would have visit with us, and to spend some time Saturday sending an energetic invitation out to them.

Just before the ritual of entering the silence, I approached Mary and told her I thought I was going to need help with the assignment. She offered to meet with me for fifteen minutes before lunch the next day. Early on Saturday morning, after yoga and breakfast, I opened the door and entered Spirit House, finding it already full of people seated cross-legged on cushions in front of nine altars dedicated to the stages of female human experience. Not wanting to disrupt their peace, I took the seat nearest the door, in front of a golden altar to the newborn. Without even closing my eyes, I soon sensed the presence of Max's twin, and knew we would visit together during the evening meditation. I left the yurt in tears, and as I looked up, I saw Mary standing on the deck of her cabin, holding a mug of tea in both hands and looking right at me. I signaled to her and she nodded and smiled—she knew I no longer needed to keep our appointment; my question had been answered.

That evening, we gathered in a larger building, and Mary led us into a meditative trance. And there he was, stepping out from between a pair of pine trees, then sitting beside me on a log in our Ohio backyard—looking much like Max but with warm, lushly fringed brown eyes (in contrast with Max's blue ones), and with dimples, like Isaac's—saying that he is always with me. Telling me his name is the same one I gave to all three of my living children as their middle name. Telling me that whenever I want to visit with him, I can go into our backyard and sit on any of the logs I'd arranged there in a circle as a sanctuary among the trees, and he would come and meet me. Since then, I have realized the location doesn't matter; I merely need to think of Aaron to feel his loving presence with me again, no matter the time or place.

I was excited to make this discovery, and to think I had a loving spiritual presence with me more constantly than any living person could be. It felt special to be so well loved. Even though I know now that every one of us has an equivalent entourage of adoring spirits around us, it was news to me at the time and made me feel less alone in the world.

Fifteen years later, I learned that my great-grandmother, Helen—who reached out to tell me about Aaron soon after he had shared my womb with Max—is also with me quite often. I like to keep her picture near me, so I can look at her likeness while I connect with her energy. When I want to connect with Aaron, I usually look at a picture of my three living children, photographed smiling with their arms around each other, taken soon after my visit to Hope Springs. We sometimes call our kids "the Aaron brothers," and joke about what future business they might establish by that name, because they all share Aaron as a middle name…but also, they are all Aaron's brothers.

Scarce Love Pie | October 2007

I was still working to integrate my new understanding of the infinite quality of love, which had come to me through the study and practice of Reiki, and was reinforced by reading contemporary authors, both recommended and stumbled upon: Thich Nhat Hanh, Louise Hay, James Redfield, Paul Coelho, Marianne

Williamson, Elizabeth Gilbert, Brian Weiss, Eben Alexander, and others. I had come to understand that love is infinitely available to every one of us. It is within us and around us, and we need only open our hearts to connect with its energy and feel the truth of this. It is the most powerful force in the universe, the most profound aspect of reality. The source of creativity. Love is the energy that brings us into our human existence and ushers us out of this life and into what lies beyond and between lives. It is the set of lessons we come into human form to learn.

When people perceive something as a scarce resource, they compete for it. The very scarcity of a thing leaves us wanting for it, feeling it can never be ours. This unfortunate but too-common belief about love triggers a dark side of human nature that begets ugly behaviors in people, but it is not their fault. So many have been conditioned to think and behave this way. The books I have read and the spirit messages I have received have helped me to forgive people who have a scarcity mentality about love—even if I ultimately decided to discontinue communication with them.

My parents were a different story. When the people whom you love and depend upon the most withhold affection in order to control your behavior, it is deeply confusing. As a child, I believed I had to be perfect in my parents' eyes to win their love. I had been exposed to literature that reinforced the idea of love as a scarce resource, a prize to be won, earned. As a college student, I journaled about my mother's disgust with me, writing about the pain it caused to realize that the person "who loves me the most" does so in spite of who I am. As I grew up, I immersed myself in literary works reflecting the same terrible perspective. And I had to make my own discoveries about love before I was able to discern that other people, including some of my elders, were still operating under this misperception. The better I came to understand love, the more I found compassion for those who perceive it differently than I do.

Our babysitter, Ivana, witnessed me overcome my stress as I prepared for visits from my parents when the children were small. I became so tense, short-tempered, and critical before their visits that I was like an entirely different person. Afterward, I would cry and apologize to Paul for having snapped at him—for having shared my misery with everyone in the house. Two years before Max's *bar mitzvah*, we endured a particularly difficult visit from my parents—the details of which I will not enumerate here, in honor of my father's spirit. As soon as they returned home to Massapequa, I called them and laid out an ultimatum so radical, I trembled from head to toe as I spoke the words: unless and until they found a way to treat everyone in our home with love, they were not welcome to visit us again. My father said he could tell I had help from my friends in crafting my speech, but he wasn't impressed by it—rather, he felt that I was very immature, and he was sad because I was making a tremendous mistake by cutting them off from their grandchildren.

I did not see or speak to my parents again for two years, and I heard through my aunts that I was blamed for the rift. I only learned my parents would be attending Max's *bar mitzvah*, five weeks after mailing the invitation, when I received their response card in the mail, devoid of handwritten remarks, on the day it was due.

Back in 1991, years before Max was born, I attempted to help my father and his sister reconcile as the three of us stood over their mother's deathbed. My Aunt Diane had been grateful for my efforts; she knew they took courage. Now, at Max's celebratory luncheon, Diane repaid her debt by leading me over to a table where my father sat, alone. A bit high from hosting Max's special day, I summoned my courage again, sat down, and spoke to my father earnestly. I looked into his face, which appeared older than I remembered, and told him what I'd been learning. I shared my realization that nothing in life mattered so much as love, but my father was not able to hear me. He said I'd hurt him by setting out conditions for their visits with me and my children, and now he was afraid to open himself up to me. He wasn't ready to trust me and didn't feel safe that I wouldn't hurt him again.

For Diane, this was just another incident she would look forward to dissecting with me, further proof that my father was not worthy of my love. Both my parents were blessed with a younger sister who was eager to confirm and corroborate any negative thought I might share about their older siblings. Both aunts could also be counted on to report anything negative they heard about me, my spouse, or my children; it was how they competed for their own slice of what they perceived as a finite love pie. Since I hadn't yet developed my boundary-setting skills, this caused me much suffering for many years. When I set boundaries with my parents, it hadn't extended to my aunts.

If anything, I became more vulnerable as they stepped forward to fill the space vacated by my parents with their enthusiastic reporting from the field. After Max's *bar mitzvah*, almost half-way through what would turn out to be a five-year estrangement, I was treated to the details of my parents' critical remarks with alacrity.

Upon returning to Connecticut from Ohio, Diane called to catch me up on the parts of the *bar mitzvah* weekend I had missed. She repeated my mother's observation that my violin playing on the *bimah* had been out of tune. My father had expressed his disappointment with me, opining that by now I should be running a Fortune 500 corporation. My parents made these and other equally reductive remarks over drinks at the hotel bar, their generation having fled Dave & Buster's once the kids' dance party got underway. Their criticism was now presented to me in the usual manner, as hearsay evidence of my parents' inadequate love.

At that moment in my life, I was busy feeding, driving, and otherwise parenting a thirteen-year-old, six-year-old, and four-year-old, while continuing to renovate our 1950s ranch home, where I hosted art classes, attended to Reiki clients, offered raw food workshops, and gave violin lessons to some of the little girls from our temple, where I played in the band at Friday night services. I dismissed my mother's remark about my not having played perfectly; I recognized that my violin playing in temple was a form of prayer, not a performance, and did not need to be perfect so long as it came from my heart. The idea of my running a large corporation was absurd, but it still hurt to know Daddy thought I hadn't achieved what he believed I was capable of—or, more accurately—what he deemed to be success. I hadn't fulfilled his idea of my potential. I had disappointed him. These were reasons to feel ashamed.

While still upset by the conversation, I called my maternal aunt, Phyllis, to process my hurt feelings, and she told me not to trust Diane; she had also been at the bar on the evening in question and heard Diane call me emotionally immature. I suppose I *was* immature, in that I still cared what my elders thought of me. I had not yet processed or discarded the belief system with which I had grown up. I remained at a distance a while longer, to carve out a bit more time and space and continue growing myself up, and loving myself, away from the influence of my earliest teachers.

The disconnect between me and my parents would continue for quite a while longer. Every time I felt an impulse to share something with them, I trained myself to call my grandmother instead, and she and I became increasingly close during her final five years, even though we didn't see each other that often. She would sometimes marvel that my mother never mentioned me when they got together, which they did frequently. She wondered aloud, telling me, "she really did love you, Nancy"—her use of the past tense landing like a rock in my stomach. It wasn't until I got a call from my sister informing me that Mama (as we called my grandmother) had died in her sleep, just before her 102nd birthday, that I traveled to Long Island and reconciled with my parents, with great trepidation.

When my parents flew to Cincinnati one last time, for Sam's *bar mitzvah*, we were on much friendlier terms than the previous visit, six years earlier. I came down from the *bimah* after delivering a speech to Sam in which I mentioned the many wonderful ways he resembled his great-grandfather, my Papa Sam, after whom he'd been named, and my father wrapped me in an embrace that was longer and tighter than any we'd experienced before. Three months later, when Daddy died, I would think back to that hug: *He knew he was going soon, and he knew I would keep his memory alive, the way I had done with Papa Sam's.*

Sam's *bar mitzvah* was also our farewell party, because the following week, we would pack up our cat, our dog, and two of our kids, and the minivan would roll out of Cincinnati for the last time. The moving truck left on the evening of a long, exhausting day, and we headed to my dear old friend Alison's house to spend our last night in Ohio, where she would move me to tears with a slideshow, set to music, of the many good times our families enjoyed together over the past seven years. Then it was off to bed before heading east to our new home and the next chapter of our lives, in Takoma Park, Maryland.

Max, who had tethered all of us to Hamilton County, Ohio all these years, was now a student at NYU—which meant that for the first time, we were free to live anywhere. When he was a baby, and I pined for New York, I never dreamed I would become so happily settled in Cincinnati, but I truly had. Our family's lives were beyond comfortable; they were richly fulfilling. Alison was the best and dearest friend I'd ever known. I also loved my Reiki clients, my piano trio, our home and garden, our friends, our community, our temple, my yoga studio, the farmers' market, the local performing arts scene, our kids' schools, pediatrician, acting coach, cello and piano teachers, and so many other facets of our existence.

But all our parents were approaching eighty back on the East Coast, where we were "from" but had not lived for two decades. It would never be easier to disrupt the children's lives than right now—before they became teenagers and got too attached to this place. It would probably never be easier for us, either. And at some future date, when our parents were older and needed us more, we would be closer to them, and that would be easier for everybody. It seemed like the right thing to do.

Moving to Takoma | Summer 2013

When we arrived in Maryland, it became clear: the massive downsizing we'd done while packing up our house was woefully insufficient; even though we'd given away so many things, we still had brought far too much. Our new home was a third of the size of our former one, and the space overflowed with furniture, an upright piano, and boxes waiting to be unpacked.

And there was the artwork... Rather than stash them behind the couch, I carried two of the largest paintings outside to our new front lawn. I leaned both canvases to face the street, one against an ancient sycamore tree, the other just below the tiny front porch, really just a momentary shelter for people awaiting entry to the house. Passersby who bothered to glance our way were now greeted by a big orange smiley face on a turquoise background floating above the words "Be Happy" and a huge red-and-purple heart, with the word "Sweet" above it that asked, "How was your day?" These were accompanied by a piece of lumber I had helped Isaac decorate with paint, coffee beans, sequins, and glass beads a few years earlier, when he was still too young to go to summer camp with his brothers. Now, I propped it against one of our two crepe myrtle trees, angled toward the sidewalk, where it asked passersby, "Hey, How You Doin'?" Accessorized with rainbow pinwheels, hot air balloon spinners, sunflower-patterned porch curtains, and fairy lights strung between two crepe myrtle trees, a joyful, loving tone was set from our first day in town.

Our sweet brick cottage, which was above average in size when it was built in 1935, is nestled at the bottom of a busy avenue, half a mile from Takoma station in DC, which sits at the top of the hill. Commuters began calling out to Paul and me when they would spot us outside as they hiked to or from the metro, thanking us for all the love we were channeling into the neighborhood. After being tucked away on a quiet cul-de-sac for nine years, nestled among people who would look at my purple hair and say "oh, bless her heart" when in fact they meant "oh, she is going straight to hell," it was wonderful to feel seen through the eyes of love.

The house was so much smaller than the one the boys had grown up in that they actually hurt themselves, over and over again, accidentally slamming into its corners and archways, as I repeated two useless utterances: "slow down" and "be careful." Bruises notwithstanding, they were both looking forward to enjoying the tradeoffs that came with a smaller home, like having access to the metro and being able to walk to school, shops, parks, and restaurants on their own.

On our third day in Maryland, after loading both boys onto a bus for sleepaway camp, I finished unpacking our boxes, gave away some bookshelves that were too tall to fit inside the house, and began painting a mural in Sam's room, transforming it into an immersive van Gogh painting—almost a decade before it became a global phenomenon. Sam's bedroom ceiling features a crescent moon and stars in the style of *De sterrennacht (The Starry Night)*. I wrapped all four bedroom walls, along with Sam's bookcase and dresser, with my adaptation of the only van Gogh painting in the Cincinnati Art Museum's collection. *Undergrowth with Two Figures* was one of the final artworks Vincent completed, and it is teeming with the energy of smaller plants growing beneath tall trees.

Paul and I took our first weekend jaunt (by metro) to the National Gallery, giddy over our proximity to countless places of wonder after years of being dependent on a minivan to get anywhere. From our new home, it was an easy hike up the hill to the station, where we could catch a train to anywhere within a 556-square-mile area, including two international airports. We saw a special exhibit on the Ballets Russes—music, dance, costumes, and sets—and I was flooded by appreciation for how much my mother had poured her love of cultural arts into me as a young girl and felt moved to invite her to visit the exhibit with me.

The exhibit was world class, a glorious confluence of several creative genres to which my mother had first introduced me: orchestral music, set design, costume design, and ballet. Mommy had been a dance major at Tuft's Jackson College for Women and worked after graduation as a dance instructor and choreographer at nearby Wellesley College. When I was a toddler, she'd helped to organize a cultural arts program in Massapequa. Standing together now, as two adults, we marveled at the genius of Nureyev, Diaghilev, Picasso, Chanel, Balanchine, Stravinsky, and Matisse. Mommy loved the Ballets Russes exhibit so much she bought the coffee-table book, but she was presumably mystified (but not curious) as to why I was crying as I watched her take in the works of art. Witnessing her appreciate things I loved gave me a taste of the connection I had always wanted with my parents, but rarely found.

After the exhibit, we rode the metro six stops north so she could see our new home, which we had needed both my parents and in-laws to help us purchase, as it was almost twice the price of our home in Ohio. She marveled at how close we now lived to the District, reminiscing about the proximity of her childhood home in Great Neck to Manhattan, where she had spent much of her teens. We emerged from Takoma station, admired the pair of grand Victorian homes at the top of Cedar Street, then stepped across the border, to Cedar Avenue in Takoma

Park, Maryland. We strolled past progressively smaller houses until at last, we reached our modest cottage at the bottom of the hill. Once inside, she hurried to phone my father, assuring him with audible relief that the house was "actually quite cute" and the street was "very nice."

While the boys were still at camp, my parents drove down together, and Daddy surveyed our new place for himself, marveling at how much I had done in a short time. I told him I didn't feel settled yet: I still had to decide what to paint on Isaac's walls, which worship congregation we would join, or where I would find a yoga studio with a sense of community like the one I'd left behind.

"Those things are not important," he said. I didn't agree. I told him that until I accomplished these goals, I wouldn't feel at home. He shrugged, accustomed to us disagreeing.

Diabetic neuropathy in his feet was making it too painful to walk very far, so we skipped the museums and visited the National Arboretum from the car, then dined with some of my mother's cousins at Sergio's—an old-school, family-owned Italian restaurant (now defunct), reminiscent of the ones we loved back on Long Island.

On Monday, my parents were back in Massapequa. Paul returned to his new job at the Veterans Administration, and I decided what mural I would paint in Isaac's room, with the goal of helping him feel relaxed and peaceful. Like me, Isaac is a fan of aromatherapy. He enjoys drifting to sleep with a lavender-infused mist wafting across the room. Under my paintbrush, hedges of lavender appeared, blooming in receding rows on the wall opposite the bed, beside which I dotted thousands of little blobs of paint in a dozen shades of purple, ranging from deep eggplant to pale periwinkle, praying as I painted that this bedroom would foster happy dreams, positive thoughts, and hold space for Isaac to experience success in the years ahead.

With the boys back from camp and settled into their new bedrooms, I began to relax a bit. Having shared the former primary bedroom in our previous home, each brother now had his own private headquarters in which to restore his spirit. I hoped they were ready to face the challenge of navigating their way around new schools, which offered stark contrast to the ones they had known. In Ohio, the boys attended small, majority-white schools, where almost everyone's parents had been born in the Midwest, except for a few Europeans and Asians who came for post-doctoral fellowships and decided to stay. In Maryland, Sam and Isaac found themselves in large, urban, minority-white schools, where half of their classmates' parents were born outside the US, many undocumented.

We chose this diverse community and school district deliberately, wishing to expand their awareness of the full tapestry of American society. The transition proved more complicated and more challenging than we had hoped, in myriad ways we hadn't anticipated, and Paul and I would listen to and process the days' events with the boys every night at the dinner table. Despite the numerous challenges, we both felt optimistic about our move being a change for the better, preparing the kids for the real world in a way that another eight years in suburban Cincinnati never could have.

Go to Sleep, Nanny Baby

A few weeks later, in September 2013, Max was a second-year theater student at Tisch School of the Arts at NYU. His nineteenth birthday was approaching, and I was packing the rest of the family for a quick trip to New York to celebrate. I was feeling excited about our plans to attend a matinee performance of my college classmate, Diane Paulus's, Broadway production of *Pippin*. It was one of Max's favorite shows; Paul had introduced him to it as a child.

After I finished organizing Sam and Isaac's essentials for the trip, my father and I had a long phone conversation extending late into the night, well past my usual bedtime. We covered some difficult topics, and he shared his concerns about various people in our family. There was a lot of darkness in our conversation, but I hung in there, listening and responding to his worries and prognostications, staying on the line until I could scarcely keep my eyes open. Hearing my exhaustion, Daddy told me, "go to sleep, Nanny baby" and said he would read a bit before turning in—making reference to the fact that he was now sleeping in shorter increments: staying up later, getting up earlier, and napping when he got home in the afternoon, "almost like a baby"—and commented about this pattern of behavior being like "bookends."

I think he was sharing with me a glimpse of his awareness that he was approaching the end of his life. The most important thing, which I will remember forever, was that the conversation ended with a rare tenderness. We both told each other "I love you." For this memory, I am grateful.

Gone, Not Gone

The next morning, my mother called. "Nancy, bad news. Your father's gone. Cardiac arrest. On the way to Bellevue." I tried to respond, but that was it; she had hung up.

I was confused. It was clear my father had died, which was shocking without being surprising, because I had been anticipating it. What wasn't clear was the rest of what she meant to tell me. Had Daddy's heart stopped while he was driving into the city to testify as an expert witness? Had his car careened across multiple lanes of the Long Island Expressway and crashed into others? What happened at Bellevue hospital, and who was there now?

My mother had called as she rushed out the door on her way into the city, where she would identify her husband's body and collect his things. She would return home with my father's watch and wedding ring, his leather handbag full of pens, eyeglasses, business cards, billfold, and other bits—all inventoried on a form, a carbon copy of which was issued to her. She would speak with the landscaper and cancel the delivery, scheduled for later in the day, of some crepe myrtle trees, like the ones my father had admired in front of our new house during their recent visit. She called her sister with the news. She called the real estate office at North Shore Towers, to see if any large, upper-floor apartments were available. She called the rabbi to arrange a graveside service for Sunday morning. She called all her closest friends to invite them to the funeral. Her phone line was busy all day.

When I finally got through to her, she said we'd have to find somewhere else to stay for the funeral; she wasn't ready to have anyone else in the house. I sent a text to Carl and Belinda, my former neighbors from Manhattan who now lived on Long Island, and they texted back right away: of course, we could stay with them. They would drive us to the funeral.

At the service, everyone took a turn with the shovel, jabbing it into the huge pile of dirt next to the grave, then dropping clumps of earth onto my father's coffin. Afterward, when my mother walked back to her car to drive home and host a meal, Carl stripped down to a polo shirt and he and Paul filled in the rest of Daddy's grave, while the kids, Belinda, and I stood around, chatting and watching. When they finished, I thanked Carl. He said, "Nance, you know I liked your father and I'm sure you also know, this is the highest *mitzvah* we can do for a person, because they cannot repay it." Grateful and *verklempt*, I nodded and hugged him.

Reading Facebook messages of condolence on the train ride up to New York, I'd been overwhelmed with regret as it occurred to me that I hadn't had enough time to make my father proud of me. It hit me like the sort of wave which, had I been entering the ocean, surely would have knocked me over. The wave was triggered by a text message sent by my college friend, Holly. Her father, also a physician and Harvard graduate, had died a few months prior, and she reached out to express her certainty that my father must have been "so proud" of me. As I read her words, I knew they weren't true. Not only had I rejected the possibility of becoming a doctor and following in his footsteps, but I had failed to do anything good enough, in his eyes, to justify that decision. I turned out to be the underachiever he had always predicted I would become. So much unrealized promise.

Eighth Spirit Messenger | September 2013—Takoma Park, Maryland

Returning home after the funeral, I received a message from Andi—a woman who had attended one of my aromatherapy classes in Ohio. She was a massage therapist and a clairvoyant. And she told me my father's spirit was reaching out to her to see if she would help him communicate with me.

"Was he a forceful...ah...er...a *strong personality* while he was alive?" she asked.

"Oh yes," I replied.

"Well, he's kind of being a pain in my ass," she said, laughing, and I found myself apologizing for my dead father's impertinence (not for the last time).

"It's okay," Andi said. "But he really wants to communicate with you. Do you have time for a reading later this week?"

"Sounds like we should do one right away," I said, and we scheduled a meeting for the next day.

When we connected on the phone the following morning, Andi opened with these words:

"So, Nancy, the first thing your father wants you to know is he is so proud of you. He really wants you to know this."

"Okay," I said, pushing the sound out past the huge lump in my throat. "Got it. Thanks."

"Also, he's sorry he didn't listen to you. He's sorry he was so stubborn. He says he was terribly...he was much more stubborn than you even knew. He says he would still be with you if he had listened to you, and he says you know what he's talking

265

about, but he wants you to know he is with you. Just talk to him. He says: 'Just talk to me. I can hear you.' He is with you."

Oh goodness, this was intense. When my father was alive—which is to say, a few days earlier—he never admitted when he was wrong. Ever. And I knew just what disagreement he was referring to. I had been brought up to never raise my voice to my father. Regardless of what I might want to say, I was required to say it with self-control. The night before my father's last birthday, we were visiting my parents at their vacation home in Palm Beach Gardens, Florida. The kids had gone to bed, and Daddy and I sat in the living room, arguing about his new diet. I had raised my voice over his interruptions, pushing back against his every assertion, then apologized—explaining I'd raised my voice because I felt concerned, afraid he was going to have a heart attack.

Daddy was diabetic, and his cardiologist had him on the Atkins Diet to lose weight. It was clear to me from my nutrition studies that eating red meat advances cardiovascular disease and leads to the dysfunction of vascular endothelial cells, which widen our veins to allow enough blood to reach our heart when we exert ourselves. Without a steady production of nitric oxide, which these cells synthesize, plaque accumulates in the blood vessels. Then, when the body demands an increase in blood flow, the lack of nitric oxide means the vessels don't widen—a combination that can be deadly.

I was relieved when Daddy greeted me the next morning with a warm embrace; we went on to enjoy a pleasant couple of hours sharing brunch at a big round table in their country club's elegant clubhouse, surrounded by my mother, my husband, my children, and several of my parents' closest friends who had moved to South Florida from New York.

When I learned I had been correct—Daddy had experienced cardiac arrest while climbing the stairs from the train platform up to the main hall of Penn Station—I understood in a flash how worthless it is to be right. A few seconds would have passed as Daddy reached the top of the stairs, before he lost consciousness and left this world. I don't know how the mind works as death comes, but as a physician, I suspect my father must have known his heart had failed him.

Daddy also told me, through Andi, he was proud of the way Paul was helping veterans. He had not seemed to appreciate the value of Paul's work as a neuropsychologist when he was alive, so this was soothing to hear.

Finally, Andi said my father was going to guide people toward me to support my healing work. From that day forward, every time I heard from a physician seeking my help in adding aromatherapy to their practice, I would attribute it to my father's influence, honor him, and thank him. I would do my best to help them—knowing this was a way of healing my father hadn't been able to embrace when he was alive—buoyed by the knowledge that I had finally made him proud.

Ninth Spirit Messenger | October 2013—Long Island

About a month after my father's death, Paul, the kids, and I visited Long Island to see my mother, aunt, and sister. My mother took us to their (other) country club for one last meal before relinquishing her membership. The club—which used an old

Vanderbilt family mansion as its clubhouse—was decked out for Halloween. And let me vouch in the affirmative: it does indeed feel odd to walk past bedsheet ghosts and life-size plastic skeletons a few weeks after burying your father. The drawing room was filled with crystal balls, tarot cards, and other tools of the intuitive trade. After the meal, as others drifted to the dessert buffet, I walked to the front of the mansion and stopped to speak with one of the intuitives.

The woman took my hand, peered at it, then closed her eyes. She described seeing me in a healer's mantle, and an image of me wearing a dark cloak popped into my head. I looked up the phrase and learned that it refers to a cloak worn by a practitioner of medicine, with many pouches in which to store herbs, salves, and other remedies. The same Google search led me to the writings of Deborah King, an energy healer, who seemed to speak directly to me as she shared the following thoughts on her website (deborahking.com), paraphrased here: In the Bible, a mantle is a garment that symbolizes a calling given to an individual by God, and a healer's mantle is said to be not only a shelter and protection, but also a source of comfort, refuge, joy, and discovery. You are welcome to take shelter under the mantle of healing. It might also be your own personal connection to the powerful forces of wellbeing, compassion, and unity.

The palm reader said the healer's mantle was being passed down to me by a recently departed ancestor. I told her she was describing my late father, who had been a surgeon and was disappointed I hadn't followed in his footsteps and become a physician.

"But you already know you're a healer, right?"

I nodded. I had been practicing Reiki for two and a half years and had been teaching my clients about whole food plant-based nutrition, restorative breathing, and aromatherapy.

"Well, I am getting that you can help people in ways he wasn't able to. You *are* continuing his work. He is very supportive of the work you're doing."

Two years later, I had a past-life regression with a woman who would later become my hypnosis teacher. At first, I thought I was recalling my past experience as a monkey, but soon realized I was a barefoot, scantily clad man, climbing along the face of a cliff, gathering leaves from a vine for a burn patient. Everything was wet and slippery from the rain. I looked down at the patient on the stretcher and suddenly felt dizzy. A moment later, I saw nothing but blue. I realized I had fallen off the cliff and lay on the ground, seeing the blue sky above me as I died. I understood that my previous life as a medicine man had been cut short, and the memory helped me reframe the urgency I felt to share information about the healing power of plants, even though trying to do so in the shadow of the FDA was making my life miserable.

Tenth Spirit Messenger | November 2013—Through Angel's Eyes

Soon after, I taught a class on aromatherapy at my best friend's house in Ohio. When we'd both lived there, Alison and I used to wish we lived closer to one another. Back then, it took less than half an hour to get to her house—we didn't realize how lucky we were. Now that I lived in Maryland, getting to Alison's entailed buckling myself into the car early in the morning and driving 500 miles, often until after sunset.

When I arrived at her home, I saw that Alison had pulled every chair she owned into the dining room, which was chock full of people eager to learn about aromatherapy. This was a heartwarming contrast to my new community, where—in response to my offering a free class about natural remedies on the neighborhood listserv—I had been brutally cyber-bullied, accused of associating with murderers and wanting to take away children's medicines, leaving them vulnerable to fatal asthma attacks on the soccer field. I had expected DC residents to be more educated and discerning than folks in Ohio, but they'd surprised me. So, despite the tiring drive, it felt lovely to receive the warm embrace of my Cincinnati community.

I sat at one end of Alison's dining table and began to speak, explaining how and why we have been cut off from our ancestral knowledge of medicinal plants, and restoring a bit of that ancestral knowledge to my students. After delivering my prepared remarks, I took questions from the audience, giving detailed instructions and sharing little-known facts about which essential oils are best suited to help us with specific challenges and how to use them most safely and effectively for each purpose: when to sprinkle oil onto salt crystals, when it's better to mix them with baking powder, when to use a diffuser, when and where to apply them topically, how to tell if the oils are adulterated, how much to dilute them.

Hours went by before the last question was answered. One of the students—a massage therapist aptly named Angel, who also helps people develop their clairvoyant and clairaudient gifts—approached me, asking if she could put her hands on me to alleviate the muscle tension from my long drive. As she massaged my neck and shoulders with two drops of frankincense mixed into a spoonful of fractionated coconut oil, Angel shared that her student Andi—the woman through whom my father had insistently requested communication with me after his death—mentioned our session. She didn't want to pry, but as Andi's teacher, she wanted to know if it had been useful. I confirmed that my session with Andi had been a true gift.

Angel bent down and whispered in my ear. "He's so proud of you, you know. He's been standing behind your left shoulder this whole time, watching you hold court. He's basking in your energy. He loves that you're doing this work and wants to help you connect with people who want to learn what you're teaching. So, let him help."

Seeking Connection

I'd discovered the power of essential oils right before we picked up and moved our lives from Ohio to Maryland. I fell in love with the way aroma transformed my healing space into a sanctuary, and I incorporated the oils more and more into my Reiki practice until I became a certified trainer, guiding people in a clinical application of the oils that felt like pure love in eight little glass bottles. I was thrilled by feedback from clients who used the oils at home as a first line of defense for everything from bug bites and burns to headaches and hangovers. Sadly, at the time of our move to Maryland, the FDA was up in arms in response to exaggerated (and illegal) claims made by amateur aromatherapists, such that a cloud of suspicion was cast over the entire industry. So, as much as I loved learning and teaching folks about essential oils in Ohio, I would have to find a different way to connect with my new community.

As ever, art and music became natural avenues. Before long, I was invited by a bassist to spend the afternoon reading chamber music with her and six other friends. As result of gathering that day to play the glorious Mendelssohn octet in E-flat major, I found a new cello teacher for Isaac and was invited into the chamber orchestra with which I perform to this day. Among the members of my new orchestra, I found friends with whom I would occasionally read string quartets and learned of other opportunities, such as accompanying singers as they performed choral works in a historic church beside the Supreme Court.

I began teaching art at a neighborhood preschool twice a month—in a manner that was so spontaneous, messy, and permissive that some of the classroom teachers soon came to consider me a nuisance. I tended to break rules, inadvertently, like when I provided glitter for an art project, unaware it had been banned from the school as a microplastic. But as a result, many parents in my community came to regard me fondly, and I became known to the children in our neighborhood, who now hailed me in public as "Miss Nancy."

One wonderful day in the spring of 2017, I led a classroom experience combining music, colored construction paper, bubble wrap, and paint. Just imagine it! Eighty children participating in a two-hour-long progressive dance party. I was so delighted that I posted about it to a Facebook group of my college classmates.

"*Please* bring this activity to our 30th!" my former roommate, Beth, commented when she saw the post. I didn't know if she was serious, but that was all the prodding I needed. I thought it was a fantastic idea and started organizing the supplies I would need to integrate the experience into our Saturday night "Back to the Future" dance party a few weeks later. I packed my kit into my suitcase, along with my embellished Doc Martens, sequined tube top, black rubber bracelets, fishnet stockings, and leopard print slip skirt. Miss Nancy was going back to Harvard!

While I enjoyed the daytime reunion activities, gathering with classmates to learn about their expertise, I was crawling out of my skin in anticipation. I could barely wait for the dance. Finally, it was time to gather under the disco ball once again. One by one, as I had done with the preschoolers, I invited my classmates to sit, wrap their stockinged feet with bubble wrap and masking tape, and coat the ticklish bottoms of their new booties with poster paint. Then I gestured for them to step onto my construction paper annex to the main dance floor, an eight-by-ten-foot rectangle beside the DJ booth. One by one, they leaped, jumped, and danced, exalting in the sensation of plastic bubbles bursting beneath their feet as they landed on the colorful paper. By focusing on the sensation of bubbles popping underfoot and, to a lesser degree, the marks their feet were making, any ounce of self-consciousness they might have felt evaporated, with their laughter, into the air. They were experiencing joy. And I was the instigator. It felt wonderful.

Later in the evening—having run out of people requesting to have their feet wrapped—I decided on impulse to lead a *hora*, inviting people who were hanging back, standing at the edge of the dance floor, to take my hand, form a circle, and move together to the music. Every one of us had by now attended our fair share of Jewish weddings and *bar mitzvahs*, and either seen or participated in a *hora*, the simplest form of a folk dance. Like the circle of life, it requires only the most basic footwork to keep yourself moving in the same direction.

Oh, what magic it was to see my classmates' broad smiles as they whipped through space together in that joyful circle—all those years we hadn't seen one another vanishing in an instant. Five years later, attendees returning for our thirty-fifth told me that the Saturday night *hora* was their happiest memory from our previous reunion.

Fifty-Seven Steps

My sorrowful meditations on my father's tragic climb up the stairs leading from the train platform into Penn Station would inspire me to produce a joyful work of art for my entire community, though I wouldn't recognize the connection for some time.

In the years following Daddy's death, I worked hard to plant myself—like a seed in soil—in my new town. In addition to securing three concurrent gigs teaching art to kids in local schools, I began offering summertime art classes in my home while Sam and Isaac were away at camp. I adored having children gather again to make art in the private space behind my home, echoing my happiest memories of creative time spent with kids on the lanai in Wyoming, Ohio.

Having learned that elementary school girls (and their parents' résumé-building ambitions) tended to outgrow me and my studio once they reached middle school, this time around, I invited toddlers to make art with me. Parents responded enthusiastically; having their small children make art at home was a messy, chaotic prospect. Evidently, nobody but me offered art classes for kids under two. I loved granting permission to little ones to make a joyful mess on my deck—covering my kitchen floor and table with newspaper and drop cloths when it rained, so it was easy enough to move art class inside.

I did paint murals for a few homeowners, but the DC area was proving to be a tough market. Local style editors, including one at *The Washington Post*, declared interior murals "risky" and told me to expect to travel great distances for work if I weren't inclined to reinvent myself. One suggested I train to become a high-end wallpaper installer. Some new friends agreed to be my first local clients, accepting a deep discount in exchange for the promise of promoting my services; rather than receiving compliments on my work, they were told how brave and daring they were.

Once I had solidly woven myself into my new community over the course of our first years there—making lasting connections through teaching, opening my home and heart to students and their parents, and gracing my clients' environments with life-enhancing health practices and artwork—it became clear to me that it was time to transform the public staircase at the end of my street.

The trouble was that the stairs had been designed to provide a safe route from the municipal parking lot below to the elementary school above—with no discernible concern for aesthetics. There were fifty-seven steps—four flights of concrete and steel railings, surrounded by nondescript red brick walls. I climbed the stairs daily with my dog, Suki, ever since our first full day in town—which happened to have occurred on the most magical day of the year: the summer solstice. Suki and I were rewarded on that first early-morning ascent with the breathtaking sight of the rising sun, centered between a pair of sculpted steel "trees" framing the entrance to the park just beyond the elementary school—its golden rays diffused through dozens of acrylic resin prisms that formed the interior of each leaf. (See Judy Sutton Moore, *Takoma Trees*.) How wonderful it must have felt to the artist, I thought, to elevate people's experience of entering the park from the mundane to the sublime.

Once school resumed in September, I would catch sight of young families clambering up the stairway to school on weekday mornings—parents and caregivers struggling to hang onto bags as they escorted their young charges along the steep ascent, some with babies strapped to their backs or chests, others with a child's scooter tucked under one arm as they climbed. I knew how challenging it was to go up those stairs while merely holding onto Suki's leash; navigating it with a kindergartener and all their gear was nothing short of heroic. My heart longed to find a way to uplift my neighbors on their upward climb.

Our mayor, Kate Stewart, announced she was holding a meet and greet at a local coffee shop so residents could approach her with ideas and questions. Mayor Kate loved my proposal of a mural for the stairs, but when I took her advice and sent it to her deputy, he replied: "Unfortunately, the city no longer has jurisdiction over the land where the stairs were built, as it was given to the school district for the purpose of constructing a safe route to school." So I walked out my front door, up the fifty-seven steps, and into the school to share this information with the principal.

"Is *that* the reason the city doesn't shovel the snow off those stairs? You know you have my blessing to paint whatever you like," she said, "but please inform your friends in city hall that I do not have the janitorial hours to keep those stairs clean, and they are definitely *not* a safe route to school when they're covered with wet leaves and ice."

"I'm sure I haven't any friends in City Hall," I told her, "but I am going to figure out a way to get this done. Don't you worry."

While puzzling over the challenge, I received a solicitation in the mail to order sweet potatoes as a fundraiser for Difference Makers, a club at the middle school for which both my younger boys had served as officers. Isaac suggested I include, along with my order form, a request to the club's advisor, Bryan Goehring, to include the stairs on a list of "passion projects" the club was organizing for the upcoming Global Youth Services Day.

Mr. Goehring said he wasn't aware of our fifty-seven steps, but I gave him the coordinates and we arranged to meet at the top of the stairs during what turned out to be a blizzard. Bryan immediately agreed to help. He added the steps to the list of projects, told me the kids' fundraising would cover any expenses associated with painting the steps in the spring—on Global Youth Services Day—and requested I design something a bunch of eager twelve- and thirteen-year-olds could accomplish.

As the winter waned and spring gingerly took hold, my design began to take shape. Around the same time, during the infamous "travel ban" of early 2017, our undocumented immigrant population was suffering from an acute fear of deportation. I heard about kids feeling afraid they would come home from school to an empty apartment because their parents might be taken away. I saw children's artwork taped to the bricks and windows of the school, proclaiming "You are loved" and "You are safe." I watched the colorful messages fade in the sun and become spattered with the rain. And I realized that our neighbors needed our encouragement and reassurance that they are beloved members of our community, regardless of their national origin.

As a symbol of inclusiveness, I decided that each of the steps would be painted a unique color. I knew this was an extravagance, so I made the rounds to local paint stores, negotiating good prices on behalf of the Difference Makers. Then I got a call from the manager of our neighborhood Sherwin Williams, offering to donate fifty-seven sample containers of paint. Amazing!

Days before the event, the forecast threatened rain, and I realized the stairs would need to be primed before the kids showed up to paint. I organized a small army of work-from-home moms, and we got the job done just in time for the primer to dry before the rain began. Then the weekend arrived, the sun came out, and Global Youth Services Day was radiant. All three of my kids showed up to lend their support. Max drove down from New York. Isaac and his friend Sarah, another former officer of Difference Makers, pitched in before heading off to co-star in a matinee of *Pirates of Penzance* at the high school. Sam made sure everyone could fasten their smock and helped distribute drinks to volunteers as they painted in the sun. Terry—our savior paint store manager—came by to see his donation being put to good use and to tell the kids they were a blessing to their community. He looked on in awe as dozens of kids hunched over their work, painting a colossal, deconstructed rainbow rising from the ground toward the sky. It was such an inspiring sight, Terry stayed all morning, heading back to his store with a big smile on his face and a proper sunburn on his bald head.

At the stroke of noon, the middle schoolers disappeared in a blur, running off to have pizza in the school parking lot. After a short rest at home, Sam and Max returned with me to the stairs to finish what the kids had started. As I surveyed the students' work, I found almost every paintbrush had been left on the cardboard to stiffen in the sun. Rather than cry over ruined brushes, I gathered them up, took some colorful yarn, looped it around their handles, and tied them to the staircases' steel railings, creating a decorative, dangling testament to how many young hands had contributed to the stairs' magical transformation. Some people say the brushes are their favorite part of the installation.

But now it was time for the real magic to begin. I sat myself down, halfway up the stairs. Equipped with a tube of black paint, a brush, a repurposed yogurt container filled with water, and a bottle of medium, I painted phrases in the few languages I knew while I put the word out and waited for news of the project to spread. Gradually—through social media posts, word of mouth, and just by spotting me out there on the stairway—local immigrants found out: an artist is on the stairs to the school, awaiting your contribution to a joy-inspired community art project.

Neighbors began arriving, I met with each person, asking them to remember a time before they moved to the United States and think of what their aunt, uncle, or grandparent would say to them if they were thinking of giving up on something important. Once they decided on a phrase, I encouraged them to borrow my brush and paint it onto one of the steps, promising to clean up any mistakes so it would look neat and professional. Most people opted to write the phrase on paper, or sent me an image of it, but some folks—including a graphic designer from Sri Lanka—sat down and painted their words right onto a stair riser.

Sitting beside them—witnessing my community members share their voices—I listened to stories about what they had endured before coming to this country. I will never forget the man from Egypt who chose to paint the phrase *"Yalla, habibi"* ("Let's go, honey" in Arabic) right below the stair where two sisters had painted *"tsa'ad akharey tsa'ad"* ("step by step" in Hebrew). When I remarked on his choice of location, he said, "Well, that's the whole point, isn't it?"; I was too *verklempt* to speak. An older gentleman told me he had survived imprisonment and threat of death in Ethiopia for his role in the recent uprising and was proud to see *"Jabbaaddhu!"*—the clarion call of the revolution—emblazoned near the top of our city's public stairs.

On the brick wall lining the stairway, I painted something that would lead people to identify the stairs as a location for selfies: stripes in the colors of the city's logo, then the number 1890 (the year the city had been incorporated), along with these words: "By lifting others up, we uplift ourselves"—which is how it came to be called the Uplifting Staircase.

After all the phrases were painted, people started reaching out to share their thoughts with me, such as the fact that this was the only place in America they had ever seen their language publicly displayed. Some families had their portraits taken on the staircase, proudly posing to showcase the step emblazoned with their native tongue. Someone else baked a banana bread and left it at my door with a handmade card, expressing love and gratitude. It was so much more than I had expected. Honestly, I'm not sure *what* I expected; I just felt compelled to do it. Now, my kitchen window is covered with colorful thank you cards and meaningful little pieces of art made by members of the community. I see them as I begin and end each day, and they serve as a constant reminder of my heart's connection to this place.

On the first day of school, a succession of families stopped on the stairs to pose with their children as they began a new academic year. Folks sent photos to their relatives back home;

some were so heartened, they decided to *move* here. As I met new neighbors, I heard how they'd chosen Takoma Park partially because of the stairs and what they communicated about our community. When I met a Trinidadian-Italian woman, newly arrived from Ireland with her two small children, she said she was overjoyed to meet the person responsible for the creation of the rainbow-colored staircase. She felt less alone upon seeing them, because she knew there were other artists here, and the colors felt like community to her.

Once the stairs were painted, the surrounding brick walls appeared drab by contrast. So the following spring, I created a GoFundMe page for a project in which all the local preschool students and their classroom teachers would help me paint a pointillistic mural on the brick walls facing Philadelphia Avenue. One class at a time, the teachers (immigrants themselves) walked groups of students to the stairs, where they took turns painting circles, ovals, and dots in many shades of green onto the brick wall. I loved seeing the youngest students' faces as they listened to me explain that someday, when they were bigger, they would climb these steps to go to school and would remember this day, when they had all worked together to make the stairway more special and beautiful.

I titled the second phase of the transformation "Positive in Nature," a cheeky reference to a wish I heard from Richard, a neighbor who had lived for forty years in the house across the street. Richard and his wife, Judy, partially funded phase two, and as he wrote the check, he said, "I look forward to finally seeing something positive in nature on that wall." When the stairs were first constructed, the city promised that a row of trees would be planted along the side wall so they could look out the window and still see greenery. But that promise was never made good. Now they would see a wall camouflaged with almost every shade of green found in nature. And during the gray days of winter, the wall is a dappled promise that the verdant days of spring and summer will return once more to Takoma Park.

The third year of the staircase transformation, I sent an email to the school's parents, inviting families to help paint the upper part of the wall to blend in with the sky. It was a joy to witness the families connect and find things in common. Other neighbors showed up too, saying they were big fans of the staircase, excited to contribute to its expanded decoration. The afternoon filled my heart to overflowing with joy, and now there are no bare bricks facing the street. The crowning joy is a mer-portrait section, high on the hillside—where a colorful purple-and-gold scaled tail is captured mid-swish, waiting for visitors to kneel above it and have their photos taken, posing as mermaids, mermen, merfolk…all are welcome here.

I was honored with an Azalea Spirit Award from the Takoma Park Historical Society because Katya Partan, a neighbor I hadn't even met yet, nominated me for having contributed something to the community that "embod[ies] the values of Takoma Park, with panache." The community voted with its heart, and I was humbled to receive the commendation in a place where so many people do a great many things to make our city a better place to live.

Seeing folks climbing my gift to the city while I walk my dog, or glimpsing a photoshoot taking place on the steps, almost always causes a little surge of dopamine, if not an actual smile. And now, it also makes me think of my dad. On a conscious level, I didn't connect the way I felt about the ugly staircase with my pain and longing to turn back time and help my father up the stairs from his train. Looking back, I realize: Daddy's sudden death at the top of a flight of stairs inspired the artistic collaboration of an entire community and manifested into a work of art that inspires the inhabitants of our fair city every day.

As I write this, I am preparing to lead another public staircase mural project in Takoma Park with a new group of middle schoolers, some of whom I taught art to when they were in preschool. I've been spending an hour every day this week scraping dirt off the stairs with a trowel and priming the concrete so that on Earth Day, the students can experience the fun of applying colorful paint—once again donated by Terry, our manager-hero at Sherwin Williams. I've also been hired to help two dozen fifth graders create a legacy mural as a gift to their local Montessori school as they graduate and move up to middle school. It is an amazing and wonderful thing to empower children with the skills to transform the space around them, and to lead them through the process of bringing joy to their communities.

Soul-Empowered Hypnosis

Not quite three years after tackling the first phase of transforming the stairs, Covid-19 arrived on our shores. During the pandemic, in-person energy healing was out of the question. So were soup demos, classroom art instruction, and dog walking. I didn't know what to do with myself.

First, I painted a cheerfully colored mural on my neighbor's garage proclaiming, "You Are Not Stuck at Home, You're Safe at Home." I offered some online classes on eating for stress resilience. My cellist son and I played duets for the neighbors, squeezed together on a brick front porch so tiny, there was no need for him to use an end pin. I offered outdoor art classes for pairs of siblings, or kids in the same learning pod, at a big table we brought from Ohio and moved into the back yard when we realized it didn't fit in our house.

While wondering what to do next, I received an email inviting me to deepen my intuition. I responded with enthusiasm and found myself in a two-month-long Zoom workshop training to learn Soul-Empowered Hypnosis. The instructor was a protégé of one of my favorite authors and teachers, Brian Weiss, MD; I had followed them both for years. Courtney led me in a past-life regression a few years earlier. Now, she introduced me and a dozen other healers to a simple way of guiding people to a state where they can commune with spirit, or with their highest self. We were an online community that met for three hours, twice a week on Zoom, signing onto computers from couches and desks as far west as Hawaii and as far east as Saudi Arabia.

Equipped with Courtney's induction script, a description of what might be about to happen, and no other training, we were sent into breakout rooms to meet our first clients! My partner endeared herself to me immediately by exclaiming in delight when she saw we'd been matched; Robbie had picked me out of the Zoom grid because of the sunlight streaming down on me from a skylight overhead. Her late father had been her sunshine—her flashlight in the darkness, she said—and the streaming light on my head and shoulders made her think of him. She told me she was in Europe, where she had lost her father to Covid a few months earlier; it was her dearest wish to connect with him. We had a magical session in which we were led by a figure who resembled her younger self through a meadow and past a series of animals, including a white dancing rabbit wearing sunglasses, until finally, we reached a great tree, and Robbie's father stepped out from behind it, shining a flashlight, which he handed to her.

Because she had shared a bit with me beforehand, the session was moving for both of us. For her, because it felt like confirmation that she and her father were still connected after his death. For me, because it was fascinating, thrilling, and surprisingly easy to hold space for such a meaningful connection. Robbie and I went on to enjoy many more sessions together, and every time I witnessed her communicating with her father's spirit, warm, happy tears cascaded down my cheeks. I fell in love with the experience of hosting family reunions on the astral plane. I also learned how to guide past-life regressions and hold space for people to receive messages from their spirit guides.

I typically hold these sessions while sitting at my grandfather's desk in the attic of our home, with an altar of essential oils and crystals that help me connect and a box of tissues for my tears. Every time I disconnect from a spiritual hypnosis client at the end of a session, my heart feels so full and I cannot stop smiling. When Paul sees me right afterward, as I come downstairs, he says he hopes I never give up doing work that lights me up from the inside the way these Soul-Empowered Hypnosis sessions do.

For a long time, I didn't want to admit I believed it was possible for people to channel spirit messages to us. I'd learned that it undermined most "educated" people's ability to respect me—to see me as a credible, intelligent person. I'm grateful to have overcome the need for others' respect; what others think of me is really none of my business.

Since the session with Andi right after Daddy's death, I continued to receive messages from multiple sources, letting me know my father was asking for my forgiveness. Frustrated by his repeated requests, I reached out to Peggy—one of my colleagues from Courtney's Soul-Empowered Hypnosis workshop—and asked if she'd be willing to guide a session for me. During the hypnosis, we asked why my father hadn't been able to be more loving and why he'd treated me the way he had.

I got this answer: *Sorry, but I was afraid of emotion.*

I heard my father's voice, Boston accent and all, and somehow received the knowledge that he had felt **cut off from love** and consequently was not able to be more loving. I had taken on the challenge of forgiveness at an intellectual level, but because my understanding was incomplete, so was my forgiveness. It would remain so until the following year, when I was guided to take a series of actions that would forever change my life.

Teachings on Love

During the retreat in 2007 where I encountered my unborn
son, Aaron, I stumbled upon the book *Teachings on Love* by the
late Buddhist monk, Thich Nhat Hanh. I helped myself to some
notebooks in the retreat center's supply closet and followed the
book's instructions to the letter. When I returned home, I had
notebooks filled with two epic love letters, which I mailed to
each of my parents, thanking them for every positive thing I
could remember receiving from them. Doing so had very little impact on my mother—my father said she threw my writing directly into the trash without reading it—but Daddy read
my letter with an open heart. It touched him deeply, and he
reached out to tell me so. My desperate, impassioned attempt at
boundary-setting had the unintended result of my not seeing or
speaking to my parents for several years just prior to that time. I
grieved about it, but I knew the boundaries I set were essential.

I did not have the faintest idea how to begin to repair our
severed relationship. It was a Buddhist monk who showed this
Jewish woman the way.

I know that I can still be a bit neurotic in my struggle to
set and maintain boundaries with narcissists, and the desire to
change this pattern invites me to continue strengthening my
practice of self-love. I have excellent intuition about people and
situations, but it can be clouded by my neurosis, which I carry with me from childhood. Perhaps my greatest challenge is
managing my expectations of other people's behavior and re-
membering that when they fail to conform to my expectations,
this has nothing to do with me.

What a magnificent lesson for every human to learn.

I have come to recognize this as my chief cause of suffering, which presents an opportunity for me to continue to develop my skills in trusting my gut, setting and maintaining boundaries, and accepting that things don't always work out the way I may want them to. These have been lifelong challenges for me—and the chief impediments to my own experience of joy, but I am encouraged by signs of my own improvement. I will continue to work on being kinder toward and more protective of my inner child, knowing that my intentions are pure.

What I have been learning ever since I sat in my yellow-and-white, grapevine-festooned bedroom listening to my Mister Rogers's records is that healing is not about becoming a better version of ourselves; it is about becoming more able to accept and love our one of-a-kind self just as we are. We cannot change harmful habits, discontinue blind behaviors, manage our fears and feelings, or break old patterns until we are able to hold ourselves with tenderness, and see ourselves with compassion.

Eleventh Spirit Messenger | 2021—Take Good Notes

After bringing up three talented thespians under my own roof and doing everything I could to support each of their many theatrical productions, I emerged from behind the scenes to play Fräulein Schneider in a community theater production of *Cabaret*. Yes, at age fifty-one, I'd been cast in a legendary role requiring me to dance, sing duets and solos, fall in love, cry, and speak with a German accent. I loved every part of it. Being in the show filled me with joy, and the cast said they felt blessed to have an Earth Mother in their midst. I liked to form a circle, stretch, and do deep breathing together before a performance and I was generous in sharing my oils—whether to alleviate pain, reduce stress, or support focus and memory.

My positive experience in *Cabaret* gave me the confidence to audition for a professional acting gig, and I was hired to portray five different women in *Incognito*, a play by the British playwright Nick Payne. The job required dancing, acting drunk, even dying on stage. I felt overwhelmed when I realized there were hundreds of lines to memorize, but I busied myself writing all of them in marker on poster-sized sheets of paper and wallpapered several rooms of the house with these pages, looking at them less and less often as Paul ran lines with me before every rehearsal.

As I worked to embody the various characters, I received a message from spirit via one of my hypnosis clients telling me to "take good notes and pay close attention." The message specified that it would be the process of preparing for my roles that would prove important in the future. This was amusing and intriguing; I laughed and wondered if perhaps I was about to be "discovered" and launched into a midlife theatrical career, playing women of a certain age.

As usual, the mysterious message proved accurate. Two of the characters I played in *Incognito* had been adopted. One of them pleaded with the pathologist who performed her father's autopsy to give her a bit of his brain tissue to perform a DNA test. Rehearsing this scene and connecting with the character's desire to know the truth of her identity, I was prompted to order a DNA kit from ancestry.com and send them a tube filled with my saliva. I also got a nudge from my former interior design colleague, Beau, who revealed that he had used this method to discover one of his Cincinnati grandparents had been Jewish. As a proud fourth-generation member of Cincinnati's insular Hyde Park society, Beau didn't think he'd even *met* a Jewish person before we met. Now, he revealed that he was dying of cancer. He said he was glad to have made his ancestry discovery before he died.

Where Did I Come From?

Almost nine years after my father was buried in a Jewish cemetery, a pair of home DNA tests revealed that Daddy, despite his having had a *bris*, hadn't had a Jewish bone in his body. Although he grew up in a Jewish community, studied and prepared to become a *bar mitzvah*, and chanted *kiddush* every Friday night of my childhood, it turns out my father is, genetically, one hundred percent Anglo-Saxon. At first, I didn't know how to process this revelation. To me, Daddy had been Jewish; I could recall the way the fringe of his *tallit* felt between my fingers as I sat beside him in synagogue. He collected antique Judaica, bought pickles by the barrel on the Lower East Side, and ordered pastrami on rye at Katz's Delicatessen as if it were his birthright.

Then I watched Hugh Bonneville in Downton Abbey and caught glimpses of my father on the screen. Once seen, it could not be unseen. My father, like the characters from the British play that inspired me to explore my true heritage, had been living "incognito" all his life. Home DNA tests were just becoming available before Daddy died, but he never had the chance to learn the secret that was so carefully kept from him: he had been the accidental, discarded descendant of one of the most well-known passengers aboard the most famous colonial settler ship in American history, the *Mayflower*.

After more than fifty years spent believing I was the grandchild of four Jewish immigrants who arrived in America near the turn of the twentieth century, it has been transcendental to uncover the missing half of my ancestry. The genetic testing revealed that in addition to sharing half my DNA with European (Ashkenazi) Jews, I share the other 50 percent with Protestant ancestors who settled the colonies of Massachusetts, New Hampshire, Maine, and Vermont. Judaism follows matrilineal descent, so I am as Jewish as I ever was, but genetically, I am half Jewish and half WASP.

I was so shocked that Paul suggested I order a second test kit from another company to see if I might get a different result. Not only were my results confirmed a few weeks later, I was also able to provide the names of many more relatives to the genealogist. In retrospect, my disbelief was ridiculous. Not only do I strongly resemble my father in many ways, my newly revealed hybrid ethnicity explains the confusion my appearance has caused so many people over the years.

I have now had over a year to digest and explore this enlightened understanding of my genetic identity. I have taken to calling the two sides of my "family" the British and Yiddish sides. Thanks to skillful work by a genealogist I've yet to meet in person, I am enjoying the process of discovering the other side of where, how, and from whom I came to be. Paul, the kids, and I have spent time in some of the beautiful places in New England where my American ancestors lived, bred, and died. We have been paying overnight guests in my great-grandparents' summer home, which is now a hotel in Kennebunkport, Maine, and recently, Paul and I visited the American Pilgrim Museum in Leiden, the Netherlands, which was closed when we arrived. Thanks to our smartphones, we were able to walk further down the canal and see where my ancestors, William and Mary Brewster, lived just before William arranged passage aboard the *Mayflower*. I was overcome, standing in this narrow alley, once hidden behind a heavy wooden door—its rusted old hinges still attached to the brick archway that now serves as its entrance. It occurred to me that my British ancestors had hidden just as furtively and fearfully as Anne Frank and her family had, a few miles to the northeast and three hundred years later, but with greater success.

These revelations about my father's origins have led me to experience a wider and deeper compassion for him. Learning about the psychological and emotional impact of secret adoption on people's lives, I've considered the many possible ramifications of my father never having learned the truth of his origins. It seems likely that he was adopted on the day of his birth, yet he never had the opportunity to process his experience of abandonment as an infant. As the mother of three human offspring, and as a vegan, I know a mammal baby bonds with its mother in utero and responds positively to her voice and her smell immediately after birth. There is an irreplaceable emotional connection there; it is deeply felt by mother and baby and causes great suffering when severed at birth.

According to Nancy Newton Verrier, in her 1993 book, *The Primal Wound*, the postnatal separation of a newborn from the biological mother imprints the human infant with a sense of abandonment and loss. Regardless of how an adoption is handled by adoptive parents, Verrier posits, the loss of the child's primordial relationship can be indelibly imprinted on the unconscious mind as a traumatic injury. Adoption trauma is an "unclaimed experience" and a "physical wound" that implants itself in the psychology of the adoptee. According to Daniel J. Siegel M.D.'s 2012 book, *The Developing Mind*, this primal wound may influence the way an adoptee acts, feels, and believes—especially if they navigate their way through life "without recognition of the influence of past experience on one's present reality."

All of this resonates for me because my late father saw the world as a harsh, punishing place, and he saw himself as responsible for toughening me up in preparation for it. And he never learned the real reason he felt so different from his adoptive family.

While researching the effects of secret adoption, which was rampant in the days before abortions could be obtained legally, I was dumbfounded when I came across an article enumerating a set of traits and behaviors I had always considered unique to my father. They were presented in a list as symptoms of a disorder common to those who were separated from their mother at birth and never received therapeutic intervention. Adults with reactive attachment disorder have trouble expressing true emotions, feelings, and needs; they tend to lack compassion and empathy. They are prone to angry outbursts, impulsivity, and distrustfulness. They often drink to excess; they may collect weapons and all manner of other things to try to feel safe. Some deny personal responsibility for their behavior and resort to the lies and manipulative, controlling behavior they learned in childhood.

My mind was blown. Everything I had always thought of as inexplicable quirks in this difficult man I had nevertheless loved and admired—or worse, interpreted as evidence of my sister and I not being loveable—were presented as symptoms, the natural consequences of his deep-rooted, lifelong pain. It was utterly heartbreaking, yet incredibly healing to learn—because, of course, it never had anything to do with us.

Daddy never had the chance to discover his truth—the root source of his deep fear of losing love, the reason he was afraid to become emotionally invested, or demonstrate affection, even in some of his most important and intimate relationships. I hate to think that my brilliant, talented, handsome, hardworking father may have questioned all his life long whether he was loved, but reading about the emotional impact of secret adoption has helped me understand the behavior behind the hidden wound he carried with him all his days.

This discovery of my father's secret, unknown even to him, reconciled in me a lifelong feeling of my own lacking and disappointment. After decades of failing to understand, I am grateful to have attained the awareness, in midlife, that all the love and support I need is right beside me. To tap into it, I need only remind myself that I am a channel for the flow of positive, loving, joyful energy streaming down from heaven to all of us on this Earth.

My mother's personality remains an enigma, but I now understand that her emotional limitations are, like his, very likely the result of wounds that have nothing to do with me. For anyone who was hurt as a child, accepting that it was never your fault is vitally important. J.K. Rowling shared in her commencement address to Harvard's Class of 2008 that there is "an expiry date" on blaming your parents for steering you in the wrong direction—excellent advice for moving on and upward, and embracing one's future. But if you have been harmed by a distorted, mangled self-image your parents fostered in you, you must also excavate how you came to hold yourself in such low esteem so that you can pick yourself up and continue becoming and doing everything you were born to be and do.

If you take nothing else from these pages, please believe this: You deserve to experience the limitless and unconditional love that surrounds you. Even now, as you read these words, you are positively enveloped by it. It is my fondest hope that you will find a way to tap into that awareness—to take it in, and keep it with you, always. You can do anything you imagine, and your inspiration is just beside you, waiting there patiently for you to notice.

Go ahead...find the joy that surrounds you.

Twelfth Spirit Messenger | 2021—Miriam Returns

On July 16, 2021—twenty-five years after first meeting Miriam and as I began writing an early iteration of this book—I hosted my friend Renee for a week-long writing retreat at my home. While chatting over morning cups of coffee on the back deck, I told her about the book *Proof of Heaven* by Eben Alexander, which I'd read eight years earlier, days before my father's death. The author is a former professor of neurosurgery at Harvard Medical School, whose understanding about the brain, the soul, and consciousness completely transformed after a near-death experience.

I told Renee that I have been receiving several of the messages featured in the book for many years now: that consciousness persists after death, that "God" is a primordial source of unconditional love, that our ancestors and departed loved ones remain present and accessible, and that we receive help and guidance from spirit when we need it most. As I told Renee about Miriam and described the impact our first session had on my life, I articulated my assumption that she had passed away, since she had been so weak the last time we spoke, years before. I searched on my iPhone for an obituary to read aloud; instead, I found evidence suggesting Miriam was alive, at the age of 86. Surprised and excited, I dialed her number and she answered! Her voice sounded frail and raspy.

"I don't know if you remember me," I began, telling her my name.

Miriam said she remembered that I had left Ohio and moved "back to New York."

"Well, not exactly. We moved to Maryland, closer to our family, many of whom are in New York. Anyway, your memory is impressive, and that is close enough that I know you do remember me."

"Of course, I do," she said. "We have spoken to each other many times."

This was true. I told Miriam I wanted to thank her for all her valuable help and advice over the years. She corrected me: It had not been her advice; she'd been channeling for me. It was up to me to make sense of it and figure out what value it held.

"Well, it did make sense and it was valuable," I told her. "I also want you to know: I am doing work now—spiritual hypnosis work, to help other people—which I never would have been led to do were it not for the messages you channeled and the way they helped guide me along my path."

Miriam said she was so happy, and grateful to hear it. Then she told me she was in tremendous pain. She'd been up since early in the morning and had asked Jesus to send her someone to help her, because she was afraid of going to the hospital. Miriam felt certain that my call was the answer to her prayers.

Feeling a bit intimidated, I asked, "How can I help you, Miriam?"

"Well, what would you do if I were one of your hypnosis clients?" she asked.

"Oh! Do you want me to do a session with you?" I knew the answer even as I asked.

"Well, I'm in my recliner. I've got my blanket over my legs. I am ready to go," she replied.

"Oh my goodness, okay, hold on a minute," I said. I felt nervous switching roles with Miriam, but I didn't want to bother her with my insecurity. I left the phone on the couch and bounded up the stairs, grabbed a notebook and a sharpie, and headed back down to the cozy basement where I'd moved to begin the conversation.

"Okay, I'm back, are you ready?" I asked.

Miriam said she was.

"Great," I said, "so go ahead and close your eyes, and begin to enjoy the feeling of having your eyes closed..."

Miriam began sharing. She said that her visions at the start of our session helped her feel peaceful, and she reported that her chest had "quit hurting" right away. She saw a blue jay and was told to "be at peace, be not afraid, I will not abandon you, as I have told you. I will take care of you as I have done since your birth."

Miriam paused. "Nancy, you are doing what you were sent to me to do. I have a hernia and breathing problems, but they are not bothering me now. They're saying to me, 'See? Beautiful flowers have grown from the seed others have planted. The seeds we plant in others can grow, with His help.' People plant seeds, and He sends the sun and the rain. He meets us halfway, but we must do our part."

Miriam breathed slowly now. "I had forgotten this," she murmured, in response to what she was receiving.

As a client, I had been accustomed to recording my sessions with Miriam, but now, I wrote as fast as I could, my sharpie racing across the page in my messiest cursive to catch every word she uttered, filling the notebook as I listened.

"We manifest through our thoughts," she reported. "Show up and remember the power of thought. Imagination is a gift. Speaking words manifests thought into the dimension of Earth.

"I am being told you called me not only to give to me but also to receive from Him, through me, so here you go:

"The days of darkness are upon you. We need the light. Many light bearers are being sent, but they are being caught up in the darkness. Nancy, you forget who you are. You've been given many gifts that are not being used. You have been given greater power. You shed the light, and I will do the work.

"Nancy, you are here to learn lessons. When you are watchful, you will learn. When you listen, you will have understanding. When silence is reached, deep silence, *then* you will hear my voice. You cannot hear before you are ready, and *then*, you will help others. Forgiveness is your current challenge.

"You are part of my work taking place now. We were meant to help one another at this time. Healing is being sent to your left leg right now, because you need some extra footing to do your work in the world."

I had recently torn my left meniscus while painting a mural on a retaining wall—too many hours focusing exclusively on what my right hand was doing, while holding a deep lunge position, not listening to the pain in my body, asking me to rest. We paused now, allowing time for my leg to receive the healing.

"Blue and purple light is surrounding you, and a blue butterfly hovers near you, to connect you to the next dimension. Teach kindness, light bearer, light the candle again, as there is much need. I will speak to your heart in the silence."

From that day on, Miriam would call me often, up until the days just before her death, often announcing—as soon as I would answer the phone—that she was actively dying, and asking if I could help her. I would step away from whatever I was doing to help her calm herself, and each time I helped her relax, restore her normal breathing, and reduce her pain. The last time I spoke to Miriam, she was in the hospital for injuries sustained during a fall.

During our calls, Miriam resumed her habit of reminding me to write my story and publish a book—as she used to do at the end of our face-to-face visits years ago— adding what struck me as a very Jewish-sounding mantra: if you help just one person, it will have been worth your trouble.

Miriam passed away recently, and because I know her spirit will not rest until I have published a book of "what I know," I abandoned my plan for a complicated advice workbook, started fresh and kept it simple, sharing memories of what I have lived through and what I have learned from my experiences.

"Oh, and one more thing," Miriam had said at the end of our reunion session. "They say you're going to want proof. They're showing me a blue butterfly...and now, they're showing me a book. It's called *Proof of Heaven*. Do you know it?"

"Oh my God—stop it, Miriam!" I exclaimed. "Not only have I read this book, but I was talking about it with my friend, Renee, the very minute before I called you!"

"Well, then, there's your proof, I guess!" she said with a chuckle, "but I think you are supposed to read it again. They are saying there are tools in it for you and that you are meant to share the ideas in it with others. This is a way you can help other people, especially those dealing with the loss of a loved one."

Saturday, as Paul and I drove to New York State to see our youngest child perform at summer camp, I listened to the latest edition of *Proof of Heaven*. As I heard Dr. Alexander recount his experience and the lessons he learned from it, I realized more fully how many of the book's concepts—which had been somewhat novel to me just eight years earlier—had become integrated into my life and work. Eben had added responses to all the people of science who had offered alternate explanations for the near-death experience he describes in the book, a valuable and informative new section which helps me share his story with scientists and physicians.

"Faith is a knowledge within the heart, beyond the reach of proof."
—KHALIL GIBRAN

The Rest of Your Life

To help you on your way to a more joyful life, I offer here my adaptation of a morning meditation practiced by His Holiness the 14th Dalai Lama. Like all good things, it does not belong to any one faith tradition. I recognize this meditation as an extended variant of a Hebrew morning prayer, *Modeh Ani*, said by many Jews upon waking, before getting out of bed, with one big difference: the Buddhist version doesn't mention the divine because the religion does not include a deity. I have edited the Buddhist text, replacing "others" with "myself":

Every day, think to yourself, as you wake up: Today, I am fortunate to have woken up. I'm alive; I have a precious human life. I am not going to waste it; I'm going to use all my energies to develop myself. To expand my heart, to achieve enlightenment for the benefit of myself. I'm going to have kind thoughts toward myself. I am not going to get angry with myself or think badly of myself. I am going to benefit myself as much as I can.

Every day, you have a blank page upon which to write. Every day, you can make a fresh start toward creating your truest, most beautiful, joyous life. We must cultivate the best in ourselves if we are to fulfill our purpose in the world. In order to do this, we must take radically good care of ourselves, and invest as much as we can in our healing, in our well-being. Women especially are taught that putting ourselves first is selfish and bad. Nothing could be further from the truth. When I've lectured on self-care, I would always say: "Self-care is not frivolous; it is essential. You cannot do your most important work in the world unless you take care of yourself." This daily care begins and ends with your body. Even if you think of your body merely as a vehicle for the soul, it must be maintained, or it will break down; you will be stopped in your tracks.

We each see our lives and our selves through the lens of inspiration or memory. Our memories continue to shift, align, and come into focus as we continue to make sense of our past. Until we reconcile our past, we will see the present and the future through the lens of that which distorts our perception of the truth.

If you take nothing else from my story, I hope you will believe that you are loved and cherished beyond measure. In the wise words of Mister Rogers, you are perfect just as you are.

You are here for a purpose only you can discover. You are part of a vast team of souls; some you will meet in your lifetime, others are watching and cheering you on from beyond the edges of your consciousness.

When I am inducing a spiritual hypnosis client into trance, I often instruct them to focus their awareness on the connection between their heart and every other beating heart on the planet, as well as to the infinite source of love, and the primal rhythm of the Universe.

Listen.

Open yourself.

Be brave enough to love yourself and claim your place in the divine.

BACK PAGES: JOY TRIGGERS

I hold in my mind's eye a vision of you as you finish this book and prepare to set it down or pass it on to a friend. I see you taking a deep breath, then exhaling, smudging yourself with sage, rubbing your skin with selenite crystal, anointing yourself with essential oils, purifying yourself with the smoke of palo santo, then maybe giving yourself a hug as you prepare to disembark from reading and embark anew on this incredible adventure called life.

As one of your loving fairy godmothers, I have some magic to bestow upon you as you prepare to continue on your way. Just as the witch* on the side of the road distributes magic pebbles to the fairy tale hero, I have some parting gifts for you, the heroine or hero of your own amazing life.

Water

Water is our mother. She is a healer whose powers sustain us and connect us with our deepest inner wisdom. On a physical level, our bodies are made mostly of water, and of all the natural

---

* *Please understand: fairy godmother and witch are just two different names for any woman who dares to denounce the norms of the patriarchy and exercise the privileges of freedom, autonomy, and outspokenness so commonplace among men.*

resources, water is the most essential to our survival. Dehydra-
tion, depending on its severity, can cause fever, high cholesterol,
high blood pressure, seizures, brain damage, organ failure, coma,
and death. Try to begin each day with a glass of water, and keep
your refrigerator stocked with fruits and vegetables with high
water content. Depending on the season, let these be staples on
your shopping list: bell peppers, berries, broccoli, celery, cucum-
ber, lettuce, melon, oranges, peaches, and squash.

On an emotional level...well, anyone who has invested in
beachfront property, a lake house, or a vacation by the shore
can attest to the value of communing with the powerful element of water. Visiting the ocean fills me with insights great
and small, even as my bathing suit fills with sand. On a typical
day at home, I often find that I do my best thinking of the day
standing in the shower or reclining in the hot tub.

In addition to growing up on Long Island in a house at the
end of a canal, with a vacation condo by the Caribbean Sea, I
was born with the sun, moon, and Mars all in Scorpio, a water
sign. Water sign people are known for being deep, emotional,
imaginative, creative. We also have a proclivity toward sensitivity and sentimentality. We are more likely to take things to
heart. We tend to hold on to people and possessions well past
their expiration date. Scorpios, in particular, are known to be
intuitive, many having innate psychic abilities. Our emotions
flow endlessly, like the waves of the ocean.

Building sandcastles is fun, and so is collecting seashells.
But bobbing alone in the vast ocean is a sublime experience, a
surefire way to feel connected to the entire universe. Every few

months, since moving to the DC area, I buy a Groupon so I can spend hours in a series of baths at a place called Spa World. If invited, I will gladly spend an entire day driving north to board a ferry to submerge myself in the waters off Fire Island or Martha's Vineyard. Whenever I immerse myself in water, especially if I give myself the gift of silence while doing so, I carry the properties of this element with me for a long time afterward.

A water feature that my spirit is often called to visit lately is at the Hillwood Estate, Museum, and Gardens—home of the late Marjorie Merriweather Post in Washington, DC. If you haven't heard of her, Marjorie was an uber-fabulous American socialite, philanthropist, and the sole heir to her father, C. W. Post, from whom she inherited the Postum Cereal Company, which became the General Foods Corporation. My favorite spot in Marjorie's gardens is a path of stepping stones spanning a koi pond, just between a rocky waterfall and a metal fish fountain. Pausing there between these two distinct ambient water sounds has proven highly therapeutic in transforming a cloudy mood to a sunny one.

Dressing Up | Sharing Beauty

I was brought up to be an eagle-eyed bargain shopper and, as a small child, honed my ability to discern quality among the racks at Loehmann's, where I trained to spot treasure amid rubble. In my mid-twenties, I would practice that skill by scouring the clearance racks at Bergdorf Goodman and Henri Bendel, scanning the floor in search of extremely long garments. While living in Cincinnati, I relied on Snooty Fox, a chain of upscale consignment stores, to satisfy my penchant for dressing up. The manager of a particular boutique revealed that there was a local lawyer who consigned many of the high-quality, gently worn items that fit me well. Without revealing the attorney's identity, she set aside her newly consigned pieces for me. Over time, I acquired a good portion of her designer wardrobe at a fraction of what she'd spent, and I still enjoy wearing these treasures.

These days, the bargains that make me happiest are found in the clearance bins at Michael's craft stores and a salvage yard called Community Forklift, as well as my local Buy Nothing group, even the Paris flea market, where I find discarded treasures—old abalone buttons, decorative champagne caps, broken antique teacups—to incorporate into my artwork. My favorite type of art since moving to Maryland, and especially since the Covid-19 pandemic, are works that surprise passersby and spark joy for them; as a consequence, I have become a specialist in retaining-wall murals, some of these incorporate mosaic along with painting. In my free time, I make small mosaic artworks on the concrete garden pavers that surround my front garden. In this way, my home has become a bit more colorful and sparkly with each passing season.

If you are a homeowner, you can spark joy for passersby in so many ways. Place seashells conspicuously in your garden, especially if you live far from the shore. Plant pinwheels with colorful glass pebbles scattered in the dirt around their base. I assure you that this combination will attract the most adorable and delighted toddlers. Plastic flowers that seem to bloom at the most unlikely time can be tacky if overdone, but if planted among roots and boulders with a light touch, they can trigger amazement and wonder.

If you are not a homeowner, you can still have a beautiful impact on your surroundings. Yarn bombing (do a search on YouTube) is a quick and easy way to jazz up dead trees, railings, or signposts wherever you may be. You can also create gueril-la mosaics: collect pieces of old crockery and gather discarded wine and beer bottles from nearby recycling bins, and apply broken pieces of each, using thin-set adhesive, to enliven an old fence post or fill some cracks in the pavement. These are just two examples of cheap, easy ways to make the world around you a bit more cheerful and full of color.

Lately, the source of beauty that most often brings me joy—which I feel compelled to take pictures of every day and share with others almost as often—is the natural beauty that surrounds me. Leaves changing color in autumn, the sun glinting off icicles encasing red berries, the first spring flowers poking through the snow and every flower that blooms for months thereafter. Being surprised by a family of deer during my morning dog walk, the way early morning light illuminates my neighbor's mosaic-tiled front steps or the moss-covered trunk of a tree. The waterfall or sweeping view of the valley that greets me at the top of a long, steep hike through the woods. Early morning walks in winter with unobstructed views of the sunrise (a spectacle in the sky as varied and glorious as any fireworks). Visiting a place without light pollution, like Maine or Martha's Vineyard, and seeing the Milky Way Galaxy spread out above you as you walk down a country road. Bike rides, hiking trails, long morning dog walks, after-dinner strolls. I love it all, and there is always something new to notice and appreciate, every single day.

DIY Fabulosity | Fancy Nancy Pants

I briefly ran a business called Fancy Nancy Pants, when I discovered it brought people great joy to extend the lifespan of a favorite pair of old jeans—otherwise relegated to a drawer because they had become threadbare, but the owners were too sentimental to discard them. I was able to rejuvenate these denim treasures using wool sweaters purchased for a dollar on sale days at Goodwill. I also incorporated vintage textiles that held great meaning for my clients—strips of cloth from a button-down shirt all three of her babies had worn, the bandana a late brother had worn on his motorcycle, a plaid jumper a grandmother bought for her teenage self during a special shopping trip to NYC. I boiled the sweaters, then cut the wool into cozy, colorful patches: hearts, smiley faces, peace signs, butterflies, fruits, and flowers. Anyone can do this, and I recommend it. I had no training or previous experience sewing, but I loved seeing my client's faces when they got their old jeans back, transformed into a work of heart.

Extending the life of anything beautiful—not just old or secondhand clothes—brings me joy. I love being the third generation to use many of the lovely things in my home. When I serve you a bowl of pistachios, you can expect me to place my grandparents' crystal ashtray just beside it, to accommodate the discarded shells. I may not sit down for breakfast, but I will typically spoon the overnight oats, berries, and cashew yogurt into my mouth from my grandmother's porcelain candy dish, its surfaces covered with hand-painted violets.

The Power of Music

Music is an elixir: it soothes us, it moves us, it is a mainline to joy. Hearing it, feeling it vibrate within me, dancing to it, I am music's minion. But ah, when I am making it—particularly with others—it resonates in my being like nothing else. Whether I'm playing my violin in a chamber orchestra, playing viola in string quartets, singing with a live karaoke band, even playing duets or singing in harmony with one other person, it is nothing short of divine.

I haven't had a professional music gig since moving back East, but I have played music for religious services, occasionally read string quartets with friends, and I am a member of an amateur orchestra that gives concerts to support local food banks. What I've observed in the world around me is that there is a musical niche for literally everyone. Whether that means joining a choir, posting an ad on your coffee shop's bulletin board to form a garage band or barbershop quartet with some of your neighbors, compiling a play list for dance parties in your living room, going to a salsa dancing event in your city, resuming piano lessons late in life, or sitting on your back deck until you remember how to play the banjo…only you and your spirit guide can know the best way back to music for you.

Hair as Freak Flag

For many years, I twisted myself into all sorts of painful knots, trying to conform to standards and expectations that weren't my own. Take my hair, for example. For many years, I kept my hair long for other people's gratification and approval, visiting the Pierre Michel salon every six weeks, spending over $200 (in 1990!) for a profusion of "natural-looking" blonde highlights on my long brown tresses. One day, soon after my first marriage ended, I decided to try to replicate the expensive results at home and purchased a boxed highlighting kit at CVS, complete with plastic bonnet and metal hook, and I did a pretty damn good job—for about one-tenth the price. In this way, I liberated myself from my high-end coiffeur habit and managed to maintain my own highlights until I cut my hair short after Isaac was born—because with three kids, who was I kidding?

One day, tired of the summer heat, I swore to my kids that if it hit 100 degrees one more time, I was going to shave my head. When the next three-digit day rolled in, I left Max in charge and took myself down the street to the barber. When I returned home, my head shaved as smooth as a cue ball, Isaac literally fell down laughing. It was priceless...and so comfortable!

When my stubble reached about a half inch in length, I bleached it. Then, as it grew longer, I experimented with different temporary colors. Today, my cropped hair is often unicorn or mermaid hued—more common now than when I first adopted it, but still rare among mortals. However, I assure you: I am just as human and complicated as you are. My locks may make me appear more joyful than many people, but as an instigator of joy, I am seeking to eradicate the disparity. I want to help everyone I meet connect more easily and sustainably with joy. And fortunately for everyone…joy is contagious.

Back when I had my hair expensively colored, it was like the crowning touch to a uniform; barely anyone commented on it. After I shaved my head and allowed my natural color to emerge, *everyone* had an opinion to express—even strangers. Gray-haired women I'd never met were constantly complimenting my salt-and-pepper coif; other women would approach me and whisper that I was still too young to "let myself go." My mother made her displeasure crystal clear: she was too young to have a gray-haired daughter. Ha! When I shut out everyone else's opinion and examined my own feelings, I found I was not yet ready to embrace gray hair in my forties, after all. But I was happy to recognize my head as a new canvas of sorts, another opportunity for creative self-expression.

My favorite thing about sporting magenta, blue, or purple hair (or all three at once) is that it brings other people joy. When a stranger calls out to me from across a parking lot or someone I pass on the street says they love my hair, it's an affirmation that I'm fulfilling my life's purpose. As for those who take one look and dismiss me, based upon their judgment of my unconventional choice, that is just fine by me—I'm sending them rays of joy as soon as their backs are turned anyway.

When young people ask me how to color their hair like mine, I tell them to wait until God gives them a blank canvas. Why strip away natural color to replace it with something artificial? Better to wear colorful clothes and accessories while your hair color decides to fade at its own pace. If you've been coloring your hair to hide your gray, let me tell you what many people discovered during the Covid-19 pandemic: letting your natural hair grow in is one of the most liberating things you can do. Remember: you were designed to be splendid, just as you are. Think of all the time and money you'd reclaim and consider celebrating by spending it in a way that brings you true joy.

Managing the Museum | The Great Giveaway

Because we moved back East before my father died, I was able to help my mother in the months and years that followed. During many gloomy visits with her in the five-bedroom house where my sister and I grew up, Mommy and I would go through my father's possessions, starting from the cavernous basement and working our way up, as she repeated, "Oh, but I can't get rid of this. It feels like I'm throwing away a life."

To spare some of her pain, I absorbed into our home things my mother couldn't bear to throw out but didn't want to take with her to her new two-bedroom apartment. I soon realized I had deluded myself in thinking it would be easier for me. To make matters worse, Paul was enchanted with many of the objects my father had collected, even those he couldn't identify. In time, I realized we needed professional help to support the process of reclaiming the space in our house, which had begun to feel more like a warehouse than a home—I started referring to our little cottage as "the museum." When people would ask why, I invited them to visit and select a souvenir to take with them.

I was struggling with a confusing sense of obligation either to keep these objects, sell them, or give them to my children—but none of these felt like the right way forward. One evening, while hosting dessert in a café at the end of a walking tour of my local public murals, I discovered that Brooke, the barista, had her own decluttering business. Brooke was a newly single mom of two young children. Ever since being one myself, I have gone out of my way to support single mothers, and Brooke had such a kind and openhearted manner, I decided to hire her on the spot.

Brooke helped me sort through the piles. We identified pieces that would become meaningful gifts for friends and relatives, and others that would spark joy for neighbors through our Buy Nothing group on Facebook. At times, Brooke has left my house with several bags and dropped their contents off at a local thrift store so they can continue to be of service. It has been a source of joy to see my father's possessions—articles of brand-new clothing he never had the chance to wear, tiny treasures he purchased as souvenirs of faraway places, or colonial-era antiques—end up in the hands of people who delight in their acquisition.

Reclaiming cluttered space in your home is a wonderful feeling—then you can create an art studio, store your bicycles, or use that open space for dancing!

Creative Matriarchy

While integrating our family into the DC suburbs and helping my two younger kids and my mother adjust to new chapters in their lives, I also had to reinvent myself—because this is what self-employed women must do when they pick up and move to a new town, hundreds of miles away from every friend, client, and anyone else in the world they've ever known. If you hadn't already noticed, I have a tendency toward the dramatic, but there I was—starting over yet again, in my mid-forties. And it was harder this time.

The children had to adjust to different schools. Though Paul found a decent job in DC, he had taken a humbling pay cut. He left behind a high-paying directorship at a private rehabilitation hospital in favor of joining the Veterans Administration, and his new post kept him busy from early in the morning until dinner time. And then there was the cost of living—so much higher in DC than in Ohio. So I used my creativity, brushed off my hustle, and found a way to maximize my contributions, both to my community and to my family.

I was fired up to find ways to spread joy and beauty in our new community, and curious to discover which of my talents would best align with our new surroundings. My enthusiasm drove me to offer a variety of services all at once—with amusing results. In a single day, I might enter someone's home early in the morning with my big black treatment table; or emerge onto the sidewalk midday to paint a retaining wall mural; then, hours later, I'd be standing in front of my home, greeting families as they arrived for a toddler art class on the back deck.

I have always preferred to manifest my own abundance, and abundance is a wealth that is all-encompassing: it's joy, laughter, purpose, and fulfillment. Of course, it includes financial wealth, because money is one of the ways we show our love and appreciation—and we all need money to survive and thrive in our society, even if we live in a commune. But the essence of abundance is the proclivity to spread the wealth, in whatever form it comes to you. To quote my younger self, as I posted on Facebook back in 2012, "If you want to know true joy, find a way to contribute to the world around you." Knowing that I am making other people's lives better—whether as a healer, a teacher, an artist, a musician who gives concerts for charity, a volunteer who packs donated food for the hungry, a leader of public artworks, or a devoted friend. Even by learning that people are still citing my cautionary article and helping women obtain better outcomes when their marriages end, helping other people live more joyful lives is the most gratifying experience I have ever known.

My faith embraces the notion that we can all do and be better. Rather than relying on God to repair the world, in Judaism we are compelled to take action and do it ourselves. As Rabbi Tarfon says in *Pirkei Avot*, commenting on a passage from the prophet Micah: "Do justly...love mercy...walk humbly. It is not your responsibility to finish the work of perfecting the world, but you are not free to desist from it either."

Consider when you have felt the most confident in yourself. Was it when things were going your way, or right after you overcame a hardship you thought might crush you? It is the moments that test us that teach us what we are capable of. We are all created in God's image, *b'tzelem Elohim*, and to me this means we are all eternal, endlessly creative, with no limit to what any of us can accomplish.

DISCUSSION QUESTIONS

1. When you think back to your earliest memories, what are the stories you remember from childhood and what values do you think you may have internalized from them? In what ways have you worked to overcome limiting messages from the literature of your childhood?

2. In what joyful ways did you exercise your individuality, even your defiance, as a child? With what response was your assertion of selfhood met? By your parents? By teachers? By other authority figures? How did those responses affect your relationship to that assertive part of yourself and to joy?

3. When you were a child, did you have role models who inspired you? Think back to fictional characters, real people in biographies, celebrities, or members of your community...how did you take steps to emulate them and with what result?

4. As you scroll through your social media feed (if you have one), what do you find you have given the most space and energy to? What do you see as having brought you the most joy (or reason to brag) over the past year, two years, five

years? Do these stories and images still spark joy for you today? How does it feel to share and savor your joy in this way? How does it feel to look back on it now?

5. Nancy finds joy as an amateur musician after relinquishing her dreams of having a career as a concert violinist. Did your reality turn out to be completely different from what you originally dreamed? If so, how are you still connected to that childhood dream? What steps might you take to increase that connection?

6. One who fears failure is likely to take no risks. Nancy made her theatrical debut after her fiftieth birthday when she found the courage and confidence to embrace the risk of failing. What would you do if you knew you would not fail?

7. On the first page of this book, Nancy shares five quotes that speak to her. What is your response to these three of those assertions?

   - *George Eliot:* "It is never too late to be what you might have been." Do you agree? Why or why not?

   - *Buddha:* "No one can save you but yourself. No one else can and no one else may. We ourselves must walk the path." Nancy seems to think that to realize our potential, we all must become our own fairy godmother, and create our own magic. How have you found this to be true in your life?

   - In the Talmud, it is written that a person who loves is

greater than a person who fears. In Judaism, there is a teaching that it is good to fear the Almighty, and live as if the eyes of the divine are always upon you. There is also a commandment to love the Almighty, with all your heart, all your soul, and all your might. Are these ideas necessarily in conflict? Why or why not?

8. At the close of her book, Nancy encourages us to be brave enough to love ourselves and claim our place in the divine. What do you think you can do to make that so, and what would help you find the courage necessary to do it?

9. Nancy says the blessings in her life occur because she allows herself to be guided by spirit. Others might say she has learned to check in with her highest self, or to trust her gut. What is another way of thinking about this? What do you do in order to connect with your highest self?

Made in the USA
Middletown, DE
03 February 2024

49034853R00186